For Merold Westphal

In memory of Johan van der Hoeven (1932–2015)

Truth in Husserl, Heidegger, and the Frankfurt School

Truth in Husserl, Heidegger, and the Frankfurt School

Critical Retrieval

Lambert Zuidervaart

The MIT Press
Cambridge, Massachusetts
London, England

This book was set in ITC Stone Serif by Jen Jackowitz. Printed and bound in the United States of America.

Library of Congress Cataloging-in-Publication Data

Names: Zuidervaart, Lambert, author.
Title: Truth in Husserl, Heidegger, and the Frankfurt school : critical
    retrieval / Lambert Zuidervaart.
Description: Cambridge, MA : MIT Press, 2017. | Includes bibliographical
    references and index.
Identifiers: LCCN 2016047139 | ISBN 9780262036283 (hardcover : alk. paper)
Subjects: LCSH: Philosophy, German—19th century. | Philosophy, German—20th
    century. | Truth. | Husserl, Edmund, 1859–1938. | Heidegger, Martin,
    1889-1976 | Frankfurt school of sociology.
Classification: LCC B3181 .Z84 2017 | DDC 121.0943—dc23 LC record available at
https://lccn.loc.gov/2016047139

10 9 8 7 6 5 4 3 2 1

Contents

5 Truth and Justification: Jürgen Habermas 103

III Truth and Objectivity 123

6 Synthetic Evidence and Objective Truth: Husserl Revisited 125

7 Transforming Truth: Heidegger and Horkheimer in Dialectical Disclosure 147

8 Conclusion: Truth and Goodness Intersect 175

Preface

This book marks an intermediate stage in a decades-long research project on the idea of truth. The project began with a master's thesis on Immanuel Kant's *Critique of Judgment* and a doctoral dissertation on Theodor W. Adorno's *Aesthetic Theory*. In both studies issues concerning nonpropositional truth guided my understanding of philosophical aesthetics, as they did in my subsequent book, *Adorno's Aesthetic Theory* (1991). I then addressed these issues further in *Artistic Truth* (2004). There I indicated that a defensible notion of artistic truth as being nonpropositional requires a more comprehensive conception of truth, one that neither reduces truth to propositional matters nor dismisses the importance of propositional truth. Articulating the details of such a comprehensive conception of truth is the ultimate aim of my decades-long research project. The current book sets the stage for this by uncovering insights from twentieth-century German philosophy. It does so by carrying out a *critical retrieval*—an approach explained in the book's introduction.

From the time of my doctoral research on Adorno in the late 1970s, I have been convinced that one cannot responsibly address questions about truth in art and philosophy without considering questions concerning truth in society as a whole. In a characteristically provocative epigram, Adorno once wrote: "The whole is the false." As I have argued in *Adorno's Aesthetic Theory* and in *Social Philosophy after Adorno*, this negative dialectical inversion of Hegel's "The True is the whole" cannot mean that Adorno's "whole"—late capitalist society—is wholly false. If there were no traces of truth in the whole, including contemporary art and philosophy, then one could not begin to decipher in what ways the whole is false. Conversely, if one wishes to point out the elements of truth in contemporary art and philosophy, then one also needs to suggest how society as a whole could be true. Moreover, to do any of this, one needs to have an idea of truth that is sufficiently comprehensive to make sense not only of philosophical and artistic truth but also of truth in other areas of social life, including science, politics, and religion. My critical retrieval of Adorno and other German philosophers aims to elicit the contours of such a comprehensive idea.

Several chapters in this book stem from previously published essays that, although originally written for specific occasions, belong to the overarching research project. These occasions span two decades, from a 1994 paper on Martin Heidegger's conception of truth, presented in a lecture series hosted by the Institut für Philosophie at the Freie Universität Berlin, to a keynote lecture on Edmund Husserl's conception of truth, given at the annual conference of Canadian Society for Continental Philosophy in 2013. The notes to various chapters provide details about such occasions and acknowledge key organizers and interlocutors. Here I simply want to express gratitude to everyone who has encouraged and supported my work, especially my students and faculty colleagues at Calvin College, the Institute for Christian Studies (ICS), and the University of Toronto. In particular, I thank Joe Kirby, a PhD candidate at ICS, for preparing the index to this volume.

Chapter 2 appeared previously as "Propositional and Existential Truth in Edmund Husserl's *Logical Investigations*," in *Symposium: Canadian Journal of Continental Philosophy* 20, no. 1 (spring 2016): 150–180. Chapter 3 is a shortened version of chapter 4 ("Truth as Disclosure") in my book *Artistic Truth: Aesthetics, Discourse, and Imaginative Disclosure* (Cambridge University Press, 2004), 77–100, and chapter 4 reproduces (with minor revisions) chapter 3 ("Heidegger and Adorno in Reverse") of Lambert Zuidervaart, *Social Philosophy after Adorno* (Cambridge University Press, 2007), 77–106; both are reprinted with permission. Chapters 5 and 7 were originally published as journal articles and appear here with minor revisions: "How Not to Be an Anti-Realist: Habermas, Truth, and Justification," *Philosophia Reformata* 77 (2012): 1–18, published by Brill; and "Truth Matters: Heidegger and Horkheimer in Dialectical Disclosure," *Telos*, no. 145 (winter 2008): 131–160, respectively. I wish to thank the editors and publishers who have given permission to use these previously published materials.

Two scholars in particular, one of them Dutch and the other American, have encouraged my work on German continental philosophy, providing inspiration through their example. The late Johan van der Hoeven, formerly Professor of Systematic Philosophy at the VU University Amsterdam, served, together with Calvin Seerveld at ICS, as the supervisor for my dissertation on Adorno's aesthetics. Highly knowledgeable about German philosophy from Kant onward and an expert in phenomenology and post-phenomenology, Johan was a leading figure in the tradition of reformational philosophy to which I belong. His fine-grained analyses of complex texts, and his generosity of spirit when interpreting them, have provided a model for the critical hermeneutics I aim to practice. As a *Doktorvater* who gently and perceptively guided my doctoral dissertation to its completion, Johan showed me how to do rigorous philosophy that is unpretentious and true to life. Both as a philosopher and as a person, he was, as the Dutch title to his festschrift suggests, "levensecht en bescheiden."

Johan's example has received reinforcement from the scholarship and collegial support of Merold Westphal, Distinguished Professor of Philosophy Emeritus at Fordham University in New York. I first met Merold at a gathering of the Society for Phenomenology and Existential Philosophy in the early 1990s, and he has taken a personal interest in my work ever since. A leading figure in continental philosophy of religion who has published seminal studies on Hegel, Kierkegaard, and the "masters of suspicion" (Marx, Nietzsche, and Freud), Merold has demonstrated that the differences between analytic and continental philosophy need not create an unbridgeable divide. He also has shown how adherence to a tradition of faith can sustain spirited philosophical exploration and debate.

Johan and Merold have inspired me to pursue a tradition-crossing inquiry into the idea of truth in the writings of Husserl, Heidegger, and the Frankfurt School. With enduring gratitude I dedicate this book to them, two exemplary and modest masters of charitable critique.

Abbreviations and Citations

Except in the cases of Husserl's *Logical Investigations* and Heidegger's *Being and Time*, citations of works listed in both English and German use abbreviations derived from the English title and give pagination first in the English translation and then in the German original, thus: ND, 153/156. Frequently translations have been modified, including the removal of original italics, as indicated by the letters "tm." Dates immediately after titles indicate when the original German editions were first presented or published. The bibliography contains additional works by Husserl, Heidegger, Horkheimer, Adorno, and Habermas.

ET: Martin Heidegger, "On the Essence of Truth" (1930), trans. John Sallis, in Martin Heidegger, *Pathmarks*, ed. William McNeill (Cambridge: Cambridge University Press, 1998), 136–154. "Vom Wesen der Wahrheit," in Martin Heidegger, *Wegmarken*, 3rd ed. (Frankfurt am Main: Klostermann, 1996), 177–202. I have also consulted, but do not cite, John Sallis's translation of an earlier edition of this essay, in Martin Heidegger, *Basic Writings*, ed. David Farrell Krell (San Francisco: Harper, 1977), 117–141.

GS: Theodor W. Adorno, *Gesammelte Schriften*, 20 vols., ed. Rolf Tiedemann et al. (Frankfurt am Main: Suhrkamp, 1970–86).

LI: Edmund Husserl, *Logical Investigations* (1900–1901), 2 vols., trans. J. N. Findlay, with a new preface by Michael Dummett, ed. Dermot Moran (London: Routledge, 1970, 2001). This is a translation of the revised German edition of 1913/1921. The two English volumes are cited as LI 1 and LI 2, respectively.

LU: Edmund Husserl, *Logische Untersuchungen*, 2 vols., in *Husserliana*, vols. 18 and 19 (The Hague: Martinus Nijhoff, 1975, 1984). *Husserliana* 18 contains the text to both the first and the second, revised editions of LU volume I and is cited here as LU I. *Husserliana* 19 contains the text to both editions of LU volume II and is divided into two parts. Part 1 of *Husserliana* 19 contains Investigations One through Five and is cited as LU II.1. Part 2 contains Investigation Six and is cited as LU II.2. Volume I of LU originally appeared in 1900. Volume II originally appeared in 1901. The revised edition of volumes I and II.1 appeared in 1913. The "partially revised" edition of volume II.2 appeared in 1921.

ND: Theodor W. Adorno, *Negative Dialectics* (1966, 1967), trans. E. B. Ashton (New York: Seabury Press, 1973). *Negative Dialektik*, in GS 6 (Frankfurt am Main: Suhrkamp, 1973), 7–412.

PT: Max Horkheimer, "On the Problem of Truth" (1935), in Max Horkheimer, *Between Philosophy and Social Science: Selected Early Writings*, trans. G. Frederick Hunter et al. (Cambridge, MA: MIT Press, 1993), 177–215. Max Horkheimer, "Zum Problem der Wahrheit," *Zeitschrift für Sozialforschung* 4 (1935): 321–364. The translation modifies one by Maurice Goldbloom in *The Essential Frankfurt School Reader*, ed. Andrew Arato and Eike Gebhardt (New York: Urizen Books, 1978), 407–443, which I have consulted but do not cite.

SZ: Martin Heidegger, *Sein und Zeit* (1927), 15th ed. (Tübingen: Max Niemeyer, 1979). Passages in translation are taken from Martin Heidegger, *Being and Time*, trans. Joan Stambaugh (Albany: State University of New York Press, 1996), but the page numbers given are from *Sein und Zeit*, as found in the margins of English translations. I have also consulted *Being and Time*, trans. John Macquarrie and Edward Robinson (New York: Harper & Row, 1962). I give preference to the Macquarrie/Robinson translation in retaining "Being" (capital "B") for *Sein* and in not hyphenating *Dasein* (which, for the most part, is not hyphenated in *Sein und Zeit* but is always hyphenated in Joan Stambaugh's translation). These modifications are made without comment in the citations and in my own text. Other relevant modifications to citations from the Stambaugh translation are marked by square brackets.

TJ: Jürgen Habermas, *Truth and Justification*, ed. and trans. Barbara Fultner (Cambridge, MA: MIT Press, 2003). *Wahrheit und Rechtfertigung: Philosophische Aufsätze* (Frankfurt: Suhrkamp, 1999). Chapters 2 and 5 in *Wahrheit und Rechtfertigung* are replaced by two new essays in *Truth and Justification*.

1 Introduction: Critical Retrieval

The idea of truth provides a leitmotif for continental philosophy in the German tradition. It is a guiding theme for its leading thinkers, from Husserl through Habermas, and it generates central debates among them. In fact, one could reconstruct the history of German philosophy since 1900 around the idea of truth, and one's reconstruction could encompass other philosophers who wrote in German but whose reflections on truth have proved more influential in analytic philosophy—figures such as Frege, Wittgenstein, Carnap, Tarski, and Popper. For all of these philosophers, whether "continental" or "analytic," positions regarding the idea of truth lie at the core of their unique contributions, their influence on other thinkers, and the seminal debates they or their students have had with one another.

This book does not undertake such a historical reconstruction. Instead it attempts what I call a *critical retrieval*. Attending to debates surrounding specific contributions in twentieth-century German continental philosophy, I seek to illuminate the issues these contributions raise and the insights they offer. Heideggerian thinking and critical theory are of particular interest here. Despite the miscommunication, opposition, and even outright hostility that have prevailed between them, the two traditions have much in common, including significant roots in the phenomenology of Edmund Husserl. This book traces the tensions that arise when one tries to gain insight into the idea of truth from both traditions, keeping in view not only their disagreements and but also their shared roots. Dialectically, I approach these as creative tensions, as potentially generative sources for a new and comprehensive conception of truth. I also begin to explore how insights critically retrieved from German continental philosophy can help one address contemporary debates in analytic truth theory.

To provide orientation for the project I have in view, let me first sum-marize the book's structure and content. Then I shall discuss the role of a critical retrieval, comment on the scope of this project, and explain why a critical retrieval is important.

1.1 Orientation

Three issues of contemporary concern provide points of orientation for my approach.[1] One is the distinction and relation between propositional truth and truth that is "more than" propositional (what I call *existential truth*). As chapter 5 explains, I use the term *propositional truth* as an umbrella for three distinct but interrelated matters, namely, the reliability of beliefs, the correctness of assertoric speech acts, and the accuracy of propositions. But I hold that there is significantly more to truth than propositional truth. A second issue concerns the relation between propositional truth and the discursive justification of propositional truth claims, as framed in analytic philosophy by debates between epistemic and nonepistemic conceptions of truth. The third issue pertains to the relation between propositional truth and the objectivity of knowledge, often presented in analytic philosophy as a conflict between realists and antirealists over the relation between propo-sitional "truth bearers" (beliefs, assertions, propositions, and the like) and purportedly mind-independent "truth makers" (objects, facts, or states of affairs, for example). Part I (chapters 2 and 3) takes up the first issue; part II (chapters 4 and 5) addresses the second; part III examines the third issue in chapter 6 and, in chapters 7 and 8, indicates how all three issues call for a new and comprehensive conception of truth.

1.1.1 Truth and Propositions
The first issue—the distinction and relation between propositional and existential truth—is both the most controversial for other truth theorists and the most important for someone who wishes to explore a comprehen-sive idea of truth. Martin Heidegger, Max Horkheimer, and Theodor W. Adorno share the intuition that truth in its most comprehensive sense is more than propositional, and they try, in their distinctive ways, to resitu-ate propositional truth within this more comprehensive idea. Their shared intuition becomes a point of contention in the next generation. Whereas Hans-Georg Gadamer rearticulates Heidegger's approach, but in a more

Hegelian manner, Jürgen Habermas restricts truth proper to propositional matters, locating it within a field of three differentiated validity claims: propositional truth (*Wahrheit*), normative legitimacy (*Richtigkeit*), and personal sincerity or authenticity (*Wahrhaftigkeit*).[2]

Many commentators overlook the fact that the intuition Heidegger, Horkheimer, and Adorno share—despite their conflicting accounts of truth—stems in part from Husserlian phenomenology. More specifically, it stems from the conception of truth worked out in Edmund Husserl's *Logical Investigations* (1900–1901). Further, this early work by Husserl provides a shared reference point for prominent French post-Heideggerians such as Emmanuel Levinas and Jacques Derrida. Because of this common source, chapter 2 introduces the issue of propositional and more-than-propositional truth by taking up the conception of truth in Husserl's *Logical Investigations*. First I review critical interpretations of Husserl by three leading post-Heideggerian philosophers: Levinas, Adorno, and Derrida. Next I examine selected passages from the *Logical Investigations*. Then I initiate a critical retrieval of early Husserl's conception of truth, one that not only evaluates his contribution in light of influential assessments by Levinas, Adorno, and Derrida but also proposes revisions to it.

These revisions are indebted in part to the work of Martin Heidegger, whose *Being and Time* (1927) dramatically reconfigures Husserl's phenomenology. The conception of truth proposed in *Being and Time* is both promising and problematic. On the one hand, Heidegger proposes a comprehensive conception that encompasses both propositional and existential truth. On the other hand, he seems to turn attaining truth into the inexplicable privilege of "authentic" existence.

Chapter 3 aims to free Heidegger's insights from their antidemocratic garb. While agreeing with Heidegger that asserting is a mode of interpreting, I take issue with his description of the supposedly derivative character of assertions. Similarly, while endorsing Heidegger's claim that the agreement between assertion and object (what I call *assertoric correctness*) derives from a more comprehensive "disclosedness," I criticize how he traces this derivation. In response, I propose to conceive of truth in general as a process of life-giving disclosure to which a differentiated array of sociocultural practices and products contribute in distinct and indispensable ways. Contra Heidegger, what distinguishes true from false disclosure is not the authenticity with which human beings face the possibility of their own impossibility (their so-called freedom toward death). Rather, it is their life-promoting and life-sustaining fidelity to that which they hold in common and which holds them in common, namely, to societal principles such as justice and solidarity. The pursuit of assertoric correctness or propositional truth is one important but limited way in which such fidelity occurs.

1.1.2 Authentication and Justification

Heidegger's emphasis on authenticity introduces a second issue of contemporary concern, namely, the relation between truth and how truth is borne out. Debates in analytic philosophy typically construe this as the question of how propositional truth relates to the discursive justification of truth claims. Philosophers with an "epistemic" conception argue that the truth of a propositional truth claim depends to a significant degree on whether someone is or can be discursively justified in claiming it. Philosophers with a nonepistemic conception reject this argument, asserting that the truth of a proposition does not and cannot depend on its justification or its justifiability. In *Being and Time*, however, Heidegger frames this issue in much broader terms. He suggests that all truth, both propositional and otherwise, depends on the authenticity (*Eigentlichkeit*) of a mode of existence—in his own language, on the authenticity of Dasein's disclosedness. This implies that, by itself, discursive justification does not suffice to bear out or authenticate truth, not even propositional truth.

Predictably, Heidegger's emphasis on authenticity does not sit well with philosophers who emphasize the *discursive justification* of propositional truth claims, regardless of whether their conception is epistemic or nonepistemic. Nor does it appeal to philosophers such as Horkheimer and Adorno, who, although they have a comprehensive conception of truth, wish to offer a *critical theory* of society. Even Heidegger, not long after he published *Being and Time* in 1927, had second thoughts. By the time he presented his public lecture "On the Essence of Truth" in 1930, which I discuss in chapter 7, Heidegger had begun to replace the notion of authenticity with the idea of letting beings be (*Gelassenheit*).

Nevertheless, Heidegger's "authenticity" points toward a structurally parallel notion in the truth conception of Theodor Adorno, Heidegger's severest critic in the Frankfurt School, namely, the notion of "emphatic experience." So an issue arises, from both sides of the Heidegger/critical theory divide, concerning the relation between truth and how truth is borne out—what I call the *authentication of truth*. Included within this issue, although insufficiently thematized by either Heidegger or Adorno, are questions about how propositional truth relates to discursive justification and how discursive justification relates to the authentication of comprehensive truth.

I take up these questions in chapter 4, where I construct a dialectic between Heidegger's *Being and Time* and Adorno's *Negative Dialectics* (1966, 1967) concerning the authentication of truth. Whereas Heidegger says authentication occurs in the authenticity of human existence (Dasein), Adorno locates the authentication of truth in emphatic experience. Portraying "authenticity" and "emphatic experience" as each other's reverse image, I argue that neither suffices to authenticate truth. Then I offer an alternative account of authentication to draw out the significance of these dialectical extremes. I describe authentication as a comprehensive attestation to truth that cannot be reduced to discursive justification: authentication is an invitational and thereby public enactment of what truth as a whole requires. Yet justification is an inescapable element of authentication. Chapter 4 tries to retain Heidegger and Adorno's concern for the comprehensive authentication of truth without either surrendering the public character of authentication or reducing authentication to discursive practices.

Compared with Adorno and the early Habermas, who together carried out a famous "positivism dispute" with Karl Popper and his students in the 1960s,[3] later critical theorists, including the later Habermas, have been surprisingly receptive to the work of leading analytic and postanalytic philosophers. Their receptivity is apparent, for example, from the title of Habermas's most sustained work on truth theory in recent years: *Truth and Justification* (1999). Whereas Habermas's early writings, such as *The Structural Transformation of the Public Sphere* (1962) and *Knowledge and Human Interests* (1968), had remained close to the unique Hegelian Marxism of the Frankfurt School, Habermas moved away from this when he began to articulate a theory of communicative action and, in that context, addressed the idea of truth. The most important historical point of contact between Habermas and Anglo-American interlocutors such as John Searle, Hilary Putnam, and Richard Rorty lies in pragmatism, especially the work of Charles Sanders Peirce.[4] Habermas shares pragmatism's appreciation for robust political democracy, which requires vigorous deliberation in a vibrant public sphere, and he finds this appreciation lacking not only in Heidegger (to put it mildly) but also in Horkheimer and Adorno.

Chapter 5 takes up the later Habermas's conception of truth in the context of Anglo-American debates about alethic realism and antirealism. After briefly tracing his movement from an antirealist and epistemic consensus theory to what he calls "linguistic-pragmatic epistemological realism," I explore the "Janus-faced" concept of propositional truth in *Truth and Justification*. Then I refine Habermas's conception by distinguishing more clearly than he does between the reliability of beliefs, the correctness of assertions, and the accuracy of propositions. I also suggest a new way to think about the linguistic mediation of facts and the disclosive character of discursive justification. By critically appropriating Habermas's insights, I aim to move beyond the realism–antirealism dispute, replacing questions of *independence* with questions of *interdependence*. I argue that truth theory needs to begin with the interdependence of "mind" and "object" and with the corporeal multidimensionality of both human knowers and that about which they acquire knowledge. A suitably "post-anti/realist" truth theory would offer a new way to understand the contested relation between propositional truth and discursive justification.

1.1.3   Truth and Objectivity

The realism–antirealism debate raises a third central issue in contemporary truth theory, namely, the relation between propositional truth and objective knowledge. The debate often revolves around the question whether purportedly mind-independent "truth makers" are required in order for propositional "truth bearers" to be true. Not surprisingly, this question pervades much of the Anglo-American literature on Husserl's conception of truth. Returning to the *Logical Investigations*, chapter 6 takes up Anglo-American interpretations of early Husserl's conception of truth and explores its significance for the objectivity debate in contemporary analytic truth theory. I argue that his conception unsettles a common polarity between epistemic and nonepistemic approaches. Unlike contemporary epistemic conceptions of truth, Husserl gives full weight to truth makers that have their own being: perceptible objects, objective identity, and states of affairs. Yet, unlike contemporary nonepistemic conceptions, he also insists on the intentional givenness of such truth makers and on the complexity of the experiences within which propositional truth claims arise.

To develop this argument, the chapter shows that early Husserl does not regard evidence in the strict sense as what justifies belief, nor does he restrict truth to propositions. The conception of truth that he proposes, with its emphasis on an objective identity between what is signitively meant and intuitively given, provides an opening beyond the impasse between epistemic and nonepistemic conceptions. Like Habermas, although in quite a different way, Husserl points toward a post-anti/realist conception of propositional truth. Indeed, the relation early Husserl posits between propositional "correctness" (*Richtigkeit*) and objective "identity" (*Identität*) allows one to regard the concept of propositional truth as part of a more comprehensive idea of truth, as suggested in chapter 2.

Chapter 7 examines what such a comprehensive idea of truth might come to. I discuss seminal essays from the 1930s by founding figures in the two post-Husserlian traditions this book explores: Martin Heidegger's "On the Essence of Truth" from 1930, and Max Horkheimer's "On the Problem of Truth" from 1935. Whereas Heidegger wonders how a postmetaphysical philosophy can disclose the meaning of Being, Horkheimer asks how a critical social theory can contribute to societal transformation.

Introducing their essays with a quote from Hegel's *Phenomenology of Spirit*, the chapter constructs a dialectical dialogue between them, suggesting that each offers insights the other lacks. Then I rework these insights into a comprehensive idea of truth as a dynamic correlation between human fidelity to societal principles and a life-giving disclosure of society. I suggest that propositional truth plays an important role in this dynamic correlation, yet truth in its most comprehensive sense cannot be reduced to propositional matters. Likewise, discursive justification makes important contributions to the authentication of truth, but authentication cannot be reduced to discursive practices. Indeed, viable accounts of propositional truth, discursive justification, and the objectivity of knowledge require a comprehensive conception of truth and authentication. That is what Heidegger and Horkheimer understood, each in his own way. As the conclusion (chapter 8) shows in greater detail, the most important contributions of Heideggerian thinking and the Frankfurt School to contemporary truth theory lie in this shared, albeit contested, understanding of truth.

1.2 Significance

1.2.1 Role

In attempting to recover this shared understanding, I do not aim to give a full-blown account of the comprehensive conception of truth toward which my critical retrieval points. Yet the project of critical retrieval can play a crucial role in the development of such a conception, in three respects.

First, no new conception on a topic as central to Western philosophy as truth is can spring fully armed, like Minerva, from a philosopher's Jupiterian brow. It must emerge from the interplay among different traditions and positions. Within this interplay, academic integrity and philosophical transparency require that one reflect on the sources of one's own conception. If one wants to advance the conversation on a topic like truth, and not simply repeat what others have said, then one needs to sort out both insights and blind spots in these sources.

A good way to do this, it seems to me, is to come to grips with texts and arguments that have proved highly generative both within another philosopher's life work and within the philosophical traditions one inhabits. Because how I think about truth is heavily indebted to twentieth-century German continental philosophy, the current book gives special attention to a few seminal works in this tradition, including Husserl's *Logical Investigations*, Heidegger's *Being and Time*, and Adorno's *Negative Dialectics*. It does not try to address the entire range of writings on the topic of truth by each of these philosophers, nor does it try to uncover historical sources in nineteenth-century philosophy, not to mention Kant and pre-Kantian philosophers. In this sense, my critical retrieval does not intend to be a historical narrative. It singles out writings whose contributions I consider both seminal and salient for a comprehensive conception of truth.

Second, the project of critical retrieval can help address the greatest challenges that face any contemporary attempt to offer a comprehensive conception of truth. Critical retrieval allows one to explore ideas, learn from disagreements, and test the validity of arguments, all with a view to finding alternative formulations.

The desire to address such challenges provides an important reason why the current book often proceeds by constructing dialectical dialogues. Methodologically, I assume that opposition between two philosophical positions on the same topic points toward potential insights one might miss if one attended to either position alone. Where the philosophers under consideration have not already articulated their opposition, then one does well to construct a debate between them, not only to bring out areas of agreement and disagreement but also to discover how each position might offer insights that the other lacks. Such dialectical construction gives one a better grasp of both positions, and it can lead to a richer articulation of one's own position, whether in partial or full agreement with one of the positions or as an alternative to both. By itself, the construction of dialectical dialogues does not yield a complete account of one's own conception on the topic in dispute. Yet it does serve as a philosophical laboratory where one can discover or rediscover the contours of one's emerging conception and can explore its potential in response to a nexus of problems (*Problematik*) among one's philosophical sources.

The project of critical retrieval does more than sort out one's sources and look for potential insights, however. In the third place, it also lets one examine the contemporary relevance of these sources and of the conception one dialectically derives from them. A deep divide between continental and analytic philosophy and ongoing attempts to bridge it currently structure the landscape of Anglophone philosophy. Those who wish to move past this divide, as I do, must consider what each side offers that the other side needs. More specifically, if the primary sources for one's conception of truth lie on the continental side, then one needs to ask what these sources offer to analytic truth theories. Accordingly, the critical retrieval pursued in this book identifies three issues of relevance for contemporary truth theories—propositional and existential truth, propositional truth and discursive justification, and truth and objectivity—and asks what twentieth-century German continental philosophy might contribute to an understanding of these issues.

This suggests that the project of critical retrieval does not pursue a merely antiquarian interest. Neither, however, does it simply extract a few nuggets of insight from continental writings and then logically refine them outside of immersion in the texts and arguments where such insights might reside. In other words, it tries to avoid two manners of doing philosophy that, in my judgment, reinforce the so-called continental divide in contemporary Anglophone philosophy. One of these I call the *sycophantic style*, which simply repeats what the masters have said. There is a constant temptation in continental philosophy to do exactly that, turning "big figures" like Heidegger and Adorno into sacred gurus and their commentators into uncritical acolytes. The opposite trap, perhaps more common in analytic philosophy, is to be constantly on the attack, not looking for worthwhile insights among thinkers outside one's own circle, and seldom acknowledging what one has learned from those whom one criticizes. This *idiopathic idiom*, if I may call it that, continually turns potential contributions into grist for the critic's own argumentative mill. Although the critical retrieval in this book pays close attention to the writings of prominent German philosophers, and although it tries to sort out arguments and counterarguments, it aims to avoid both the sycophantic style and the idiopathic idiom. It tries instead to point toward an alternative conception of truth that has relevance for both sides of the contemporary divide in Anglophone philosophy.

So I regard critical retrieval as a crucial stage in the development of a comprehensive conception of truth. By selectively focusing on generative writings, a critical retrieval helps uncover important ideas about truth in German continental philosophy. By constructing dialectical dialogues, it helps establish the potential fruitfulness and validity of these ideas. And by attuning the discussion to issues in contemporary truth theory, it probes the potential relevance of the comprehensive conception toward which it points.

1.2.2 Scope

One could acknowledge all of these advantages yet remain unconvinced that the project as I have described it has the proper scope. On the one hand, my proposed critical retrieval might seem insufficiently attentive to the vast literature, both primary and secondary, that surrounds the authors and works I have singled out for attention. On the other hand, by discussing five major figures and several of their most difficult and complex works, I might seem to risk not delving with sufficient depth into any one. Further, one could easily argue that other twentieth-century authors and works should be included, such as Walter Benjamin or Herbert Marcuse or Hans-Georg Gadamer, or that one cannot really understand twentieth-century contributions without taking up such precursors as Kant, Hegel, and Nietzsche. In other words, the proposed critical retrieval might seem overly narrow, overly broad, or historically superficial.

My first response to such worries is simply to say, "Guilty as charged." Although the chapters in this book address some of the secondary literature, refer to other writings by each primary author, and point occasionally to important contemporaries and historical precursors, I do not aim for comprehensive coverage in any of these respects. Anyone who expects such coverage will be disappointed. Whether the more limited coverage

I do provide is adequate, readers will need to judge for themselves. The proof, as they say, is in the pudding. Or, to paraphrase what Adorno said in a different context: one's performance legitimates one's method, and that precludes the supposition of a method.[5]

My second response is to explain the model for my approach. My model is neither commentary nor historiography but rather a text-based imma-nent critique. More specifically, I aim to carry out what my first book on Adorno described as immanent criticism with metacritical intent.[6] Taking all five primary authors to be wrestling with the same "problematic" of truth as a comprehensive idea, I try to uncover the issues this idea raises *within* their most seminal writings on the topic, gradually weaving my own responses into a proto-conception both indebted to these writings and critical of them. In a critical retrieval, as I envision it, "immanent critique becomes metacritique—a combination, often precarious, of dependence upon, and transcendence of, the object of criticism."[7]

In taking this approach, the current book has affinities with a number of other studies that try to reclaim crucial insights into truth or closely related concepts from one or more of the five philosophers I discuss. I think, for example, of Pierre Keller's careful examination of the notions of experi-ence in Husserl and Heidegger that sorts out connections between their conceptions of truth as well as problems in Heidegger's conception.[8] I also think of the ambitious attempt by Nikolas Kompridis to reclaim a Heideg-gerian notion of world disclosure in order to develop a more robust critical theory than what Habermas provides.[9] Also, a number of Heidegger schol-ars in recent years have provided lucid and illuminating reconstructions of his conception of truth that rescue it from the most telling objections and demonstrate its relevance for contemporary philosophy. Mark Wrathall, for example, not only shows the notion of truth as unconcealment (*Unverbor-genheit*) to be a guiding thread through the labyrinth of Heidegger's earlier and later writings but also brings it into productive dialogue with contribu-tions by analytic philosophers such as Donald Davidson.[10] Denis McManus uncovers the roots of Heidegger's conception of truth in Husserl's *Logical Investigations* and explores many illuminating points of contact with the later Wittgenstein, while taking issue with the pragmatist interpretations of Heidegger that have become common in Anglo-American philosophy.[11] One could easily expand this list to include books on closely related top-ics by such Heidegger scholars as William Blattner, Steven Crowell, John

Haugeland, and Stephen Mulhall.[12] The current project has benefited greatly from such studies.

I know of no previous attempts, however, to bring Husserl, Heidegger, Horkheimer, Adorno, and Habermas together in one study devoted to the topic of truth.[13] No doubt there are many reasons for this, including the complexity of each author's contributions, the historic tensions among them, and the difficulties of making their contributions intelligible to a wider audience. Nevertheless, there are two compelling sorts of reasons to make an attempt. One is historical in character; the other is more systematic.

Historically, it makes a great deal of sense to see the contributions of both Heidegger and the Frankfurt School as critical outworkings of Husserlian phenomenology. While Heidegger's uneasy indebtedness to Husserl is beyond doubt, Husserlian phenomenology is in fact an important historical source of critical theory as well. Horkheimer, Adorno, and Marcuse, the three most influential philosophers in the Frankfurt School, each engaged with Edmund Husserl's thought as a significant alternative to the neo-Kantianism that dominated their German philosophical environment.[14]

Herbert Marcuse underwent the most obvious influence, having studied in Freiburg with both Husserl and Heidegger, and having continued to cite and write on Husserl much later into his career. Marcuse's 1932 Habilitationsschrift on Hegel's ontology[15] is clearly indebted to the work of his mentor Martin Heidegger. Adorno, however, writing in the first volume of the Frankfurt School's journal of record, thought the book decisively deviated from Heidegger's teachings, moving away "from the 'meaning of Being' to the disclosure of beings, from fundamental ontology to philosophy of history [*Geschichtsphilosophie*], from historicity to history."[16]

Theodor W. Adorno wrote his doctoral dissertation on Husserl during the early 1920s, resumed this work at Oxford University in the 1930s, published an article on Husserl in the *Journal of Philosophy* in 1940, and incorporated much of this into his 1956 *Zur Metakritik der Erkenntnistheorie*.[17] For Adorno, Husserl's importance lay in having pushed bourgeois philosophy to its breaking point, just as Arnold Schoenberg had done for Western concert music.

Max Horkheimer's interest in Husserlian phenomenology, while shorterlived than Adorno's, was more than a passing fancy. He first met Adorno when Horkheimer gave a paper on Husserl in Hans Cornelius's seminar in the early 1920s. On Cornelius's recommendation, Horkheimer then went to Freiburg to study with Husserl for two semesters. While at Freiburg, Hork-heimer also attended Heidegger's seminar, famously writing to a friend, "Heidegger is one of the most significant personalities who spoke to me." In a later interview, however, Horkheimer said he was "more impressed by Husserl."[18] Horkheimer's papers on Husserl during the 1920s show that he deeply admired Husserl as a critic of positivism, relativism, and scientism. Hence it is not surprising that two decades later *Dialectic of Enlightenment* quotes from the published portion of Husserl's *The Crisis of European Sciences* to support Horkheimer and Adorno's critical diagnosis of the modern reification of thought.[19]

Like Heidegger, then, Horkheimer and Adorno regarded Husserl as having made the most important contemporary attempt to overcome the aporias of neo-Kantianism. Critical theory is, in part, the "offspring" of that attempt. Hence it makes sense historically to look for both continuity and conflict among these philosophers on the topic of truth. Moreover, the fact that Jürgen Habermas, the most prominent philosopher in the second generation of critical theory, arrives at his own truth theory via criticisms of not only Heidegger but also Horkheimer and Adorno, makes the historical rationale even stronger.[20]

At this point, however, the historical rationale shades into a more systematic set of reasons. On my view, the idea of truth makes up a pervasive problematic (*Problematik*) in philosophy since the 1900s, and this problematic has specific contours among the conflicted offspring of Husserlian phenomenology. By "a problematic" I mean that the idea of truth is a historically evolving set of interlocking issues, issues that are not easily resolved and that continue to call for resolution. One can indicate the issues at stake by way of the polarities that often frame philosophical debates about them: realism versus antirealism, for example, and objectivism versus relativism,[21] and idealism versus (historical) materialism.[22]

My own systematic understanding of philosophy suggests that one needs a holistic and pluralist conception of truth to address these issues. I find this suggestion both provoked and borne out by Husserl, Heidegger, and the Frankfurt School. Hence, in uncovering the alethic issues that arise in their most seminal works, I hope to develop and deepen a conception that can address the interlocked issues at stake in the idea of truth. To do this, I have selected writings that particularly merit such systematic attention, with a special emphasis on Husserl's *Logical Investigations* and Heidegger's *Being and Time*. For both historical and systematic reasons, then, it makes sense to focus on these authors and these works. The history of German continental philosophy since 1900 and the prospects for an adequate contemporary conception of truth come together in the problematic they articulate.

1.2.3   Relevance

I am under no illusions about the prospects for this admittedly ambitious undertaking. Many contemporary philosophers—too many, unfortunately—think either the analytic or the continental tradition has little of worth to offer the other side. Moreover, many contemporary philosophers—surprisingly many, I would say—find the idea of truth either unimportant or ideologically suspect. If all of them were right, then the envisioned retrieval of insights into truth from German continental philosophy would be pointless. Its aim to be relevant would be irrelevant, and its dialectically reconstructive efforts would be either unimportant or ideologically suspect.

Short of providing the expansive account of truth toward which my critical retrieval points, I probably cannot give an adequate response to such reservations. Nevertheless, let me offer three sets of reasons why it is relevant to attempt a tradition-crossing critical retrieval. All of these reasons have to do with the importance of truth itself.

In the first place, the idea of truth is central to philosophy and, more broadly, to academic endeavors. A primary purpose of scholarly pursuits has been—and, for many scholars, continues to be—to seek and understand the truth. If this is so, then it is worthwhile to figure out what can count as truth and why truth merits our scholarly efforts. All of the philosophers highlighted in this book—Husserl, Heidegger, Horkheimer, Adorno, and Habermas—understand this point, even though they have different conceptions of truth as well as different critical stances toward Western philosophy and toward established academic institutions. To the extent that the pursuit of truth remains a leading and legitimate purpose for doing academic work and for having academic institutions, it is worth one's while to consider the contributions these philosophers have made and to recover their insights for a comprehensive conception of truth.

In the second place, the idea of truth has significant ramifications beyond the academy in other practices and institutions of public life. Despite widespread disillusionment over the prospects for personal integrity in a highly mediatized society, for example, people still expect truthfulness from their closest colleagues and intimate acquaintances, and they express disappointment when their expectations are not met. Similarly, we are not always satisfied with mere "truthiness" from our journalists, politicians, and courts of law but hold them to higher standards of "truth." So too, conflicts among religious adherents and between various religions usually involve opposing claims to revealed truth, even though one cannot reduce the political and economic dimensions of these conflicts to such claims. Moreover, many debates concerning cultural and legal authority in education, health care, and environmental policy involve conflicts over which institutions and practices have a better claim to truth: Religion or science? Traditional or alternative medicine? Business corporations or government agencies?

The philosophers discussed in this book recognize such societal ramifications to the idea of truth. They understand that debates about the idea of truth are not merely academic exercises. They also recognize the pressures placed on this idea by political, economic, and technological forces.[23] If one agrees that truth is important in public life, then it makes sense to attempt a critical retrieval of their insights on this topic.

Third, the idea of truth has played a leading role in the development of Western culture since antiquity. Together with closely related ideas such as justice and freedom, it has entered the self-understanding of those who inhabit this culture, and it has decisively shaped modern and contemporary aspirations for a democratic society.[24] The idea of truth has also provided a focal point for critiques of Western culture and for resistance to antidemocratic tendencies. In all of these ways, it has acquired great historical significance, not only as a legacy that participants in Western culture can ill afford to ignore but also as a normative guideline for sociocultural transformation in the future.

Because Husserl and his successors understand such historical significance, they consider philosophical debates about truth to be culturally important. Their various attempts to specify what truth is and why it matters belong to larger critiques of Western culture. To the extent that their cultural criticisms are on target, and to the extent that these criticisms revolve around their conceptions of truth, their insights into truth merit careful scrutiny by anyone who thinks philosophy should contribute to the critique and renewal of Western culture.

Hence I think the proposed critical retrieval is relevant because the idea of truth is important, and it is important for academic, societal, and cultural reasons. Of course, anyone who is conversant with contemporary philosophy will recognize that many fellow philosophers doubt whether their work either can or should make significant contributions to the wider academy, to public life, and to Western culture. Such doubts help constitute the current crisis in philosophy itself, a crisis signaled a few decades ago by the title of an illuminating anthology: *Philosophy: End or Transformation?*[25] I am convinced that philosophy, as practiced and institutionalized in the Western academy, needs to be transformed, and that the transformation of philosophy is significant for cultural and societal change. Central to the transformation I envision would be a revitalized conception of truth. My critical retrieval of German continental philosophy serves the pursuit of a transformed and transforming idea of truth.

I Truth and Propositions

2 Propositional and Existential Truth: Edmund Husserl

"Philosophy" … stands for the idea of orienting human life as a whole toward truth.
—Ernst Tugendhat[1]

Ernst Tugendhat has claimed that Edmund Husserl's conception of truth offers an important alternative to two divergent tendencies in recent philosophy. On the one hand, many analytic philosophers are content with a minimalist notion of propositional truth, along the lines of Alfred Tarski's formula "'p' is true if and only if p." According to Tugendhat, formulas like this are "precise and pertinent [*zutreffend*], but trivial." They do not explicate the correspondence between proposition and fact that they nonetheless assume. As a result, they obstruct any inquiry into "a possible expansion of the concept of truth beyond the narrower domain of propositional truth [*Aussagewahrheit*]."[2]

On the other hand, continental philosophers who expand the concept of truth beyond the propositional end up with such vague and indeterminate conceptions that they cannot adequately account for the usual notion of propositional truth. Martin Heidegger, for example, with his conceptions of disclosedness (*Erschlossenheit*) and unconcealment (*Unverborgenheit*), expands the concept of truth to encompass all of human comportment (*Verhalten*), making truth "practical, historical, existentiell."[3] But, according to Tugendhat, Heidegger never gives a satisfactory answer to the question: Exactly how does this expanded concept relate to propositional truth?

Hence contemporary truth theory separates into two divergent tendencies: a precise and pertinent specification of propositional truth that is constricted, trivial, and tautological; and a properly expansive approach to truth that is vague and insufficiently specific about propositional truth. Tugendhat considers both tendencies highly problematic. Each in its own way surrenders "the idea of critical responsibility," he claims.[4] And this idea is central to philosophy itself: "'Philosophy,' in the broadest and ... most original sense of the word, stands for the idea of orienting human life as a whole toward truth, i.e., for the idea of living in critical responsibility."[5]

Tugendhat thinks Husserl's phenomenological conception of truth has the potential to take us past this impasse. For Husserl's explication of propositional truth makes possible "a deliberate [*schrittweise*] and critically testable [*kontrollierbare*] expansion" toward existential truth, toward truth as it is lived in true friendships and truthful conduct, for example, and not simply as it is asserted. Even though Husserl does not really account for the relationships among truth, history, and human practices (*Praxis*), "for the first time since German idealism" Husserl understands human life in its entirety as "oriented to truth," and he regards philosophy as "the radicalization of this relation to truth [*Wahrheitsbezug*]."[6]

Tugendhat first published his study in 1967, having successfully submitted it one year earlier as a Habilitationsschrift to the University of Tübingen's Faculty of Philosophy. Although the divergence he noted then has not disappeared, a similar description today would need to be more complicated. After the 1960s, minimalism about truth in analytic philosophy diversified into deflationism and pluralism, and Heideggerian expansionism gave way to Derridean deconstruction and Habermasian critical theory. Moreover, the revival of pragmatism and the development of feminism and other forms of liberatory theory make the contemporary "truthscape" much more colorful than the one Tugendhat described. Nevertheless, the challenge he posed has not gone away. Perhaps, likewise, Husserl's phenomenological conception of truth has retained its potential as a way to address this challenge.

That, at least, is what this chapter explores. I plan to ask whether, and to what extent, Husserl's conception of truth can help philosophers connect the concept of propositional truth with a more comprehensive, life-oriented idea of truth, without short-circuiting either side.

My focus is on the account Husserl gives in his early two-volume work *Logical Investigations* (1900–1901).[7] Despite the refinements, revisions, and rearticulations Husserl offers in subsequent writings such as *Ideas I* (1913) and *Formal and Transcendental Logic* (1929), the account of truth in the *Logical Investigations* provides the core to his conception.[8] This account is also a crucial source for Heidegger's expansive conception of truth, as has been pointed out not only by Tugendhat but also by more recent commentators such as Daniel Dahlstrom.[9]

I do not intend merely to exegete Husserl's text, however. I try to begin a critical retrieval. To explain what I mean by "critical retrieval," and to position my interpretation within a wider field of reception, I first summarize critical readings of Husserl by three influential post-Heideggerian philosophers: Levinas, Adorno, and Derrida.[10] Then I examine selected passages in Husserl's *Logical Investigations*. Finally, based on this examination, I discuss the contributions and limitations of early Husserl's conception of truth.

2.1   Post-Heideggerian Criticisms

Strikingly, three of the most influential post-Heideggerian philosophers have taken up the conception of truth in the *Logical Investigations*, within wider engagements with Husserl that helped establish their own philosophical programs. Emmanuel Levinas, who had recently studied with Husserl and Heidegger in Freiburg, published *The Theory of Intuition in Husserl's Phenomenology* in 1930 and reissued it in 1963. In France at the time, his short monograph was one of the first systematic interpretations of Husserl's published writings.[11] Theodor Adorno, who had completed a Frankfurt University doctoral dissertation on Husserl in 1924,[12] began a new monograph in the mid-1930s on the "antinomies" in Husserlian phenomenology. Intended as a doctoral dissertation to be submitted at Oxford University under the direction of Gilbert Ryle, it was completed and published in 1956, under the title *Zur Metakritik der Erkenntnistheorie: Studien über Husserl und die phänomenologischen Antinomien*, and later translated into English under the misleading title *Against Epistemology*.[13] Jacques Derrida published *Speech and Phenomena*, his critique of Husserl's theory of meaning, a decade later, in 1967,[14] in the same year as Derrida's *Of Grammatology* and one year after Adorno's extensive critique of Heideggerian ontology in *Negative Dialectics*. Each philosopher has his own angle of approach.[15]

2.1.1   Emmanuel Levinas

Levinas offers the most sympathetic reading, giving an immanent interpretation of Husserl's published writings[16] while raising reservations along the way. Clearly indebted to Heidegger's work in the 1920s, especially *Sein und Zeit*, Levinas interprets Husserl's project as an attempt to understand

the meaning of being and to uncover the ontological basis for both epistemology and the phenomenological method. As Levinas says with respect
to Husserl's concern about the transcendental constitution of the world,
"knowledge of Heidegger's starting point may allow us to understand better Husserl's end point." Even Husserl's early attacks on psychologism and
naturalism aim to arrive at a new conception of being, Levinas claims.[17]

This implies, in turn, that the concept of truth presented in Husserl's
Logical Investigations is not simply an epistemological or logical concept.
Rather, it is at bottom an ontological concept. It pertains to the being of
the intuited objects toward which judgments and other signitive acts are
aimed: "Truth does not become possible with judgment; on the contrary,
judgments presuppose the primary phenomenon of truth, which consists in
facing being. ... Making a judgment about an object is only a new mode of
facing it." According to Levinas, Husserl found this "primary phenomenon"
in "intuition ... as an intentionality which reaches being."[18] In transforming
the notion of truth, Husserl simultaneously transforms the notion of being,
turning it into "nothing other than the correlate of our intuitive life."[19]

Levinas's main reservation about this transformation is that Husserl continues to regard intuition as "a theoretical act," such that his concept of
intuition—and, by implication, his concepts of being and truth—is intel-
lectualistic and "possibly too narrow." This can give rise to a charge of logicism that Levinas considers misplaced.[20] In the book's conclusion, Levinas
states that Husserl's purported logicism or his purported scientism is not the
source of such intellectualism. The problem is not that Husserl privileges
logic or takes geometry and the natural sciences as the model for philosophical inquiry, but rather that he makes philosophy seem "as independent
of the historical situation of man [*sic*] as any theory that tries to consider
everything *sub specie aeternitatis.*"[21] Husserl's intellectualism concerning
intuition stems from his ahistorical conception of human existence.

2.1.2   Theodor W. Adorno

Adorno is among the critics who charge Husserl with logicism. His monograph on Husserl aims to uncover the antinomies in Husserl's thought in
order to elicit the ideological character and societal role of philosophical
idealism. As he says up front, "Husserl's philosophy is the occasion and
not the point of this book."[22] Rather, the point is to uncover and move
beyond the antinomies of idealism that return in Husserl's phenomenology

and remain under disguise in Heidegger's ontology. By "idealism" Adorno means a philosophy that affirms an identity between subject and object, thereby assigning constitutive priority to the epistemic subject. He regards idealism as the dominant philosophical ideology in capitalist society since Descartes, and he implicitly juxtaposes it with historical materialism as he understands and pursues it. Adorno sees Husserl's unfolding philosophical project as a dogged but failed attempt to transcend idealism idealistically.[23]

The first step along this path is what Adorno calls the "logical absolutism" of Husserl's *Logical Investigations*. Noticing what Levinas describes as intellectualism, Adorno says that a philosophy like Husserl's, which regards science as the ideal for human thought, cannot avoid the tensions that arise when it tries to remain philosophical. These tensions give expression to underlying tensions in capitalist society. More specifically, Husserl absolutizes the products of formal logic and thereby inadvertently, yet effectively, both expresses and ratifies the larger societal process of reification that Georg Lukács, updating Marx's critique of commodity fetishism, diagnosed in the 1920s.[24] Like the bourgeois economist who treats commodities as freestanding things and forgets their origins in human labor, Husserl turns highly formal propositions into irreducible "states of affairs," ignoring their historical origins, social context, and existential meaning, and then treats all phenomena in a similar fashion: "Logical axioms, elevated to propositions in themselves, offer the model of fact-free, pure essences [*Wesenheiten*] whose grounding and description phenomenology as a whole chose as its task and equated with the concept of philosophy."[25]

According to Adorno, Husserl's logical absolutism generates a highly problematic conception of truth.[26] On the one hand, Husserl formalizes and isolates the subject's contribution to truth, turning it into supposedly pure propositional "truths" that float free from any sociohistorically mediated experience and become ideal essences. On the other hand, the objectivity of truth, which Husserl labors mightily to preserve, gets reduced to the internal contents of consciousness. The sociohistorical mediations of both subject and object go missing, along with the dialectical character of their interrelation, making it impossible to conceive of truth as a "force field" (*Kraftfeld*) or "constellation." Husserl, he says, "sees only a rigid choice between the empirical, contingent subject and the absolutely necessary ideal law, purified of all facticity. He fails to see that truth does not emerge in either the one or the other, but it is a constellation of moments that cannot be reckoned as a 'residuum' of [either] the subjective or the objective side."[27]

2.1.3 Jacques Derrida

Whereas Levinas applauds Husserl's emphasis on intuition but worries about his intellectualism, Adorno highlights and rejects Husserl's "logical absolutism," but mostly ignores his emphasis on sensuous intuition.[28] Derrida, by contrast, takes issue with the entire "metaphysics of presence" that, on his interpretation, permeates Husserl's phenomenology, including his accounts of intuition, logic, and truth. Husserl's concepts of "sense, ideality, objectivity, truth, intuition, perception, and expression" have a "common matrix," Derrida says, namely, "being as *presence*: the absolute proximity of self-identity, the being-in-front of the object available for repetition, the maintenance of the temporal present, whose ideal form is the self-presence of transcendental *life*, whose ideal identity allows *idealiter* of infinite repetition. The living present ... is thus the conceptual foundation of phenomenology as metaphysics."[29] Accordingly, contra Levinas, the intuitionist side to Husserl's conception of truth is not to be celebrated, and, contra Adorno, the logicist side is not to be highlighted. For Derrida, both Husserl's emphasis on intuition and his apparent privileging of logic stem from his prior attachment to the traditional Western metaphysical and epistemological project of anchoring meaning, especially linguistic meaning, in the subject's direct relation to an ever-present object. The guiding norm of Husserl's phenomenology in general, and of his concept of truth in particular, is "knowledge, the intuition that is adequate to its object, the evidence that is not only distinct but also 'clear.' It is the full presence of sense to a consciousness that is itself self-present in the fullness of its life, its living present."[30] To uncover this norm, and to show why it is deeply problematic, Derrida deconstructs Husserl's theory of signs (*Zeichen*), tracing this theory back to the *Logical Investigations*, the text where it first takes shape.[31]

Although, like Adorno, Derrida is critical of Husserl's conception of truth, neither he nor Adorno actually discusses the Sixth Investigation's chapter on truth and evidence (chapter 5). In fact, Derrida never cites this Investigation, the longest of the six, where Husserl offers "Elements of a Phenomenological Elucidation of Knowledge." That omission points to an important difference between Adorno and Derrida. Whereas Adorno criticizes Husserl's *Logical Investigations* for absolutizing the products of formal logic and thereby cutting them off from actual subjects and objects, Derrida, referring specifically to Husserl's later *Formal and Transcendental Logic* (1929), suggests that Husserl's "pure logical grammar" is overly tied to a subject–object relation.[32] Perhaps one can summarize the difference here between Derrida and Adorno as follows: Derrida appears to reject the epistemological project *tout court*, but Adorno wishes to transform it via a metacritique. In that sense, Adorno remains closer to Levinas, the only one who actually discusses Husserl's chapter on truth and evidence, and does so at some length.[33]

We see, then, that Levinas, Adorno, and Derrida provide three markedly different, indeed, three mutually incompatible interpretations of Husserl's conception of truth: as intuitionist, as logicist, and as outright metaphysical, respectively. Nor does any one of these prominent post-Heideggerian philosophers refer to the interpretations of the other two.[34] This history of reception complicates the task of someone who wishes to explore whether Husserl's conception of truth in the *Logical Investigations* can help us face the challenge posed by Tugendhat, that is, to offer a precise and defensible conception of propositional truth in conjunction with a more comprehensive and life-oriented idea of truth that is neither disconnected from propositional truth nor impossibly vague. One needs not only to contend with conflicting interpretations by three prominent post-Heideggerian philosophers but also to take seriously the critical worry that unites all three, namely, that, in the end, Husserl did not really break away from a primarily propositional conception of truth, and therefore he either accepted the metaphysical underpinnings of propositional truth as traditionally understood (Derrida) or failed to expand the concept of truth in the direction of historical human practices (Levinas) or sociohistorical tendencies (Adorno).

Confronting this complex hermeneutical situation, I propose to initiate a critical retrieval. A critical retrieval tries to reclaim crucial insights from a previous philosopher's thought by responding to legitimate criticisms raised by others. In the case of early Husserl's conception of truth, this involves closely reading the relevant texts and evaluating their contribution in light of assessments by others. It also requires a critical evaluation of the objections and worries others have raised. In what follows I take up representative passages in the *Logical Investigations* and partially respond to the readings of Husserl by Levinas, Adorno, and Derrida. My wider purpose, however, is to work toward a redemptive critique of Husserl's conception of truth, a critique simultaneously indebted to his conception and critical of it, by sorting out the objections raised by other philosophers who share a similar debt.

2.2   Phenomenology of Knowledge

Husserl's conception of truth in the *Logical Investigations* implies criticisms of three tendencies that were prevalent in his context, especially among empiricists and neo-Kantians. First, the prevalent conceptions of truth restrict it to judgments and propositions. Second, they give a psychologizing account of judgments and do not understand the intentionality of human experience. Third, they ignore the truth of that which makes judgments and propositions true. To resist these prevalent tendencies, and to offer a more robust conception of truth, Husserl develops a multidimensional account of intentional acts, including nonjudgmental and nonpropositional acts of intuition. He ties the notion of propositional truth to the intentional experience of truth. And he insists that the object *meant* when one passes a judgment about it must also be *given* in the right way, a givenness that, in itself, is not propositional.

2.2.1   Meaning

As Derrida rightly points out, Husserl launches his phenomenological account of knowledge and truth from the discussion of "Expression and Meaning" in his First Investigation.[35] Husserl conceives of meaning as the ideal correlate to an intentional relation between a conscious act and its object. Linguistic expressions have meaning insofar as they function within such a relation. To say they "have meaning," however, can be ambiguous. For Husserl, this does not mean that an expression manifests the actual experience of the person who uses it, even though the use of an expression can do that. Rather, the meaning an expression expresses is its ideal content: what it says (*besagt*) regardless of who uses it and on what occasion. Moreover, by way of this meaning, this ideal content, an expression refers to the "objective correlate" (*Gegenständlichkeit*) that is meant in the meaning and is expressed by means of this meaning ("die in der Bedeutung gemeinte und mittels ihrer ausgedrückte *Gegenständlichkeit*," LU II.1, 52; LI 1, 197). So the meaning of an expression is the combination of what it says (its ideal content) and its referring to an objective correlate—roughly the combination of what Frege distinguished as "sense" and "reference."[36]

To further establish the meaning of "meaning," however, Husserl also distinguishes "meaning-intention" (*Bedeutungsintention*) from "meaning-fulfillment" (*Bedeutungserfüllung*). We can use an expression to mean something, and in meaning something, we can refer to an object. Yet the expression's relation to an object can be unfulfilled—the expression can function in an act of mere meaning-intention. For the relation to be fulfilled, the expression must function within an act that gives it its object, and this can only be an intuitively based act of meaning-fulfillment. Everything in Husserl's account of meaning hangs on his distinguishing between meaning-intentions (*Bedeutungsintentionen*) that are intuitively empty (*anschauungsleer*) and those that are intuitively fulfilled, between meaning-conferring acts (*bedeutungsverleihende Akte*) and meaning-fulfilling acts (*bedeutungserfüllende Akte*), between meaning-intention and meaning-fulfillment. It is, he says, a "fundamental distinction" (LU II.1, 44; LI 1, 192).

Applying such distinctions to the cognitive usage of language, one can summarize Husserl's preliminary account of meaning as follows. Although we often use words and grammatical constructions to gain knowledge about various matters, the use of language does not suffice. The employment of language in acts of meaning-intention does not, in and of itself, provide cognitive access to the subject matter we wish to grasp. For this, we need intuitive acts of perception or imagination that can function in correlation with meaning-intentions within acts of meaning-fulfillment. Only in conjunction with intuitive, meaning-fulfilling acts can our use of linguistic expressions provide cognitive access to the referents of our language usage—synthetic linguistic-intuitive access, if you will, both to objects as actually perceived or imagined and to their ideal correlates. As we shall see, a coinciding of meaning-intention with meaning-fulfillment provides the core to Husserl's conception of truth. The background to this conception resides in his accounts of intentional experience, meaning-fulfillment, and intuitive fullness.

2.2.2 Intentional Experience

What Husserl calls "intentional experience" (*intentionales Erlebnis*) is the main topic of Investigation Five. Human experience is intentional, he says, insofar as it is an experience *of something* toward which it is *aimed or directed* (LU II.1, 391–393; LI 2, 101–102). Our conscious experience of feeling or wishing or perceiving, for example, is directed toward some object. What we experience can be called intentional objects. How we experience them is in intentional acts such as feeling, wishing, and perceiving.

To account for such acts, Husserl introduces two specifications: the *quality* of an act and the *matter* of an act. Taken together the quality and matter of an act make up its intentional *essence*. The quality of an act is what distinguishes it as the type of act it is, whether, for example, it is an act of feeling or of wishing or of perceiving. Quality pertains to its "general act-character" (LU II.1, 425; LI 2, 119). The matter of an act pertains to its content or "mode of objective reference" (LU II.1, 427; LI 2, 120). The matter of an act is what both "gives it reference to an object" and determines "the precise way" in which the object is intended: "The matter ... not only determines *that* [the act] grasps the object but also *as what* it grasps it" (LU II.1, 429–430; LI 2, 121).[37] Hence, for example, the quality of the act of my seeing a green house would be its being an act of perception, not an act of imagination or judgment. The matter of this act would be its perceptual content—the way in which the house presents itself (e.g., visually) and as what it is presented (as perceptually green, not red, for example, and as a house, not a car).

The quality–matter distinction lets one see how acts that differ in quality can have the same matter. For example, I can both *perceive* a house as being green and *judge* it to be green. These acts of perceiving and judging differ in quality, but they have the same matter. Conversely, acts that have the same quality can differ in their matter. To use Husserl's example, if I assert "2 × 2 = 4" and I assert "Ibsen is the principal founder of modern dramatic realism," the two acts involved have the same "judgment-quality" even though they differ significantly in matter (LU II.1, 426; LI 2, 119). Not only do they have different "objects" (numbers and a person, respectively) but they also "determine" their objects in different ways (in terms of relations and in terms of properties, respectively, according to Husserl's categories).

Using the quality–matter distinction, Husserl introduces two systems of classification that frame his discussion of knowledge and truth. In the first place, he distinguishes between objectifying acts and nonobjectifying acts. *Objectifying* acts let an object be present to consciousness in a determinate fashion. Perception, imagination, and judgment are examples of objectifying acts. It does not matter whether what is perceived, imagined, or judged is an object or a state of affairs, and whether it is intended as actually existing or not. All such acts objectify objects—let them be present—and all have or can have what Husserl calls "an epistemic essence [*erkenntnismäs-siges Wesen*]" (LU II.2, 626; LI 2, 246). *Non-objectifying* acts, by contrast, such as "joys, wishes, [and] volitions [*Wollungen*]" (LU II.2, 519; LI 2, 169), do not present objects even when they are directed at objects. Because of this, they lack a characteristic of objectifying acts that is essential for knowledge, namely, what Husserl will describe as "fulfillment-syntheses." We can talk about our joys and wishes, for example, but enjoying and wishing as such do not confer or fulfill meaning in relation to (intended) objects, Husserl claims. And although enjoying and wishing must be founded (*Fundierung*) on objectifying acts such as perception of the object enjoyed or desired, our joys and wishes cannot provide the objectifying basis for other intentional acts. Accordingly, early Husserl's phenomenology of knowledge and truth leaves aside all nonobjectifying acts.

In the second place, Husserl distinguishes within the large class of objectifying acts between those that have a semantic essence and those that do not. All meaning-conferring acts that either do function or can function in conjunction with (*bei*) expressions have a "semantic essence [*bedeutungs-mässiges Wesen*]" (LU II.1, 431; LI 2, 122–123). To judge something to be a green house and assert this would be to engage in an act that has a semantic essence. Ideationally abstracting the semantic essence of a particular meaning-conferring act yields an ideal meaning (*Bedeutung*). This ideal meaning is what gives a judgment (*Urteil*) or assertion (*Aussage*), for example, its identity across many individual assertoric acts. No matter how many times you or anyone else might assert with respect to the same object "This is a loaf of bread," what is asserted retains "an identical meaning repeated *as* the same in the many individual acts, and represented [*vertreten*] in them by their semantic essence" (LU II.1, 435; LI 2, 125, tm): all such individual assertoric acts have exactly the same quality and matter.

Objectifying acts that have a semantic essence are what Husserl calls signitive acts or acts of signification. All the rest—that is, objectifying acts that do not have a semantic essence—are what he calls intuitive acts or acts of intuition. So, for example, if I perceive a house as green without saying it is green (i.e., without judging or asserting it to be green), then I engage in an act that lacks a semantic essence. It is an intuitive act. For Husserl, the two main sorts of intuitive acts are perception and imagination. These are objectifying acts, for they let the objects of perception and imagination be present to consciousness, but they are not signitive acts.

2.2.3   Synthesis of Knowing

The objectifying–nonobjectifying and signitive–intuitive distinctions are at work throughout the Sixth Investigation's "phenomenological elucidation of knowledge." There Husserl argues that knowledge arises from the coincidence between objectifying signitive acts and objectifying intuitive acts in synthetic acts of fulfillment (and frustration). Synthetic acts of fulfillment yield what he calls "the synthesis of knowing [*Synthesis des Erkennens*]," and this cognitive synthesis is the "characteristic form of fulfillment" for objectifying acts in general. Indeed, all signitive and intuitive acts aim at a "unity of fulfillment" that has "the character of unity of identification" and possibly "the narrower character of a unity of knowledge, i.e., of an act to which objective identity corresponds as the intentional correlate" (LU II.2, 582–586; LI 2, 216–218, tm). Although not every identification yields knowledge, knowledge—that is, the synthesis of knowing—is the overriding goal of objectifying acts.

Here we begin to see the epistemological implications of Husserl's earlier distinction between meaning-intention and meaning-fulfillment. Take, for instance, Husserl's example of the judgment of perception (*Wahrnehmungsurteil*) expressed in the words "There flies a blackbird!" The expressed meaning (*Bedeutung*) of this act does not lie in an intuitive act of perception per se, since the utterance and judgment can retain their meaning in the absence of any perception (LU II.2, 550; LI 2, 195). Rather, the meaning resides in the signitive act of making this judgment. At most, the act of perception helps determine the meaning, and the act of judgment relies on the perception in order to have the intended meaning fulfilled: "The perception [*Wahrnehmung*] that gives [us] the object and the assertion [*Aussage*] that thinks and expresses the object by way of the judgment [*Urteil*] … must be kept completely separate, even though, in the case of the perceptual judgment under consideration, they stand in the most intimate interrelationship, in the relationship of mutual coincidence [*Deckung*], of the unity of fulfillment" (LU II.2, 556; LI 2, 199, tm).

At the same time, however, Husserl insists that the signitive act itself would remain a mere meaning-intention, intuitively empty, if it were not rendered intuitive (*Veranschaulichung*) within a perceptually based act of meaning-fulfillment in which the object is intuitively given. Accordingly, he argues for the importance of distinguishing the signitive act of meaning-intention from the "full act of cognition [*Erkenntisakt*]" (LU II.2,

570; LI 2, 209, tm). Signitive and intuitive acts, when they coincide, are parts of a larger whole, namely, of fulfillment or of knowledge as a complex act.[38] When fulfillment and cognition occur, the "free" signitive part becomes "bound," so that it is no longer a mere meaning-intention. When, for example, I say "This house is green," my "act of meaning-intention," which is connected with an "empty symbolic presentation," can become "so peculiarly inwrought or infused" into a complex act of cognition—for example, knowing this house is green—that, although the meaning-intention's "semantic essence" remains intact, the signitive act's "character, in a certain sense, does undergo a modification" (LU II.2, 571; LI 2, 209, tm).

By the same token, there is more to the act of cognitive fulfillment than mere meaning-fulfillment. For perceptual acts also seek fulfillment. Unlike a signitive act, however, an act of perception fulfills itself "through the *synthesis of thingly identity* [*sachliche Identität*]: the thing [*Sache*] establishes itself through its 'self,' insofar as it shows itself from various sides and, in this, is always one and the same." Although any "external" object can be perceived in multiple ways and in partial ways, the act of perception inherently aims to be the "self-appearance" (*Selbsterscheinung*) of the object. Moreover, a perception that intends an object seeks a perception that would fulfill it, so that the act of perception aims at an "ideal synthesis," a "complete coincidence," between the "purely perceptual contents" of the intending and fulfilling perceptions (LU II.2, 588–590; LI 2, 220–221).[39]

Accordingly, cognitive fulfillment requires both meaning-fulfillment and perceptual fulfillment, and its goal is "absolute knowledge," understood here as "the adequate self-presentation of the object of knowledge [*die adäquaten Selbstdarstellung des Erkenntnisobjekts*]"—of the thing itself (*die Sache selbst*). In itself, a meaning-intention cannot approximate this goal. Only by being rendered intuitive (*Veranschaulichung*) can a meaning-intention participate in synthetic fulfillment that sets the intended objects more or less "directly before us [*direct vor uns hinstellt*]" (LU II.2, 597–598; LI 2, 226–227).

Certain acts of fulfillment are closer to the goal of knowledge than others are, however. Husserl traces differences in degrees of fulfillment—and in degrees of epistemic perfection—back to the relative "fullness" (*Fülle*) of the intuitive act. What gives relative fullness to acts of fulfillment is the extent to which the intuitive content of an act of perception or imagination approximates the corresponding content of the intended object. As an ideal, adequate perception would have maximal richness, liveliness, and substantiality—it would be "the self-apprehension [*Selbsterfassung*] of the full and whole object" (LU II.2, 83–84; LI 2, 238, tm).[40] Such degrees of fullness occur in conjunction with synthetic acts of identification in which intentions can find fulfillment. When a signitive act coincides with an intuitive act, "the intuitive act 'gives' its [relative] fullness to the signitive act," at least to the extent that the intuitive fullness coincides with "correlative parts of the signitive intention" (LU II.2, 615; LI 2, 239). Not every such synthesis involves an increase in fullness, however. That is why we must distinguish between acts of "mere identification" and acts of fulfillment.

2.3 Conception of Truth

The coincidence between meaning-intention and meaning-fulfillment provides the core to early Husserl's conception of truth. Truth has to do with a two-sided agreement involving both meaning-intention and meaning-fulfillment. On one side, it pertains to the coinciding of two qualitatively distinct types of acts, one of which confers meaning and the other of which fulfills the intended meaning. This coinciding occurs in synthetic acts of identification. On the other side, truth pertains to the agreement of the object as it is meant with the object as it is intuitively given. This agreement on the side of the object is the identity we experience as truth.

What unites these two sides is the ideal of adequation, as the title to chapter 5 in the Sixth Investigation indicates: "The Ideal of Adequation: Evidence and Truth" (LU II.2, 645–656; LI 2, 259–267). Reformulating the traditional conception of truth as the adequation between thing and thought (*adaequatio rei et intellectus*), Husserl regards adequation as the ideal of knowledge, which, as we have seen, arises in intentional experience via objectifying signitive and intuitive acts.

The preceding discussion of fulfillment points toward two types of adequation: (1) between the act of intuition and the imagined or perceived object and (2) between the act of synthetic fulfillment, in which intuitive and signitive intentions coincide, and the objective identity this synthetic act intends. Strictly speaking, only an act of perception, and not an act of imagination, can live up to the first ideal of adequation, by giving us the object itself (*die Sache selbst*) and not simply its image (LU II.2, 646–647; LI 2, 260). Moreover, the second type of adequation depends on the first.[41]

2.3.1 Truth Concepts

From this understanding of adequation as an ideal Husserl derives his first two concepts of truth. The first is the concept of objective identity. The second is the concept of evidence (*Evidenz*), which he also calls the "'experience' of truth ['*Erlebnis' der Wahrheit*]" (LU II.2, 652; LI 2, 263). Because, as I discuss in chapter 6, much of the literature on early Husserl's concept of evidence confuses it with whatever can justify a propositional truth claim, I prefer to discuss this second concept as the ideal of inter-active coincidence.

Truth as objective identity concerns the objective correlate to synthetic acts of identification and fulfillment. Husserl distinguishes here between truth as a state of affairs (*Sachverhalt*) and truth as objective identity (*Identität*). As we shall see, the notion of truth as a state of affairs presupposes Husserl's subsequent account of categorial intuition. Setting this notion aside for now, we can say that truth as identity is the objective correlate to a synthetic, coinciding act of identification (*Korrelate einer deckenden Identifizierung*). As an ideal, truth as objective identity would be the complete agreement (*Übereinstimmung*) between the signitively meant object and the intuitively given object as such (LU II.2, 651–652; LI 2, 263). This objective agreement, this identity, this truth is what one experiences when one successfully carries out a synthetic and fulfilled act of identification. Moreover, one can experience this truth, this objective identity, in a prereflective manner.[42]

As an ideal, truth as inter-active coincidence (what Husserl calls "evidence" in the strict sense) would be the act of "the most complete [*vollkommensten*] fulfillment-synthesis, which gives the intention, e.g. the intention of judgment, the absolute fullness of content, that of the object itself. The object is not merely meant, but rather it is in the strictest sense *given*, given just as it is meant and made one with the meaning [*in eins gesetzt mit dem Meinen*]" (LU II.2, 651; LI 2, 263, tm). This is truth as the objectifying, identifying, and most complete synthesis of coincidence (*Deckungssynthesis*) between signitive and intuitive acts, and it has its objective correlate in "being [*Sein*] in the sense of truth" or, more simply, "truth" as objective identity (LU II.2, 651; LI 2, 263, tm). Truth as inter-active coincidence would occur to the extent that a synthetic act of identification lives up to the operative ideal of adequation, which involves both the relative fullness of intuition and the degree to which the signitive intention is intuitively fulfilled. To the extent that truth as inter-active coincidence occurs, we can have an experience of truth as objective identity.

The third and fourth concepts of truth introduced by Husserl pertain, respectively, to the fullness of the intuited object and the correctness of the signitive intention with respect to the object identified. There is a legitimate sense, Husserl claims, in which we can say the intuited object is true when it is given intuitively just as it is signitively meant. To the extent, for example, that a perceived object provides "ideal fullness" for my identifying the house as green, this object is true "as that which makes an intention true" (LU II.2, 652; LI 2, 264). Alternatively, we can say of our signitive intention that it is true with respect to the identified object. It is true "to its true object." Although broader than the usual notion of propositional truth, this concept explains what it means to say than an asserted proposition is true. It is true—that is, correct (*richtig*)—if it "'directs' itself to ['*richtet' sich nach*] the thing itself, it says that it is so, and it really is so." The ideal of truth as correctness is that a proposition can be completely fulfilled and thereby completely adequate to its true object (LU II.2, 653; LI 2, 264).

These four interrelated concepts of truth—as objective identity, interactive coincidence, intuitive fullness, and signitive correctness—provide specific content to the claim that truth is the ideal of adequation that governs knowledge. The first and third concepts pertain to the truth of what contemporary philosophers call "truth makers," and the second and fourth concepts pertain to the truth of "truth bearers." According to Husserl, true knowledge requires an agreement both between what I would call epistemic object functions (identity) and between what I would call epistemic subject functions (coincidence). It also requires the adequacy of the object as given for these subject functions (fullness) and the adequacy of the subject functions for the given object (correctness).

By distinguishing these four concepts and granting each its legitimacy, Husserl provides a robust alternative to the narrowness of the prevailing theories in his day, theories that restricted truth to propositions, misconstrued intentionality, and ignored the truth of so-called truth makers. His more expansive conception also challenges minimalist truth theories in our own day. Husserl's four-dimensional conception of truth is expansive enough to anchor propositional correctness in a broader truth, to highlight the intentional character of knowledge and its constitutive acts (including perception), and not only to recognize but also to emphasize object-sided truth (identity and fullness), with respect to which propositions can be true (correct) and cognitive acts can be fulfilled. Indeed, the remainder of §39 ("Evidence and Truth") secures these gains by offering three refinements to Husserl's conception of truth: he distinguishes and relates propositional correctness and more expansive truth; he shows how his approach can accommodate narrower conceptions that restrict truth to judgments and propositions; and he indicates how his broader conception counters the relativism that all too easily undermines theories of propositional truth when these involve psychologizing accounts of judgments.

The first refinement is especially important as a response to theories that would restrict truth to propositional truth.[43] Husserl argues that the one-dimensional predicative identity syntactically posited in an assertion ("The house 'is' green") is not the same as the multidimensional objective identity synthetically posited in the multidimensional act of identification (The house-is-green that is signitively meant coincides with the house perceived as green). Nevertheless, predicative identity is bound up in such objective identity and, in the absence of objective identity and of the synthetic act that identifies it, a correct proposition could not contribute to true knowledge. In directing itself (*sich nachrichten*) to its true object, a correct (*richtig*) proposition seeks intuitive fulfillment, as does the signitive act in which a proposition is asserted.

If propositions and assertions seek fulfillment by way of an act and object of intuition, however, how can an intuition serve to fulfill the "is" in a simple assertion of the form "x is y"? That, essentially, is the topic of the next chapter in the Sixth Investigation, the famous chapter 6, titled "Sensuous and Categorial Intuition." Husserl's response expands the notion of intuition to include nonsensuous or supersensuous (*übersinnlich*) acts and objects, even as he insists that these, too, are genuine acts and objects of perception and imagination, not acts and objects of signification.

2.3.2 Categorial Intuition

As in his earlier discussion of meaning-fulfillment, Husserl begins with the simple judgment of perception and perceptual assertion (*Wahrnehmungsaussage*). If, for example, I successfully assert "The paper is yellow," do only the signified paper and its signified color find fulfillment via the perception of the paper as yellow? Or does the "is" also find fulfillment, say, in a "predicative being" (*prädikatives Sein*)? If it does, how can this fulfillment be perceptual? To raise the question more generally, how can the formal moments in signitive acts reach fulfillment—moments expressed using words such as "a," "some," "not," "and," "or," including what Husserl labels "categorial forms" such as the copula ("is") (LU II.2, 657–661; LI 2, 271–273)?

Husserl claims that all fulfillment properly so called is intuitive. He also argues that the fulfillment of such formal moments cannot be sensuous. Nor can we explain it in a Lockean fashion by saying that predicative being and other logical categories such as unity, plurality, and totality arise from our reflecting on certain mental acts (*psychische Akte*) in which we combine, unify, or distinguish perceptions. No, if the "is" of an assertion is to find fulfillment, then the predicative being it expresses must itself be given, and the logical category of "being" must intend such a given object. Husserl calls such predicatively intended objects "states of affairs." To be given, a state of affairs, although it is not sensuously perceptible, must in some sense be intuitively given (LU II.2, 669–670; LI 2, 279–280). Moreover, such a state of affairs can be "true" in the sense of Husserl's first concept of truth: true as true being or being true (*Wahrhaft-sein*).

Husserl calls this mode of intuition "categorial."[44] Categorial intuition is not simply analogous to sensuous intuition, however. It is genuinely intuitive—that is, genuinely perceptual, imaginative, or both—and it occurs within every fulfillment in which formal meanings are intended. Husserl's primary reason for expanding the notion of intuition to include categorial intuition is the "essential homogeneity" (*wesentliche Gleichartigkeit*) of the function of fulfillment. The formal and supersensuous character of categorial intuition does not make it any less fulfilling than or any different in this role from stuff-like (*stoffliche*) and sensuous perception and imagination. Every fulfilling act in general is an intuition; the intentional correlate of any intuition is an object (*Gegenstand*); and every act that fulfills in the manner of "confirming self-presentation" (*bestätigende Selbstdarstellung*) is a perception. For it is characteristic of perception that something appears as "actual" (*wirklich*) and "self-given" (*selbst gegeben*), unlike "essentially related acts" such as "imaginative making present" (*bildliche Vergegenwärtigen*) and "purely significative thinking of" (*rein signifikatives Darandenken*). Even universal states of affairs can rightly be said to be "perceived" (*wahrgenommen*): we have insight into them (they are "*eingesehen*"), and they can be intuitively detected (*erschaut*) (LU II.2, 670–673; LI 2, 280–281).

Nevertheless, Husserl says we need to distinguish between sensuous and categorial intuition and between their respective objects. Although every act of perception aims to grasp (*erfassen*) its object directly—to grasp the object itself—the sensuous objects of sensuous perception are "real" (*real*) objects of the "lowest level of intuition," and the categorial objects of categorial perception are "ideal" (*ideal*) objects of "higher levels" of intuition. Moreover, the objects of sensuous perception constitute themselves in a straightforward (*schlichter*) manner. They are "immediately given" in a single-rayed act. The objects of categorial perception, by contrast, are based on such immediately given, sensuously perceptible objects. Categorial objects, which also appear as actual and self-given, are given in more complex acts. Such many-rayed categorial acts either include or presuppose a basic and straightforward act of sensuous perception, and they allow something to appear that could not be given in the basic act of sensuous perception that founds them. Categorial objects—states of affairs and the like—"can come to appearance 'in person' ['*selbst*'] in such founded acts." Only due to founded acts of categorial intuition can expressed and assertoric thought (*das aussagende Denken, wo es als Ausdruck fungiert*) find fulfillment. The truth (i.e., correctness) of an assertion aims at a "complete accord" (*vollkommene Anmessung*) with such acts of categorial intuition (LU II.2, 674–675; LI 2, 282–283).

Elaborating the distinction between sensuous and categorial acts, Husserl argues that in sensuous perception the object "appears 'in one blow,' as soon as our glance falls upon it" (LU II.2, 676; LI 2, 283). Sense perception is straightforward, does not require its own "synthetic acts," and is never founded in another act, even though it provides the foundation for many other acts, including acts of categorial intuition. Acts of categorial intuition, by contrast, are founded acts, and they are not straightforward. Instead, they are articulating and relational acts (*gliedernde Akte*). They make explicit an object's parts, which we implicitly and straightforwardly perceive, and bring them "into relation, whether to one another or to the whole." This does not mean that first we perceive the object straightforwardly and then perceive it in an articulating fashion, however. Rather, we perceive the object within "overarching act-unities" within which the relations of the parts constitute themselves "as new objects" (LU II.2, 681; LI 2, 286–287, tm). Thus, for example, the categorial perception of green as a feature of a house explicates, and relies upon (i.e., is founded upon), the straightforward sensuous perception of a house as green. Similarly, the categorial perception of this house as standing to the right of that house explicates and relies upon the sensuous perception of both houses on a particular occasion. In both examples, the act of categorial intuition makes present a specific state of affairs that can be identified in conjunction with a signifying act of assertion: "This house *is* green," "This house *is to the right of* that house."[45]

Although Husserl goes into much greater detail about categorial intuition, including "universal intuition"—that is, the categorial intuition of universals such as kinds and properties (LU II.2, 690–693; LI 2, 292–294)—I have summarized enough of his theory of categorial intuition to uncover its primary motivation. As Husserl himself indicates, the theory is required in order to give a complete account of "knowledge as the unity of fulfillment [*die Erkenntnis als Erfüllungseinheit*]" (LU II.2, 695; LI 2, 295). Normally, he says, we achieve such unity of fulfillment on the basis not only of straightforward sensuous perception but also of categorial intuition. Hence, to account for the coincidence of signitive and intuitive acts and the identity of meant and intuited objects—loosely, to account for the relation between thought (*Denken*) and intuition (*Anschauen*)—we need to include categorial intuition within our account (LU II.2, 695; LI 2, 295). Indeed, Husserl's conception of truth requires his theory of categorial intuition.

All of this implies that a true—that is, correct—proposition will be directed toward an intuited object, including a predicatively intended state of affairs that is categorially intuited. It also implies that, if the intended object in question is true—that is, if it provides ideal fullness—its categorial intuitive formation will be adequate to the predicative signifying act in which the proposition functions or can function, typically an act of assertion. Early Husserl anchors propositional correctness in a more expansive conception of truth. In this way, his conception of truth clears a path through the impasse between trivially minimalist and vaguely expansionist conceptions of truth.

2.4   Contested Concepts

Nevertheless, the post-Heideggerian concerns of Levinas, Adorno, and Derrida make one wonder whether the path Husserl has cleared is a viable one. Specifically, to what extent can early Husserl's conception of truth connect, without short-circuiting, a precise concept of propositional truth and a more comprehensive and life-oriented idea of truth? As I indicated earlier, Levinas applauds Husserl's emphasis on intuition as giving us access to true being, but he criticizes the "intellectualism" of Husserl's account, its distance from historical praxis. Adorno charges Husserl with a "logical absolutism" whose conception of truth ignores the sociohistorical mediation and dialectical interrelation of subject and object. Derrida rejects the entire "metaphysics of presence" that he finds throughout Husserl's conceptions of meaning, intuition, and truth.

I think there is something to each of these criticisms. Early Husserl's conception of truth does rely on an insufficiently historical concept of intuition, both sensuous and categorial. It pays too little attention to the sociohistorical mediations of subject and object in their dialectical interrelation. And it assumes that the presence of the object and the subject's being present to the object are central to truth as such. Moreover, these concerns get registered in modifications that Husserl introduces to his phenomenology of knowledge in later writings, and each is addressed in Heidegger's conception of truth as authentic disclosedness, the topic of the next two chapters.

It is one thing to identify these problematic tendencies, however, and quite another to provide a viable alternative. By viable alternative I mean a conception of truth that successfully explicates and links propositional and existential truth. So far as I can tell, Levinas, Adorno, and Derrida do not provide such an alternative, and Heidegger's conception is at best only potentially viable, insofar as he does not offer a sufficiently precise concept of propositional truth, as Tugendhat has argued.[46] Here, then, is the challenge we face: to undertake a critical retrieval of early Husserl's conception of truth, one that reclaims important insights by responding to legitimate objections. I propose to begin such a critical retrieval by reconsidering three contested concepts within Husserl's conception: fulfillment, coincidence, and givenness.

2.4.1 Fulfillment

Like Heidegger, all three of our post-Heideggerian critics agree that the emphasis on intuition, including categorial intuition, is highly characteristic of Husserl's conception of truth, for better or worse. The context for this emphasis is Husserl's account of meaning-fulfillment. He begins with the premise that signitive acts and intuitive acts are not only intentional (i.e., object-directed) but also fundamentally distinct. For Husserl, the question of truth revolves around the issue of whether and how signitive acts, including propositional assertions, can be intuitively fulfilled.

What is fundamentally right about Husserl's insistence on intuitive fulfillment, it seems to me, is the insight that, for the most part, linguistic and
logical practices attain truth only in conjunction with other practices and
on their basis. Further, that toward which we direct our linguistic and logical practices, and in relationship to which such practices are meaningful,
is inherently multidimensional. Hence, for us to achieve true knowledge of
practical objects (i.e., the objects toward which we direct our practices) and
to do so via language and logic, such objects need to be available to us in
nonlinguistic and nonlogical ways.

The problematic aspects to Husserl's emphasis on intuitive fulfillment
arise for three reasons. First, as Hans-Georg Gadamer has suggested, Husserl employs an epistemologically restricted notion of intuition, reducing
it in the first instance to immediate sensuous perception and imagination
and then expanding it to include categorial intuition, which he nevertheless models along the lines of sensuous intuition.[47] Second, Husserl ignores
an entire range of object-related practices that are neither perceptual nor
imaginative in his sense but are not simply linguistic or logical either—the
practices, for example, that help constitute political interactions, economic
transactions, and ethical relations. Third, and in conjunction with the first
two problems, early Husserl fails to acknowledge the sociohistorically situ-
ated and sociohistorically active character of human experience in all its
dimensions, including what he describes as intuitive and signitive acts. This
failure goes to the heart of his conception of intentional experience, as both
Levinas and Adorno recognize.[48]

If my observations are on the right track, then the early Husserlian
account of intuitive fulfillment requires significant reformulation. It needs
to be expanded to include a much wider range of human practices and
practical objects. On this reformulation, the required fulfillment of "signification" in many cases could be based on "intuition" in Husserl's sense. But
the fulfillment often would include practices and objects that are neither
intuitive nor signitive but instead involve ways in which objects are available for various other social practices, in a broad sense. This would mean,
for example, that my asserting "That is a dastardly deed" would find fulfillment not simply in my perception of the deed (which might barely exist if
the deed were reported rather than observed) but in relationship to a moral
stance and moral practices that I share with other people.

2.4.2   Inter-Active Coincidence

As this example suggests, Husserl's concept of subject-sided truth as inter-active coincidence also merits further reflection. Husserl regards such coincidence as a synthetic act of identification in which the meaning-intention of signitive acts is completely and intuitively fulfilled. Husserl's account correctly describes such synthetic coincidence as something we accomplish in relationship to multidimensional objects and with regard to the identity these objects display across at least two of their interrelated dimensions. If I assert "This house is green," for example, my act of asserting this can be borne out as being correct if my interlocutor and I not only perceive the house as green but also predicatively posit it (or regard it, in the interlocutor's case) as being green, and we find our predication sustained by our perception.

Notice, however, that my example inserts an interlocutor, while Husserl's account of subject-sided truth is notably silent about the interlocutor's role. This difference points to a significant gap in the early Husserl's account: he does not sufficiently consider the role of intersubjective communication in the achievement of subject-sided truth. In fairness to Husserl, one could of course point out that the *Logical Investigations* do not aim to explicate empirical interactions and accomplishments but aim instead to uncover the transcendental grounds of such interactions and accomplishments. Never-theless, even if he has in view what he later calls "transcendental subjectiv-ity," the fact remains that Husserl's transcendental subjectivity is an I and not a we. This is clear from how the later Husserl takes up issues of inter-subjectivity when he discusses the transcendental grounding of logic[49] and the relation between pre-predicative experience and predicative judgment.[50] There he approaches intersubjectivity as something constituted by the tran-scendental ego, not as an ego-constituting transcendental intersubjectivity. Husserl's aim is to ground both logic and predicative judgment in what he calls "transcendental subjectivity"—not a "subjectivity which finds itself in a world ready-made" but "a subjectivity bearing within itself, and achieving, all of the possible operations to which this world owes its becoming."[51] That is why, in tracking down "the original act of judgment," he also says that, methodologically, we must set aside issues of intersubjective validity and "act as if the operations were precisely *my own* completely original acquisi-tions, without any … reference to a community already there." Indeed, we must "completely disregard the function of the act of judgment in communication and the fact that it always presupposes preceding communication precisely in the way in which its objects are pregiven."[52]

By contrast, it seems to me that intersubjective communication is a constitutive feature of predication as such. In most cases when signification occurs—specifically, when assertoric practices occur—we are communicating with others, and our signitive practices must be intersubjective. Moreover, such cases are typical, not exceptional. Transcendentally, they would make little sense if one stripped away the interlocutor's role. Simply insisting that multidimensional coincidence is a synthetic act of objectification, accomplished in principle by a single epistemic subject, ignores this communicative context. Nor does Husserl's turning coincidence into an *ideal* remove the problem. For the ideal as he understands it remains one that in principle holds for an epistemic subject and not for communicative agents in practical interaction.

In response to this problem, I propose to regard inter-active coincidence not as a single-subject *act* but as an *intersubjective process*. Coincidence is, as Husserl partially suggests, a process in which shared linguistic and logical practices dynamically correlate with relevant nonsignitive practices and with respect to a commonly available practical object in its relevant signitive and nonsignitive dimensions. Typically, however, it is not a process carried out by a single agent. It involves at least two agents in communicative interaction, both of whom participate in the same signitive and nonsignitive practices, and both of whom find the object disclosing itself in the same dynamically correlated signitive and nonsignitive ways. Hence, for example, when I assert "This house is green" or "That is a dastardly deed," I do so expecting that you share my perception or assessment, that you can make the same assertion in these circumstances with respect to the same object, that the point of my making the assertion is for you either to agree or disagree, and that your agreement or disagreement will be relevant for the correctness of this assertion. When these expectations are met and you agree with the assertion, the communicative interaction within which the assertion occurs is such that the correctness of the assertion can be borne out.[53] This proposed account does not make the asserted truth relative. Rather, it undercuts the move toward relativism by building intersubjectivity and relevance into the very structure of subject-sided truth.

2.4.3 Givenness

Husserl's ultimate defense against relativism, and against skepticism too, lies in his insisting on the intuitive givenness of the object. The object is given, he says, to our sensuous and categorial perception and imagination, with greater and lesser degrees of fullness; the truth of our signitive acts ultimately means that they are adequate to what is intuitively given. Conversely, the object as intuited must be true in order for our linguistic and logical practices to be true.

Tugendhat claims that Heidegger loses track of this Husserlian insight and, as a result, ends up with a vague and expansive idea of truth that no longer explicates propositional truth. If Tugendhat is right, then an appropriation of Husserl's "intuitive givenness" is fundamental for a response to the challenge Tugendhat poses. Adorno is most keenly aware of this, as is apparent from his own insistence on the "priority of the object."[54] Derrida, by contrast, regards this Husserlian emphasis as hopelessly mired in the metaphysics of presence, and Levinas seems to soften it by reading Husserl as a proto-Heideggerian.

The issue comes down to this: Do practical objects in their relation to human practices always already have their own identity, and is this identity such that how they function in our experience impinges on our practices and in some sense makes it possible for our practices to be true toward them? With Husserl, I want to answer yes. Yet I would not restrict the scope of such "givenness" to perceptual and imaginative functions. Indeed, the very notion of "givenness" is insufficiently dynamic, insufficiently attuned to the sociohistorical character of both practical objects and human practices. Moreover, the notion presupposes an ideal of adequation that is itself an insufficient model of truth, as all three of our post-Heideggerian critics would agree.

Having said all that, however, one still needs to develop an illuminating account of how practical objects can "be true" or "truly be" (*Wahrhaftsein*, in Husserl's terminology), such that the relations they sustain with us enable human practices, including assertoric practices, to be true with respect to them. Let me suggest that, despite Tugendhat's criticisms of Heidegger, the notion of intuitive givenness needs to be recast along the lines of Heidegger's "handiness" or "readiness to hand" (*Zuhandenheit*) or of practical availability, in my own terms. The modification of two Husserlian claims is crucial in this regard, provided we extend them beyond merely intuited objects. First, the identity of practical objects consists in a dynamic coherence among their various functions in relation to human practices of identification. Such practices will always include linguistic and logical practices of the sort Husserl labels "signitive acts." Second, the identity of practical objects is not given to them by our identifying them, nor is it made possible by the linguistic and logical practices that are a necessary part of such identification. Rather, their identity is what makes it possible for us to identify them, and this identity discloses itself when our identifications, necessarily including relevant linguistic and logical practices, are successful—that is, when they are true.[55]

Applying these modified claims to the topic of propositional truth, we can say Husserl is right to insist that predicative identity is not the same as synthetic identity, even though synthetic identity usually includes predicative identity. I would put this point as follows. When we make assertions about a practical object, we engage in predicative identification, and the object's predicative availability makes this possible. To the extent that such assertions are true, however, the object must also be available in nonpredicative ways in nonpredicative dimensions of our practical experience. Moreover, such nonpredicative ways of availability—at least those that are relevant with respect to the assertion—must align with the object's predicative identity. I call this "objective" alignment on the occasion of a predicative identification "predicative self-disclosure."[56] Predicative self-disclosure is what the practical object to which we refer allows us to specify on such an occasion with respect to nonpredicative ways in which the object is available to us. Rather than talk of the object's presence and givenness, we can speak of its availability and self-disclosure. And rather than restrict its availability to intuitive givenness, we can acknowledge the many practical ways in which objects function in relation to human practices. That will allow us to index assertoric correctness concerning practical objects to the dynamic coherence between their predicative and nonpredicative functions as well as between our own predicative and nonpredicative practices.

Hence I propose to begin a retrieval of Husserl's insights by expanding "fulfillment" to include a much wider range of practices and practical objects; by reformulating "coincidence" as an intersubjective process; and by replacing "intuitive givenness" with the notion of predicative self-disclosure. Although such revisions respond to the legitimate objections of Levinas,

Adorno, and Derrida, they also imply criticisms of these post-Heideggerian critiques, criticisms that stem in part from my response to the conception of truth in Heidegger's *Being and Time*—the topic of chapters 3 and 4.

My proposed revisions point to an expanded conception of truth that replaces the ideal of adequation with a dynamic correlation between socio-historical practices and what these practices disclose. Achieving propositional truth is only one part of this disclosive correlation, as Husserl recognized in his own fashion. Yet, as he also recognized, in a society such as ours, multidimensional and dynamic disclosure seldom occurs in the absence of correct assertions about practical objects that are available to us in more than predicative ways. When worked out in greater detail, perhaps this account of truth can help meet the challenge Tugendhat posed. Perhaps it will connect a precise concept of propositional truth with an expansive and life-oriented idea of truth.[57]

3 Truth as Disclosure: Martin Heidegger

Assertion is not the primary "locus" of truth, but ... is based ... in the *disclosedness* of Dasein.
—Martin Heidegger[1]

The conception of truth proposed by Martin Heidegger's *Being and Time* is both provocative and problematic. On the one hand, in going beyond Husserl's phenomenological account, Heidegger provides a way to reconnect technical accounts of propositional truth within logic, epistemology, and philosophy of language with the cultural practices and social institutions from which such accounts take distance. He does so by developing an ontological alternative to a pervasive "logical prejudice" in Western philosophy,[2] an alternative to the "propositionally inflected" character of many conceptions of truth.[3] On the other hand, Heidegger takes such a dim view of "everydayness" and public communication that attaining truth becomes the inexplicable privilege of "authentic" existence. This privileging of authentic existence ensnares his conception in the self-referential incoherence of theorizing what, according to his own theory, cannot be theorized.[4] The promise and the problems of Heidegger's proposal are meshed. To redeem its potential, one must criticize its inherent flaws and ideological functions.

I hope to show that *Being and Time* offers important insights to a comprehensive conception of truth, more than could be acknowledged by Theodor W. Adorno, whose critique of Heidegger shapes my own interpretation. My aim is to begin to fashion an alternative conception that frees Heidegger's insights from what I consider to be a reactionary garb. As will become apparent, my alternative is to conceive truth as a process of life-giving disclosure, marked by human fidelity, to which a differentiated array of sociocultural practices and products can contribute in distinct and indispensable ways. Linguistic claims and logical propositions belong to such an array, but so do the nonpropositional practices and products of art, for example.

Let me first summarize Heidegger's argument for conceiving truth as disclosedness (section 3.1). Then I shall consider his claims that assertion or statement (*Aussage*) is a derivative mode of interpretation (section 3.2) and that Dasein's disclosedness is the primary locus of truth (section 3.3). I shall argue that assertion is indeed a mode of interpretation, but it is not derivative. I shall also argue that the larger truth of assertion does stem from its role in life-giving disclosure, even though, contra Heidegger, the disclosedness of human existence is not the primary locus of truth.

3.1   Heidegger's Disclosedness

Section 44, titled "Dasein, Disclosedness, and Truth" (SZ, 212–230), gives the central presentation of Heidegger's conception of truth in *Being and Time*. This section simultaneously concludes the book's first division, titled "The Preparatory Fundamental Analysis of Dasein," and the sixth chapter in this division, titled "Care as the Being of Dasein." It not only summarizes and deepens Heidegger's analysis of "being-in-the-world" as the "basic state of Dasein" but also marks a transition to interpreting this state as thoroughly temporal in Division II (titled "Dasein and Temporality"). In this doubly laden context, Heidegger argues that the primary locus of truth is not propositions or assertions or discursive claims. Rather, the primary locus is the disclosedness of that being (Dasein) which, among other activities, understands and formulates and discusses assertions. While making this argument, Heidegger transforms the correspondence theory of truth, traditionally formulated as the *adaequatio rei et intellectus*, into a conception of "disclosedness" (*Erschlossenheit*) and "discoveredness" (*Entdecktheit*).[5]

Heidegger aims to ask about the meaning of Being. He approaches this question by analyzing and interpreting Dasein (i.e., human being) as that entity for whom Being is a question. He distinguishes Dasein from entities such as tools that are "at hand" or "handy" (*zuhanden*) as well as from entities such as scientifically defined properties that are "objectively present" (*vorhanden*). He also analyzes the three directions taken by Dasein's "being-in-the-world" (*In-der-Welt-sein*): "being together with the world," "being-with" others, and "being-one's-self." In more traditional language, which Heidegger carefully avoids, he distinguishes three types of relations— subject–object, subject–subject, and subject–self—only to argue that they form a unitary structure founded in Dasein's "being-in." Their unity becomes apparent from the terms he uses to summarize Dasein's orientation in the first two types of relations: taking care (*Besorgen*) of that which is handy, and concern (*Fürsorge*) toward fellow human beings. Both orientations rest in a more fundamental care (*Sorge*). Moreover, Dasein's dealings are guided by circumspection (*Umsicht*) toward the handy and by considerateness (*Rücksicht*) and tolerance (*Nachsicht*) toward others. These guides are made possible by the sight (*Sicht*) that characterizes Dasein's being-in per se. Such sight is what Heidegger calls understanding (*Verstehen*). Together with attunement (*Befindlichkeit*) and talk (*Rede*), understanding is one of three "equiprimordial" modes or structures (*existentialia*) of Dasein's being-in (SZ, 161).[6]

Two fundamental points affect everything Heidegger writes about understanding and talk. First, both understanding and talk are modes of Dasein's disclosedness. Second, since Dasein's disclosedness follows the orientation of care, and since temporality (*Zeitlichkeit*) is "the ontological meaning of care" (section 65), temporality characterizes both understanding and talk (section 68). Let me briefly elaborate each point.

The first point pertains to the essential openness that characterizes Dasein. Unlike other entities, Dasein not only occupies a field of relationships but also holds itself open in these relationships. For Dasein, that which is at hand resides in a significant totality of relevance (*Bewandtnis*), even when Dasein experiences or analyzes what is at hand, in abstraction from its relevance, as something merely objectively present. So too, Dasein's selfhood is always constituted by coexistence with others for whom what is at hand has significance, even when we regularly experience ourselves as indifferent members of a mass public (as *das Man* or "the they"). In other words, human beings are essentially open to their world and fellow human beings: the world lies open to human dealings and, even amid inauthenticity and indifference, human beings remain open to themselves and one another. In Heidegger's own words, Dasein (literally "there-being") "bears in its ownmost being the character of not being closed. The expression 'there' means this essential disclosedness. Through disclosedness, this being (Dasein) is 'there' for itself together with the Dasein of the world. ... By its very nature, Dasein brings its there along with it. ... *Dasein is its [disclosedness]*" (SZ, 132–133).

The second point pertains to the kind of temporality that underlies understanding and talk, respectively, and unites them in the structure of care.[7] Heidegger arrives at the theme of temporality by examining "anticipatory resoluteness" as the authentic and most primordial truth of Dasein (SZ, 297). He claims that understanding, which always projects Dasein's potentiality-of-being (*Seinkönnen*), is essentially futural, even when understanding is inauthentic. In contrast to understanding, talk, which articulates the disclosedness constituted by understanding and attunement, does not have an essential temporalization, whether future, past, or present. "Factically," however, the "making-present" that characterizes inauthentic understanding has "a *privileged* constitutive function" in ordinary talk (SZ, 349). Crucial in this context is the claim that both Dasein's disclosedness and its "basic existentiell possibilities" of "authenticity and inauthenticity" are "founded in temporality" in the manner described (SZ, 350). By extension, the futural character of understanding and the anticipatory resoluteness of authentic understanding provide preconditions for the disclosure of other entities.[8]

Reconstructed primarily from sections 31–34 and 44, Heidegger's argument against propositionally inflected correspondence theories of truth, and for his own conception of truth as disclosedness, involves accounts of understanding, assertion, and talk. Dasein understands itself, others, and its world, he says, by projecting its own potentials and possibilities from within its own factual context. Understanding is characterized by projective thrownness or thrown projection. Through projection, understanding (*Verstehen*) lets entities be encountered in their discoveredness (*Entdecktheit*) by Dasein in its disclosedness (*Erschlossenheit*). Such an encounter is developed in interpretation (*Auslegung*) as a working out (*Ausarbeitung*) of projected possibilities. When directed at understanding the world, as distinct from oneself or others, interpretation works out the purposes for which something exists by elaborating its embeddedness in a purposive whole. It always does so on the basis of a prior understanding, and often in a pre-predicative manner. More specifically, Heidegger argues that such "circumspect interpretation" rests on the three projective involvements that understanding has with the world: fore-having, fore-sight, and fore-conception (*Vorhabe*, *Vorsicht*, and *Vorgriff*), which could also be translated as prepossession, preview, and preconception. An interpretation is never a neutral gathering of bare facts. According to Heidegger, there is a circle in all interpretation, even in so simple an act as finding the right hammer for a particular task. "Every interpretation which is to contribute some understanding must already have understood what is to be interpreted" (SZ 152). That is the ontological basis for a familiar hermeneutical circle in the interpretation of texts.

Heidegger's account of projective understanding and its interpretive elaboration forms the basis for his approach to propositional truth. His approach treats assertion or statement (*Aussage*) as a derivative mode of interpretation (*Auslegung*), which itself is an outworking (*Ausbildung*) of understanding.[9] Assertion is derivative because of the abstraction it requires from the holistic context in which interpretation ordinarily occurs. Assertion points out or indicates an entity in abstraction from its purposive involvements. Through such "pointing out" (*Aufzeigen*), assertion "determines" (*bestimmt*) something (predication—*Prädikation*) and communicates this indication and predication to others (communication—*Mitteilung*). At the same time, unlike ordinary circumspect interpretation, which approaches a hammer, for example, as something serviceable within a context of relevance, assertion forces the hermeneutical "as" back to "the uniform level of what is merely objectively present. ... This levelling down of the primordial 'as' of circumspect interpretation to the as of the determination of objective presence is the specialty of the [assertion]" (SZ, 158). So assertion involves a transition from handiness to objective presence or, in non-Heideggerian terms, from pragmatic usefulness to predicative identity.

A similar concern about the transition from handiness to objective presence marks Heidegger's account of talk (*Rede*) as a second equiprimordial mode of Dasein's disclosedness. Talk makes possible the communication of shared attunements and common understandings, he claims. It gets expressed in language (*Sprache*), and it articulates meaning.[10] For Heidegger it is crucial that whatever is intelligible has already been articulated (*gegliedert*), even prior to being interpreted and asserted: "[Talk] is the articulation [*Artikulation*] of intelligibility. Thus it already lies at the basis of interpretation and statement [*Aussage*]" (SZ, 161). Likewise, the making of assertions is only one of the many ways in which we communicate in talk. Assertoric communication is a special case of a more comprehensive "articulation of being-with-one-another understandingly" (SZ, 162). But such articulation of what we have in common usually occurs in inauthentic ways. In a mass society, where Dasein is thrown "into the publicness [*Öffentlichkeit*] of the they" (SZ, 167), talk ordinarily occurs as idle talk (*Gerede*), which closes off our being-in-the-world and covers over the "innerworldly beings" (SZ, 169) to which we are nevertheless related. So too understanding ordinarily occurs as a restless, distracted, and uprooted curiosity (*Neugier*) that makes it impossible to decide "what is disclosed in a genuine understanding, and what is not" (SZ, 173). Such idle talk, curiosity, and ambiguity manifest the "falling prey" (*Verfallen*) to public existence that characterizes Dasein in its inauthentic mode of being-in-the-world.[11]

These accounts of understanding, assertion, and talk provide the impetus to Heidegger's critique of modern epistemology and of the premodern metaphysics from which it arose. The modern conception of truth treats assertion (*die Aussage*) or judgment (*das Urteil*) as the locus of truth, he claims. The modern conception also defines truth as the judgment's agreement (*Übereinstimmung*) with its object (*Gegenstand*). Heidegger then gives a novel, albeit Husserl-inflected, account of what such agreement comes to. Contrary to Descartes or Kant, Heidegger argues that the agreement between a judgment and an object does not mean that mental representations (*Vorstellungen*) get compared among themselves or in relation to the so-called real thing. Rather, it means the asserted entity "shows itself *as [that] very same thing*." The truth of an assertion is a being-true (*Wahrsein*), in the sense of the assertion's discovering the asserted entity as it is in itself (SZ, 218).[12] An assertion's being-true is its capacity to discover, its to-be-discovering (*Entdeckend-sein*). This capacity, in turn, depends ontologically upon Dasein's basic state of being-in-the-world (SZ, 219).[13] The truth of assertion reaches back via interpretation "to the disclosedness of understanding" (SZ, 223). More specifically, just as discovering (*Entdecken*) and the discoveredness (*Entdecktheit*) of entities are grounded in the world's disclosedness (*Erschlossenheit*), so the assertion's capacity to discover (*Entdeckend-sein*) is grounded in Dasein's disclosedness (*Erschlossenheit*), without which the world would not be disclosed.

Along this rather circuitous route, then, we return to the central point of Heidegger's analytic of Dasein, namely, that in all relationships, and in every mode of their being, human beings are essentially open. That essential openness is also the key to Heidegger's general conception of truth. For "only with the disclosedness of Dasein is the *most primordial* phenomenon of truth attained. … In that Dasein essentially *is* its disclosedness, and, as disclosed, discloses and discovers, it is essentially 'true.' Dasein *is* '*in the truth'"* (SZ, 220–221). This existential condition, if you will, is what Heidegger finds missing both in modern notions of correspondence between judgment and object, or between proposition and fact, and in premodern notions of an adequation between intellect and thing. These notions miss the open-ended connections that sustain both sides within a larger whole and that make any "correspondence" possible. They also miss the complexity and risk that truth involves. For, according to Heidegger, Dasein's disclosedness is both authentic (i.e., governed by Dasein's "ownmost potentiality-of-being," SZ, 221) and inauthentic (i.e., governed by "public interpretedness," SZ, 222). Hence Dasein is equiprimordially not only in the truth but also in untruth. Yet inauthenticity and being in untruth are made possible by disclosedness and discoveredness, and truth must be wrested from the inauthenticity of Dasein and the concealment (*Verborgenheit*) of entities.

To summarize: Heidegger thinks that propositionally inflected correspondence theories cover up the ontological foundations from which any agreement between assertion and object derives (SZ, 223–226). Contrary to such theories, "[Assertion] is not the primary 'locus' of truth," but is itself grounded in the primary locus of truth, namely, in Dasein's disclosedness. Dasein's disclosedness is "the ontological condition of the possibility that [assertions] can be true or false (discovering or covering over)" (SZ, 226). Moreover, since disclosedness is essential to Dasein's being, *"all truth is relative to the being of Dasein"* (SZ, 227). This does not mean that truth is left to subjective discretion or is constituted by a transcendental subject. Rather, it means that without Dasein's ontological disclosedness there would be neither authenticity nor inauthenticity, neither discovering nor covering over, neither discoveredness nor concealment, and neither true assertions nor false ones.[14] Truth is relative to Dasein's *being*, not to Dasein's will nor to its consciousness.

In this way, Heidegger thinks he has found a path beyond either absolutism or skepticism with regard to truth. Neither the dogmatic claim that there are eternal truths nor general skepticism about truth has an adequate ontological basis, he says. Both positions overlook the reciprocal and foundational relationship between truth and Dasein: just as truth belongs to the core of Dasein's being, so Dasein exists for the sake of truth. Moreover, such reciprocity extends to Being, toward whose understanding Dasein, in its disclosedness, is predisposed. "'There is' [*Es gibt*] Being—not beings—only insofar as truth is. And truth *is* only because and as long as Dasein is. Being and truth 'are' equiprimordially" (SZ, 230).

Some readers have accused Heidegger of "subjectivizing" truth, in the sense of reducing it to a condition or quality of human existence: after all, he does claim that all truth is relative to Dasein's being. Yet this accusation ignores his explicit opposition to subjectivism and his marked preference for substantives such as "disclosedness" and "discoveredness" over verbs such as "disclose" and "discover." That leads other readers to claim that Heidegger turns truth into a state of Being, one for which Dasein's being-in-the-world is crucial but perhaps not decisive. Accordingly, the fatal flaw in Heidegger's conception, one that deepens in his later writings, might lie in his both dehumanizing and structuralizing a dynamic process of disclosure. It seems to me that neither the first nor the second reading by itself does justice to the scope of Heidegger's project and to an unavoidable tension in his own conception of truth. There is a sense in which Heidegger both subjectivizes and dehumanizes truth. To derive an adequate alternative, one must wrestle with both tendencies in their dialectical tension.[15] I shall develop this "fore-conception" by criticizing Heidegger's accounts of assertion (section 3.2 below) and disclosedness (section 3.3). These criticisms will allow me to begin to articulate my own general conception of truth as one that, like Heidegger's, is neither propositionally inflected nor a correspondence theory.

3.2 Assertion and Interpretation

Heidegger lays out the derivative character of assertion in order to deconstruct the ontological foundations of propositionally inflected correspondence theories of truth. In the process, he makes a number of claims that, when taken together, diminish the role of assertions in the pursuit of truth and belittle their significance. Although such may not have been the clear intent of his formulations, arguably it has been their dominant effect. It has led to readings that exaggerate *anti*propositional tendencies in Heidegger's conception of truth that go beyond the *more-than*-propositional emphasis that I endorse. Let me first sketch two examples of how Heidegger can be read to this effect, and how alternative readings could counter what may not have been his clear intent. Then I shall analyze the claim that assertion is a derivative mode of interpretation.

Heidegger points out that the making of assertions (*Aussagen machen*) is only one of many practices within talk (alongside commanding, wishing, interceding, etc.—SZ, 161–162), and that self-expression, hearing, and keeping silent are constitutive of talk (SZ, 162–165). Here he can be read as saying that the making of assertions is not nearly as important as traditional philosophy and linguistics have claimed, and that other practices and "existential possibilities" are more important to ordinary language than is the making of assertions. But on a different and, I think, preferable interpretation, the main point about asserting would be that it normally occurs in connection with these other practices and as a way to actualize such existential possibilities. It is precisely because of such embeddedness, and because of the role of assertions in pursuing intersubjective understanding, that the making and discussing of assertions become crucial to public "talk" and deserve the special attention of philosophers and linguists, no matter how misguided previous accounts may have been. The task, then, would not simply be to free grammar from logic, as Heidegger puts it (SZ, 165), but also to liberate logic from its reification of the practice of making assertions.

Similarly, when Heidegger argues that the agreement of assertion and object derives from the disclosedness of Dasein and the discoveredness of entities, he embeds a thinner epistemological correspondence between subjective product and independent object in a thicker ontological harmony between the state of Dasein and the state of other entities. Described by Heidegger as a relation commonly understood as merely "objectively present" (SZ, 224), the thinner correspondence comes to appear less important for truth than the thicker harmony. This despite the fact that Heidegger's account of the thicker harmony seems to remain within the modern correspondence theory's subject–object paradigm, to which he explicitly objects. On a different and more fruitful reading, however, the crucial "agreement" would not be between the assertion and the object. It would occur instead among those who make assertions about the object, as well as between the process of making assertions and recognized principles for intersubjective conversation. Such an alternative, with its emphasis on the search for intersubjective "agreement" in accordance with recognized principles, can be extracted from Heidegger's account of "being-in-the-world" as including "being-with" others. Yet his critique of correspondence theories and his locating of truth in Dasein's disclosedness make little of intersubjective relations. In fact, his initial orientation to circumspect interpretation of the handy, combined with his disparaging view of the public sphere, makes it difficult to extract this alternative without violence.

What, more specifically, needs to be said about the purported derivativeness of assertion or statement (*die Aussage*)? To examine this topic, let me introduce a distinction and make a related comment. In the first place, the intelligibility of Heidegger's claims depends on a distinction between the making of assertions as a cultural *practice* and the availability of assertions as cultural *accomplishments*. Heidegger tends to elide this distinction. I shall mark it by using "asserting" and "assertion" as technical terms, respectively, for the practice and the accomplishment at issue. In the second place, the derivation of asserting and assertion from (the practices and accomplishments of) interpretation does not entail that the asserted (*das Ausgesagte*) simply acquires a definite character when asserted. Rather, the asserted can already array itself (or offer itself) in definable ways, and this array can impinge upon interpretation, even when interpretation is nonassertoric. Although such arraying and impinging do not by themselves give the asserted a definite character, neither does the asserted's becoming definable simply depend on its being asserted.[16] The reasons for making this comment will emerge from my more detailed discussion of the purported derivation of *die Aussage* from interpretation (*Auslegung*). Let me turn first to Heidegger's account of what I have distinguished as asserting and assertion, before I examine his account of the asserted.

3.2.1 Asserting and Assertion

Heidegger distinguishes three significations of the term assertion (*die Aussage*): pointing out (*Aufzeigung*), predication (*Prädikation*), and communication (*Mitteilung*). Of these, pointing out, which lets an entity be seen from itself (SZ, 154), is the primary signification. Heidegger considers predication to be founded in pointing out, which is broader, and he describes communication as an extension of pointing out and predication. The primacy he assigns to "pointing out" becomes apparent from his unifying definition of assertion as "*a pointing out which communicates and defines* [*mitteilend bestimmende Aufzeigung*]" (SZ, 156). He does not define assertion as predication that points out and communicates or as communication that points out and predicates. So too, he does not describe assertion as a mode of talk but as a mode of interpretation.

Heidegger's account of interpretation has a prior orientation to the purposive conduct of craftspersons and the users of tools. This orientation shapes the contrast Heidegger draws between the categorical statement "the hammer is heavy," understood by logicians to mean "this thing, the hammer, has the property of heaviness," and related formulations common to ordinary talk: "'Initially' there are no such statements in heedful circumspection. But it does have its specific ways of interpretation which ... may take some such form as 'the hammer is too heavy' or, even better, 'too heavy, the other hammer!' The primordial act of interpretation lies not in a theoretical sentence, but in circumspectly and heedfully putting away or changing the inappropriate tool 'without wasting words'" (SZ, 157). Given this prior orientation to purposive conduct, Heidegger analyzes assertion primarily as a practice rather than an accomplishment, and one that is originally purposive, although tending toward abstraction: "The [assertion's] pointing out is accomplished on the basis of what is already disclosed in understanding, or what is circumspectly discovered. The [assertion] is not an unattached kind of behavior which could of itself primarily disclose beings in general, but always already maintains itself on the basis of being-in-the-world" (SZ, 156). By emphasizing the practice of *asserting* and its ontological roots in Dasein, Heidegger creates the impression that *assertions as such*, as accomplishments, are cut off from the totality of human involvements with the world, and that theoretical assertions are the farthest removed.

Unfortunately, Heidegger's approach presupposes a problematic hierarchy of originality according to which the accomplishment derives from the practice, and a more explicit and more definite practice derives from ones less explicit and less definite. Only such a hierarchy can explain why predication should be considered "narrower" than pointing out (rather than, for example, more precise and inclusive), or why asserting "x is y" should be thought to arise via modification from circumspect interpretation (rather than simply constituting one type of purposive conduct, perhaps, or shaping or even giving rise to circumspect interpretation). While I acknowledge, with Heidegger, that, once accomplished, an assertion can be discussed and analyzed in its own right and in abstraction from the occasion and circumstances for making the assertion, this fact in itself does not warrant the view that accomplished assertions are cut off from other human involvements with the world.

In addition, the force of "pointing out" depends on its connections with predication and communication. I see no reason to think that a pre-predicative and noncommunicative pointing out would have any intrinsic connection with asserting and assertions. Consider, for example, Heidegger, alone in his shop, simply pointing his finger at a hammer while thinking "The hammer is too heavy." He might be pointing something out, but he would not be asserting anything, nor would any assertion become available as an accomplishment. Far from being founded in pointing out, predication is that which allows any pointing out to become assertoric. Insofar as asserting is an illocutionary act that requires an interpretable utterance in a public language, a private thought not communicated to anyone else, no matter how "pointed," would be neither predicative nor assertoric. What allows the entity to be "seen from itself" is not the pointing out as such, but rather the predication by way of which something can be taken as something distinct from something else.[17] Furthermore, predication as a practice cannot get off the ground in the absence of predications as accomplishments: not only does the practice often consist of formulating and discussing predications, but also such formulation and discussion necessarily refer to previously accomplished predications.

My criticisms have implications for two corollaries to Heidegger's position that assertion is a derivative mode of interpretation. The first corollary is that assertion has the same thrown projection that characterizes understanding as a mode of Dasein: "Like interpretation in general, the [assertion] necessarily has its existential foundations in fore-having, fore-sight, and fore-conception" (SZ, 157). Viewed from one direction, this characterization of assertion is unobjectionable: to the extent that it is an interpretive practice, the making of assertions draws on a hermeneutical fore-structure. This hermeneutical account of asserting contains an important insight, and it distinguishes Heidegger's truth theory from most propositionally inflected accounts. Viewed from another direction, however, Heidegger's characterization detaches assertions as such from their conversational texture and demotes their predicative status. He does not emphasize sufficiently that the hermeneutical fore-structure on which asserting draws is itself shaped in part by the predications already available in conversation and language. Nor is such predicative preshaping of the hermeneutical fore-structure a mark of falling prey. It is, one could say, ontologically unavoidable, even for "authentic" existence. Yet Heidegger is right to resist the tendency for accomplished assertions, when singled out for discussion in contexts of argument or theory, to float free from their hermeneutical matrix. He is also correct to counter any privileging of accomplished assertions in the formation of that matrix.

The second corollary is that, according to Heidegger, assertion characteristically turns the "existential-hermeneutical as" of circumspect interpretation into an "apophantical as." Heidegger describes this transition as the "levelling down of the primordial 'as'" (SZ, 158). The term "levelling down" (*Nivellierung*) captures the gist of Heidegger's account. He does not call the transition from the hermeneutical to the apophantic a "heightening" or an "enriching" or a "making more precise." He says that under the impact of assertions the "as" of circumspect interpretation gets "cut off" (*abgeschnitten*) and "forced back" (*zurückgedrängt*), that it "dwindles" (*sinkt herab*) (SZ, 158). Such strong language presupposes that the fullness of pre-predicative interpretation is somehow paradigmatic for all interpretive practices, and that the apophantic "as" peculiar to assertion is primarily a modification of the hermeneutical "as." If instead, as I have suggested, one anchors the making of assertions in conversation and ordinary language, and if one ties the possibility of asserting to the availability of predications, then the transition from interpretation to assertion need not involve a leveling or dwindling. The transition would be not so much a *modification* as a *movement* from one level to another, not a leveling but a leap. Accordingly, the leveling would lie not in the transition from *hermeneuein* to *apophansis* but in Heidegger's account of the transition. In fact, this is where I think the leveling lies.

3.2.2 The Asserted

Heidegger's leveling undermines his account of what gets asserted (*das Ausgesagte*). Although his account promises to break with epistemic subjectivism and the representational theory of knowledge that has dominated modern philosophy, it also introduces ambiguities that take a toll on his conception of truth.

Heidegger rightly insists in various places that what is asserted is not a "representation" (*Vorstellung*), neither a mental object nor a state of consciousness (SZ, 62, 154, 217–218). At the same time, the asserted is not the "content" or "meaning" of an accomplished assertion (SZ, 155–156). Much less is the asserted a free-floating proposition that "exists" independently of assertoric practices and accomplishments (SZ, 159–160). Rather, what is asserted, he argues, is the entity itself in a certain mode of its givenness. For example, when one says "The hammer is too heavy," what is asserted—and in this is allowed to "be seen from itself" or "discovered for sight"—is the hammer itself, a "being in the mode of its being at hand" (SZ, 154). The hammer is put forward (*ausgesagt*) and is explicitly determined as being "too heavy" for some purpose. And in uttering this assertion, one is sharing with others the hammer as so "seen" with such a definite character: "As something communicated, what is spoken [*das Ausgesagte*] can be 'shared' by the others with the speaker [*mit dem Aussagenden*] even when they them-selves do not have the beings pointed out and defined in a palpable and vis-ible range. What is spoken [*das Ausgesagte*] can be 'passed along' in further retelling. ... But at the same time what is pointed out can become veiled again in this further retelling, although the knowledge and cognition grow-ing in such hearsay always means beings themselves and does not 'affirm' a 'valid meaning' passed around" (SZ, 155).

In elaborating this analysis, Heidegger is of two minds. On the one hand, he wants to say that the asserter does not constitute or create the asserted in its specific character as asserted, but rather lets the entity stand out as it is in itself in a certain mode of its givenness. The hammer simply *is* too heavy or too light or too large for some purpose, and the asserter simply points the hammer out (or lets it be seen) in this regard. On the other hand, because Heidegger insists on the derivativeness of assertion, he also wants to claim that, as predication and communication, assertion does something to the asserted: predication "narrows" (*Verengung*) the asserted, "determines it" (*bestimmt*), and makes it "*explicitly* manifest" (*ausdrücklich offenbar zu machen*); and communication shares the asserted with others (*teilt ... mit dem Anderen*) (SZ, 154–155). In principle, assertion turns some-thing at hand, such as the hammer, into something objectively present (or lets it turn into such) and veils its handiness (or lets this become veiled): "Something *at hand with which* we have to do or perform something, turns into something 'about which' the [assertion] that points it out is made. ... Within this discovering of objective presence which covers over handiness, what is encountered as objectively present is determined in its being objec-tively present in such and such a way. Now the access is first available for something like *qualities*" (SZ, 158).[18] Heidegger seems to claim both that the asserted entity simply presents itself and that asserting affects the asserted.[19]

Heidegger's account of the asserted argues correctly that the accomplished assertion is about an entity (or a range of entities) in a certain mode of its givenness. This "aboutness" is not a third thing in addition to the assertion and the entity; indeed, it is not a thing at all. Rather, "aboutness" simply indicates the mutual mediation of the assertoric practice and that toward which one can engage in this practice.[20] Moreover, Heidegger rightly suggests that the entity asserted allows itself to be asserted and even, in a sense, calls forth the assertion.

To indicate the entity's "givenness" for assertoric practice, let me reintroduce "predicative availability" as a technical term.[21] The term suggests that, among the many ways in which entities are available (Heidegger: at hand) for human practices, they also offer themselves to us in a way that lets us make assertions about them. We do not impose such availability upon them, nor does our assertoric practice alone create their identity, even though asserting can help shape their identity, for better or worse. At the same time, the predicative availability of entities is only one of the many ways in which they can engage us. It is also one way in which many entities, lacking predicative capacities and practices of their own, cannot engage one another: nails are not predicatively available for hammers, and a hammer cannot engage other hammers in their predicative availability.

Heidegger's account of predicative availability goes astray when he tries to ground the asserted in the discovered. This attempt leads him to claim *both* that the asserted entity is predicatively and nonpredicatively available *and* that, when the entity is asserted, its nonpredicative availability becomes veiled or, as it were, undiscovered. Two problems come to the fore. In the first place, predicative availability comes to be seen as a distorting or an opposing of nonpredicative availability, rather than simply another mode of availability that can support nonpredicative modes and receive support from them. By contrast, I would argue that, rather than covering up the hammer's nonpredicative availability for hammering, for example, the hammer's availability for being predicated as "too heavy" makes its nonpredicative availability more broadly and precisely accessible. In the second place, Heidegger assigns assertoric practice a constitutive or constructive force that belies its limited "space" in the range of human practices. Heidegger sometimes suggests that asserting determines (*bestimmt*) the asserted, and that the true assertion discovers the entity. It would be better, I think, to say that asserting discovers not the entity as such but the entity in its predicative availability. Hence, in my own terms, asserting is an interpretive practice, as Heidegger suggests, but it is not derivative from other interpretive practices, nor is it possible without reference to already accomplished assertions. So too, the asserted is available in many nonpredicative ways, as Heidegger's account of handiness indicates, and its predicative availability neither opposes nor occludes the asserted entity's multifaceted and nonpredicative availability. My alternative formulation has a direct bearing on Heidegger's conception of truth as Dasein's disclosedness, the topic of the next section.

.

3.3   Correspondence and Disclosure

When he analyzes the derivative character of assertion in section 33, Heidegger has in view the position, advanced in section 44, that Dasein's disclosedness, not assertion, is the primary locus of truth. To establish this position, the three subsections of section 44 (a) explore the ontological foundations of traditional correspondence theories that regard truth as the agreement of assertion and object (SZ, 214–219), (b) demonstrate the derivative character of such theories (SZ, 219–226), and (c) analyze the kind of Being that truth as disclosedness possesses (SZ, 226–230). Without rehearsing every step in Heidegger's extended argument, I shall follow his outline to discuss (1) the connection between truth and the correctness of accomplished assertions, and (2) the connection between assertoric agreement and Dasein's disclosedness. Several clues for my critical reading of section 44 come from the work of Ernst Tugendhat.[22]

3.3.1   Correctness and Truth

In harmony with my own criticisms of Heidegger's account of the asserted, Tugendhat argues that the first subsection of section 44 slides through three different formulations of the truth of an assertion, implicitly taking distance from Husserl's conception of truth, to arrive, without sufficient argumentation, at Heidegger's own characteristic idea of truth.[23] In moving from Husserl's static conception of the assertoric act as a mode of intentionality to a more dynamic conception of assertion as a mode of disclosedness, Heidegger capitalizes on an unexamined ambiguity in the concept of "uncovering" or "discovering" (*Entdecken*): "In the first instance, [discovering] stands for pointing out (*apophainesthai*) in general. In this sense every assertion—the false as well as the true—can be said to [discover]. Nevertheless, Heidegger [also] employs the word in a narrow and [precise] sense according to which a false assertion would be a covering up rather than [a discovering]. In this case … the truth lies in [being-discovering] [*Entdeckendsein*]; however, what does [discovering] now mean if it no longer signifies pointing out [*Aufzeigen*] in general? How is *aletheia* to be differentiated from *apophansis*?"[24] Tugendhat replies that Heidegger gives no answer, for he "fails to expressly differentiate … between the broad and the narrow meaning of [discovering]."[25]

Against Heidegger, Tugendhat insists that the truth or falsity of an assertion cannot lie merely in its discovering or covering up an entity, but must lie more specifically in how such discovering or covering up takes place. Just as the true assertion discovers the entity *as the entity is in itself*, so the false assertion "[covers up] [*verdeckt*] the entity as it is in itself, and it does this in that it [discovers] it in another way than the way it is in itself."[26] Although Heidegger is right to ground the truth of assertions as correctness (*Richtigkeit*) in the truth of entities as discoveredness or (in the term he later prefers) unconcealment (*Unverborgenheit*), he simply bypasses Husserl's insight that the truth of entities is not their givenness as such but rather their self-givenness, a "superior mode of givenness."[27] As a pointing out that aims at truth, assertion tries to measure the entity's givenness against that entity's self-givenness. Hence, Tugendhat argues, assertion must be directed not simply by the entity as it shows itself but by the entity as it manifests itself *in itself*: "Self-sameness is the critical measure of unconcealedness [*des Entbergens*]. Only if this second meaning of being-directed is recognized in its autonomy can it profitably be clarified with the help of the first; so that one can say that the false assertion covers up the entity and that only the true assertion genuinely unconceals [*entbirgt*] the entity—that is, as it is in itself."[28] According to Tugendhat, it is only because Heidegger first ignores the distinction between givenness and self-givenness, and then equates truth with discovering as *apophansis*, that he can subsequently regard untruth as an aspect of truth rather than as something opposed to truth.

To provide terminological markers for Tugendhat's criticisms, I shall distinguish between the "correctness" of an accomplished assertion and the "predicative self-disclosure" of the asserted entity in its predicative availability. By "predicative self-disclosure" I mean a process whereby an entity, in its predicative availability, offers or manifests itself in relevant accord with nonpredicative aspects of its availability.[29] I agree with Heidegger (using my own terminology) that both assertoric correctness and predicative self-disclosure are grounded in a more comprehensive mediation of disclosive practices and systatic availability.[30] But I also agree with Tugendhat that, to connect this mediation with the concept of truth, one must have a way to distinguish between true and untrue "discoverings," "unconcealments," and the like.

At the same time, I want to avoid Tugendhat's tendency to anchor the distinction between true and untrue in the "self-givenness" of the asserted entity. Although an accomplished assertion about an entity does aim to discover the entity as that entity manifests itself "in itself," not all accomplished assertions are about entities, nor is such discovering sufficient for the assertion to be correct, nor does an entity's manifesting itself occur in isolation from other entities. Accomplished assertions can be about processes or actions rather than about entities (e.g., "To err is human"); the correctness of accomplished assertions depends in part on how they are formulated and used, and not merely on how they "accord" with what is asserted; and the entity's manifesting itself occurs in relationship to other entities, including those entities (i.e., human beings) to whom the entity is manifesting itself. Moreover, many of the entities about which we make assertions have a historical character that precludes their having a permanently fixed identity. As I suggested in the previous chapter, the Husserlian notion of self-givenness has a static quality that belies the dynamics uncovered, albeit only partially, by Heidegger's notion of discoveredness. To avoid the static connotations of "self-givenness," I have adopted the term "predicative self-disclosure."

All that having been said, an account is still required for the predicative self-disclosure of asserted entities and the correctness of accomplished assertions. Earlier I introduced the term "predicative availability" to refer to the fact that entities (and not only entities) offer themselves to us in ways that let us make assertions about them. I also said that asserting something discovers the entity in its predicative availability. Now it can be added that, when correct, an accomplished assertion discovers the entity in its predicative availability in a manner that accords with other relevant ways in which the asserted entity is available. Imagine, for example, that a carpenter says "too heavy, give me the other one" in a certain context. If correct, her (implicit) assertion "The hammer is too heavy" discovers the hammer as something of which relative heaviness can be predicated. It discovers this in a way that accords with the (un)suitability of the hammer for the task at hand.

Accordingly, asserting can go wrong in two ways: (1) by failing to discover the entity in its predicative availability and (2) by discovering this in a manner that fails to accord with other relevant ways in which the entity is available. The first way usually results in assertions that are "false" in the sense of being misleading or misplaced (e.g., claiming "The hammer is too heavy" when the tool in question offers itself for predication not as a hammer but as a pipe wrench). The second way usually results in assertions that are "false" in the sense of being incorrect (e.g., claiming "The hammer is too heavy" when the hammer in question is very well suited for the task and for the carpenter in question).

Those are not the only ways in which asserting can go wrong. For example, the asserter can misspeak or can respond inappropriately to a question or can deliberately lie. In addition, the "fore-structure" of a speech community can be such that false assertions are routinely made about an entire range of entities, due, for example, to ideology or what Habermas calls "systematically distorted communication."[31] Hence, viewed from the side of assertoric practice, the measure of assertoric truth cannot be a single criterion such as the traditional "correspondence with the object" or the Heideggerian "discovering the entity [(just as it is) in itself]." Rather, the measure must be a complex of considerations that might not be specifiable as necessary and sufficient conditions.

Satisfying this complex depends in part on the entity's predicative self-disclosure. In the usage proposed above, "predicative self-disclosure" refers specifically to the asserted entity in its predicative availability. This usage acknowledges that entities disclose themselves when they are neither asserted nor predicatively available. In fact, if entities did not disclose themselves in nonpredicative ways for nonassertoric practices, most of them would be incapable of predicative self-disclosure. This is an indispensable insight to be retained from Heidegger's account of handiness. But my usage of "predicative self-disclosure" also notes that entities do disclose themselves when they are asserted and are predicatively available.

The predicative self-disclosure of an asserted entity lies in its offering itself for predicative practice reliably and in accordance with other ways in which the entity is available. The self-disclosing entity offers itself not simply "just as that entity is in itself," as Tugendhat claims, but rather just as that entity is available to us in some other respect. When the hammer discloses itself as something about which one can correctly claim "The hammer is too heavy," it offers itself just as that hammer is available for a particular task of carpentry, say, for setting nails. As is the case with asserting, an entity's predicative self-disclosure can misfire in a couple of ways: (1) either the entity can withdraw from the assertoric field, in which case it becomes or remains predicatively unintelligible (although most likely available in other ways), or (2) the entity can offer itself for predicative practice but not just as it is available in some relevant way, in which case the entity becomes predicatively confusing. In the first case, we might find ourselves "unable to say anything," in the sense of being unable to make an assertion about the entity. In the second instance, we might find ourselves "not knowing quite what to say," in the sense of finding our assertions about the entity repeatedly "off the mark." Although neither of these misfirings may be prevalent in our dealings with hammers and the like, they occur frequently in our dealings with one another.

My account of assertoric correctness and predicative self-disclosure has the advantage of differentiating *aletheia* from *apophansis* without either resorting to a static notion of self-givenness, à la Tugendhat, or turning incorrectness and predicative hiddenness into aspects of truth, à la Heidegger. At the same time, this account serves to strengthen the Heideggerian intuition that assertoric correctness or propositional accuracy, although an aspect of truth, is neither the sole or primary locus of truth nor the key to a comprehensive conception of truth. Clues to a more comprehensive conception of truth occur when Heidegger grounds the "agreement of assertion and object" in Dasein's disclosedness.

3.3.2   Agreement and Disclosedness

Midway through section 44, Heidegger tries to show how the purported agreement of assertion and object derives from Dasein's disclosedness, and thereby to transform traditional conceptions of truth as correspondence. To do this he traces a path from ordinary language to what could be called theoretical metalanguage. His account goes roughly as follows (SZ, 223–226).[32] Dasein expresses itself in talk, Heidegger says, as a being whose relationship to entities always involves the discovering of entities. Although the practice of asserting is only one mode of such self-expression, it allows Dasein not only to express its capacity to discover entities but also to express itself *about* discovered entities and to communicate how these are discovered. Indeed, an accomplished assertion has an "aboutness" in which (*in ihrem Worüber*) the assertion preserves the discoveredness of the entity asserted. Once expressed by Dasein, the accomplished assertion itself becomes something at hand and further discussable. The entity's discoveredness also becomes handy. Yet the accomplished assertion, which preserves discoveredness, continues to sustain a relation to the asserted entity.

Here, however, the original connection between Dasein's ability to discover (*Entdeckendsein*) and the discovered entity begins to go underground. Heidegger claims that subsequent discussion of the accomplished assertion exempts Dasein from discovering entities in an original way, even though in such discussion Dasein does enter a relationship with those entities whose discoveredness the assertion preserves. In such discussion at one remove, which is common in public talk, the assertion's handiness gets covered up. Correlatively with this covering of the assertion's handiness, the discoveredness of the asserted entity becomes an objectively present conformity between the accomplished assertion and the asserted entity. Hence the original connections among Dasein, entities, and assertion get reduced to an objectively present agreement between an objectively present assertion and an objectively present object. One could say the original connections become that correspondence between proposition and fact which propositionally inflected correspondence theories regard as the very essence of truth. "Truth as disclosedness and as a being toward discovered beings—a being that itself discovers—has become truth as the agreement between innerworldly things objectively present" (SZ, 225). Truth as disclosedness—the most fundamental condition of human existence—has become a mere agreement between assertion and object: comprehensive truth has become merely propositional truth. Moreover, this objectively present agreement *seems* primary and not derivative because Dasein ordinarily understands itself in terms of what it encounters as objectively present. Traditional metaphysics and modern epistemology simply strengthen such an understanding.

By reconsidering "correspondence" or "agreement" along these lines, one can learn from Heidegger why propositionally inflected correspondence theories have enough plausibility to make the idea of more-than-propositional truth seem implausible. One can also see why Heidegger thinks his own conception of truth as disclosedness is ontologically prefer-able. Yet Heidegger's highly instructive explanation for both the plausibil-ity and the inadequacy of correspondence theories employs a questionable premise at the outset. Let me elaborate.

Earlier I questioned two corollaries to Heidegger's claim that assertion is a derivative mode of interpretation: that assertion has the same thrown projection as understanding has, and that assertion "levels" the existen-tial-hermeneutical "as" into an apophantical "as." Heidegger's derivation of agreement from disclosedness brings to light a third and equally ques-tionable corollary. The third corollary is that the sharing and discussing of accomplished assertions spares Dasein a direct encounter with entities themselves in "'original' experience" and thereby helps turn accomplished assertions into objectively present things (SZ, 224). Deep in the fore-struc-ture of Heidegger's phenomenology lies the image of authentic existence as having direct dealings with equipment and with that which equipment makes available—the image of *homo faber* as the attentive craftsperson who can get on with his or her work "without wasting words." The image sug-gests that the more indirect and mediated our dealings become, the more we drift from authentic understanding, interpretation, and talk. Once one abandons this image, already ideologically loaded in the 1920s, one becomes dubious about the entire notion that public talk spares us a direct encounter. There are two reasons for this: first, no experience of entities is direct and original, and, second, public talk mediates even the most "origi-nal" experience. Heidegger's account of assertion remains caught in the dream of eidetic intuition, despite his shifting Husserlian phenomenology from the realm of theoretically perceived noemata to the realm of circum-spectly interpreted entities.[33]

The dream of a direct encounter clouds Heidegger's account of the con-nection between agreement and disclosedness. His account begins with the assumption that Dasein's original self-expression and orientation and dis-covering are such that the entities discovered are truly discovered and that their discoveredness itself is true. Hence Dasein's disclosedness can itself be described as truth. As Tugendhat points out, however, to describe disclosed-ness as truth is to preclude asking how Dasein's disclosedness can be truly disclosive and how it can be false. Even if the agreement between assertion and object is derivative from a more primordial truth, that from which such agreement derives must be such that it can itself be distinguished from untruth. As it stands, Heidegger's account of the connection between agreement and disclosedness could just as readily be given for the lack of agreement between assertion and object. And that leads Tugendhat to accuse Heidegger of abandoning the idea of critical consciousness: "If truth means unconcealedness as Heidegger understands the word, then everything depends on the fact that an understanding of the world actually opens up, not that we scrutinize it [such understanding] critically."[34]

Yet Tugendhat's alternative also will not do, since it seems intent on deriving any broader conception of truth from an account of assertoric correctness or propositional truth.[35] There is something fundamentally right, it seems to me, about Heidegger's refusal to reduce truth to the correctness of assertions or the discoveredness of entities. He is correct not to exclude the ontological stance of those beings for whom truth itself, like Being, is a question and can never not be a question. Heidegger has successfully removed this question from the realms of Platonic perfection and Cartesian certainty. He has relocated it in those regions of human striving and disillusionment where getting things right often involves also getting them wrong, and where genuine discoveries seldom occur without difficult self-sacrifice.

So we appear to have arrived at an impasse: we can neither derive correspondence from disclosedness nor make propositional truth the key to a general conception of truth. Escaping this impasse is crucial for elaborating a comprehensive conception truth that withstands propositionally inflected denial, yet retains the questions of propositional truth that a Heideggerian affirmation of truth as disclosedness occludes. We must find ways to link assertoric correctness with a more comprehensive conception of truth without either reducing truth to correctness or simply absorbing correctness into comprehensive truth. Both Tugendhat's emphasis on critical consciousness and Heidegger's emphasis on existential disclosedness must undergo dialectical correction. Nothing less would satisfy the demands of a comprehensive conception of truth.

3.3.3 Life-Giving Disclosure

One way out of the impasse is to recognize principles according to which human self-expression, orientation, and discovering can be more or less true. Just as "correctness" indicates such a principle for the practice of asserting, so parallel principles obtain for other ranges of human practice, such as resourcefulness in the production and use of goods and services, or solidarity in the development of human communities, or justice in the governance of social institutions. It would make no sense, of course, to equate adherence to such societal principles with the achievement of assertoric correctness or propositional "truth." Yet there may be a more comprehensive sense of truth according to which "being in the truth" requires fidelity to that which people hold in common and which holds them in common. That which holds them in common are societal principles of the sort already mentioned. That which people hold in common may or may not be in line with such principles. Yet their holding something in common requires appeals or gestures toward such principles, even when the appeal is self-serving or the gesture is ideologically distorted. Moreover, for the principles to hold people in common, people must themselves hold something in common. Correlatively, infidelity to the commonly holding/held amounts to "being in untruth." From this description it appears that Dasein's "disclosedness" is itself a site of social struggle over principles for human existence. Whether the commonly holding/held sustains and promotes life is always implicitly at issue.

A second, complementary way out of the impasse is to replace the notion of disclosedness, as an ontological state of essential openness, with the notion of life-giving disclosure, as a historical process of opening up society. By "life-giving" I mean a process in which human beings and other creatures come to flourish, and not just some human beings or certain creatures, but all of them in their interconnections. Clearly this is, in Adorno's terms, an "emphatic idea," or, in Hegel's terms, a speculative concept. It must go beyond any specific societal formation, even though what counts as "flourishing" always derives its content from specific circumstances and experiences. Hence, for example, to envision a society in which no one is poor and the environment is not polluted would let the idea of life-giving disclosure acquire content, through negation, from contemporary society, where poverty and pollution persist. Given such content, the idea of life-giving disclosure would point toward cultural practices and social institutions that promote greater equity in the ownership and distribution of economic resources. It would also point toward societal arrangements that do not turn creaturely habitats into mere resources for myopic exploitation.

In transforming Heidegger's notion of disclosedness into one of life-giving disclosure, I emphasize fidelity to societal principles that people hold in common and that hold them in common. But I do not wish to anchor these principles in an unchanging and universal "human nature." I see them as shared reference points that have emerged historically through clashes between societies and within them.[36] Indeed, fidelity to the commonly holding/held and life-giving disclosure are indissoluble correlates. Just as the telos of such fidelity is to promote a process in which human beings and other creatures come to flourish, so life-giving disclosure depends in part on the degree to which cultural practices, social institutions, and entire societal formations align themselves with societal principles such as solidarity and justice. As life-giving disclosure, truth occurs in part by way of people being true—pursuing fidelity—in the various dimensions of their social existence. But only in part, since such disclosure also occurs both beyond and despite our principles and alignments. There is always more to truth than our "being in the truth," whether in our theoretical assertions or in our political engagements.

My emphasis on fidelity to the commonly holding/held recalls an etymological link between "truth" and "troth" that Heidegger had discovered before he wrote *Sein und Zeit*. Although one does not want to make etymology do the work of philosophical argument, it is at least noteworthy that "truth" derives from the Old English word "treowth"—"fidelity"—which is also a source of the word "troth." Moreover, "true" is commonly used to mean steadfast, loyal, honest, or just, and one archaic meaning of "truth" is fidelity.[37] If one regards the more comprehensive sense of truth as a process of life-giving disclosure in dynamic correlation with fidelity to societal principles, then one can see the pursuit of assertoric correctness as one important but limited way in which truth occurs. Similarly, the failure or refusal to pursue assertoric correctness can be regarded as contrary to truth, not only in the sense of leading to assertoric "falsehood" but also in the sense of undermining other ways in which fidelity to societal principles is to be practiced. For the persistent avoidance or rejection of assertoric correctness would render unlikely or impossible the pursuit of resourcefulness, solidarity, and justice. In that way, propositional truth is indispensable to life-giving disclosure, even though truth in this latter and more comprehensive sense exceeds assertoric correctness, just as it exceeds specific types of nonpropositional truth such as artistic truth.

Such an approach has several advantages over the account given by Heidegger. In the first place, a more comprehensive conception of truth need not preclude distinguishing truth from untruth. Rather, it can make available a number of respects in which to draw such a distinction. Second, there is no need to see the discussion of accomplished assertions as more remote from primordial truth, since such discussion is simply one of several ways in which the pursuit of truth occurs. Third, truth does not turn into a state of Dasein's being. It can be seen as a dynamic, multifaceted, and fragile calling in which everyone always has a stake and to which no one can avoid making a reply. Fourth, the agreement between assertion and object, which itself is only one component of assertoric correctness or propositional "truth," would no longer direct our understanding of what truth is like, not even in the inverted Heideggerian sense that comes from trying to show how such agreement derives from disclosedness. The relation of epistemic subject to epistemic object that strongly colors Heidegger's account of disclosedness would no longer be the point of departure for a general conception of truth.

At the same time, the proposed conception respects Heidegger's insistence on the temporal character of truth. The principles already mentioned are not timeless absolutes but rather historical horizons. They are historically learned, achieved, contested, reformulated, and ignored, and their pursuit occurs amid social struggle. Moreover, the description of these principles as "commonly held" does not mean that they are always and everywhere recognized, or that they provide the heavy artillery of common sense. Rather, it means that when people in modern societies find themselves pushed to the extremes of their self-understanding and their shared talk, they cannot avoid a struggle over these very principles. And contemporary struggles over resourcefulness, solidarity, and justice cannot but rely on efforts to make correct and corrigible assertions in ongoing public debates.

That is why I have criticized Heidegger for underestimating the role of predication in assertion, and for portraying predicative availability as a distorting of nonpredicative availability. Heidegger is right to try to ground the correctness of assertions in a more comprehensive mediation of disclosive practices and systatic availability. For this attempt to succeed, however, the pursuit of assertoric correctness must be seen as appealing to one of several societal principles in accordance with which the disclosure of culture, society, and human life can be more or less true. Contra Heidegger, as the next chapter argues in greater detail, what helps distinguish true disclosure from false is not the authenticity with which human beings face the possibility of their own death. Rather, it is their life-promoting and life-sustaining fidelity to societal principles that they hold in common and that hold them in common.[38]

II Authentication and Justification

4   Truth and Authentication: Heidegger and Adorno in Reverse

A transformed philosophy … would be nothing but full, unreduced experience in the medium of conceptual reflection.

—Adorno, *Negative Dialectics*[1]

The critical retrieval of Heidegger's conception of truth, begun in the previous chapter, is partially indebted to the critique of *Being and Time* in Adorno's *Negative Dialectics*. More needs to be said, however, both because Heidegger's conception turns on a not yet examined notion of authenticity and because Adorno's own alternative is closer to *Being and Time* than his harsh criticisms suggest. Indeed, the dialectical extremes of twentieth-century German philosophy touch in their conceptions of truth. More specifically, they touch in their conceptions of how truth is authenticated. Whereas Martin Heidegger says this occurs in the "authenticity" of Dasein, Theodor Adorno locates the authentication of truth in "emphatic experience."

I wish to explore this dialectic using Heidegger's *Being and Time* and Adorno's *Negative Dialectics* as my primary sources. Like Heidegger and Adorno, I consider truth to be a comprehensive idea that cannot be reduced to notions of assertoric correctness or propositional accuracy. But I also regard correctness and accuracy as indispensable dimensions of truth. Similarly, I take authentication to be a comprehensive attestation of truth that cannot be reduced to discursive justification or verification. Yet justification and verification are inescapable ingredients of authentication.

My exploration has three stages. First I summarize and criticize Heidegger's account of authenticity. Next I examine Adorno's appeal to emphatic experience. Portraying "authenticity" and "emphatic experience" as each other's reverse image, I claim that neither one suffices to authenticate truth. Then I draw out the significance of these dialectical extremes by proposing an alternative account of authentication.

4.1   Existential Authenticity

As we saw in the previous chapter, Heidegger's *Being and Time* argues that the disclosedness (*Erschlossenheit*) of Dasein is the primary locus of truth. This means that propositional truth, or the truth of assertions, is not the primary locus. Rather, whatever truth accrues to assertions and to the practice of making assertions stems from the fundamental openness that characterizes human relationships with other entities, with fellow human beings, and with one's self. Moreover, the accuracy of our statements and claims stems from the "discoveredness" (*Entdecktheit*) that characterizes entities in relation to the disclosedness of the world Dasein inhabits. Accordingly, "only with the disclosedness of Dasein is the *most primordial* phenomenon of truth attained. ... In that Dasein essentially *is* its disclosedness, and, as disclosed, discloses and discovers, it is essentially 'true.' Dasein *is* '*in the truth*'" (SZ, 220–221).

For philosophers who maintain the primacy of propositional truth, Heidegger's emphasis on the disclosedness of Dasein has unsettling consequences. For example, Ernst Tugendhat, as we have seen, claims that Heidegger surrenders the concept of truth, even though he continues to use the word. This occurs because Heidegger equates truth and disclosedness without asking what distinguishes truth from untruth in various modes of disclosedness: "Heidegger has given the word truth another meaning. The broadening of the concept of truth, from truth as assertion to all disclosedness, becomes trivial if all that one sees in truth as assertion is the fact that it discloses in general."[2] As a result, Tugendhat claims, Heidegger also surrenders the idea of critical consciousness. Yet Tugendhat recognizes the appeal of a conception "that, without denying the relativity and lack of transparency of our historical world, ... once again made possible an immediate and positive relation to truth: an alleged relation to truth that no longer stakes a claim to certainty, yet which also no longer poses a threat to uncertainty."[3]

There is something to Tugendhat's criticism. Yet, as I began to show in the previous chapter, Heidegger's conception has resources not only to counter this criticism but also to provide a more satisfactory account of assertoric correctness or propositional truth than the one Tugendhat assumes. Without rehearsing my arguments here, let me point out that Heidegger's discussion of truth has greater nuance than Tugendhat seems to recognize. At a minimum, Heidegger introduces five ways in which truth can be distinguished from untruth.[4] (1) The discoveredness of entities can be distinguished from their being covered up. (2) The disclosedness of the world and of Dasein can be distinguished from their lack of disclosedness. (3) The authenticity of Dasein's disclosedness can be distinguished from the inauthenticity of Dasein's disclosedness. (4) Dasein's falling prey within its disclosedness can be distinguished from Dasein's reclaiming itself from falling prey. (5) The illusion (*Schein*) and distortion (*Verstellung*) into which discovered entities sink (relative to Dasein's falling prey) can be distinguished from their having been wrested from concealment. Provided such distinctions and their recognition need not have the same apparent rigor and certainty as the difference between the correctness and incorrectness of a simple assertion, Tugendhat's complaint is too crude. Whereas Tugendhat seems intent on deriving any broader conception of truth from an account of assertoric correctness, Heidegger aims to derive assertoric correctness from a more comprehensive ontology of truth.

4.1.1 Authentic Disclosedness

Contra Tugendhat, Heidegger does not so much surrender the idea of critical consciousness as transpose it into the demand for authenticity. That is where the fulcrum to his ontology of truth lies. On the one hand, the discoveredness of entities and the disclosedness of Dasein are conditioned, at least in part, by the authenticity with which Dasein seizes upon Dasein's "potentiality-for-being-in-the-world" (SZ, 228). On the other hand, Dasein can reclaim itself from falling prey and can wrest entities from illusion and distortion only to the extent that Dasein's own disclosedness is authentic. Heidegger signals the pivotal role of authenticity when he describes the possibility of authentic disclosedness: "This possibility means that Dasein discloses itself to itself in and as its ownmost potentiality-of-being. This *authentic* disclosedness shows the phenomenon of the most primordial truth in the mode of authenticity. The most primordial and authentic disclosedness in which Dasein can be as a potentiality-of-being is the *truth of existence*. Only in the context of an analysis of the authenticity of Dasein does it [the truth of existence] receive its existential, ontological definiteness" (SZ, 221). The significance of the concept of authenticity is borne out by Heidegger's subsequent discussion of Dasein's "authentic potentiality-for-being-a-whole" (*das eigentliche Ganzseinkönnen*) in Division II ("Dasein and Temporality," SZ, §§45–83). There he states that his discussion results in a more complete grasp of that truth of Dasein which is "most primordial" because "it is *authentic*" (SZ, 297).[5] Tugendhat, with his phenomenological notion of "self-givenness," gives too little attention to Heidegger's emphasis on authentication.

Without detailing Heidegger's elaborate "primordial existential interpretation" of Dasein in Division II, let me briefly summarize his account of authenticity (*Eigentlichkeit*). His account calls attention to three topics: the ontological status of authenticity, the existential conditions of authenticity, and the primary characteristics of authentic disclosedness.

To begin, Heidegger regards authenticity as ontological. The concept of authenticity pertains primarily to Dasein in its modes of existence, in its potentiality-of-being or ability-to-be (*Seinkönnen*), and not to actual attitudes, behaviors, accomplishments, or beliefs. Earlier, Heidegger had distinguished three equiprimordial modes of Dasein's existence: understanding, attunement, and talk. Of these three, understanding provides the primary (but not sole) locus of authenticity and inauthenticity. This implies that authenticity has a projective character and is future oriented. In its projective orientation to the future, authentic understanding aims at Dasein itself. Authenticity has to do with Dasein's understanding itself in terms of its ownmost (*eigenste*) possibility or potential rather than in terms of the world and others. When Dasein understands itself in this way, Dasein anticipates death. It anticipates death as that ownmost possibility which would render Dasein's existence impossible. This anticipated possibility is private, individualizing, unavoidable, certain, and indefinite. Authentic existence amounts to Dasein's being-its-self in an impassioned "freedom toward death."[6]

This sheds light on the existential conditions that make authenticity possible. Since, to be authentic, Dasein must understand itself in terms of its ownmost possibility, nothing outside Dasein can make authentic existence possible. Rather, authentic existence is made possible by Dasein's own choice. It is made possible by Dasein's choosing to choose Dasein's ownmost potentiality-for-being-its-self rather than choosing to remain lost in the "they" (SZ, 267–268). This potentiality-for-being-its-self is attested by conscience

(SZ, 279). Indeed, such choosing to choose amounts to our wanting to have a conscience. Wanting to have a conscience is itself an understanding of Dasein's being directly called "to its ownmost potentiality-of-being-a-self" (SZ, 269, 287–288). Moreover, the call of conscience is the call of care, a call Dasein gives to itself in its alienation from the public world (SZ, 275–277). The self-given call of conscience summons Dasein to understand its own being-guilty as the null basis of its own potentiality-of-being (SZ, 283–288). Choosing to choose Dasein's ownmost possibility and hearing Dasein's own conscience are the existential conditions of authenticity.

Accordingly, Heidegger characterizes authentic disclosedness (*Erschlossenheit*) as "resoluteness" (*Entschlossenheit*). He assigns three primary characteristics to Dasein's authentic potentiality-of-being (*eigentliches Seinkönnen*). These characteristics link back to the three equiprimordial modes of Dasein's disclosedness, to understanding, attunement, and talk. Authentic potentiality-of-being consists in (a) wanting to have a conscience (i.e., authentic self-understanding), (b) readiness for anxiety (*Angst*) as an attunement, and (c) reticence (*Verschwiegenheit*) or keeping silent (*Schweigen*) as a mode of talk. Taken together, these characteristic manners of understanding, attunement, and talk make up "resoluteness" as the "distinctive and authentic disclosedness" of Dasein (SZ, 295–297).[7]

Perhaps we can say that resoluteness is what authenticates truth in Heidegger's conception. He puts it this way: "Now, in resoluteness the most primordial truth of Dasein has been reached, because it is *authentic*" (SZ, 297). As the authenticating of Dasein's truth, resoluteness modifies the discoveredness of entities, the disclosedness of the world, and the concern of Dasein's being-with others (SZ, 297–298). Resoluteness even "appropriates untruth authentically" (SZ, 299). It reveals the authentic truth of existence. To this truth there corresponds an "equiprimordial being-certain" (*Gewissein*) whereby Dasein unflinchingly and flexibly maintains itself in the actual factical situation disclosed by resoluteness (SZ, 307–308).[8]

Such certainty has little to do with having the present under control or the past in our grasp. For resoluteness "is authentically and completely what it can be only as *anticipatory resoluteness*" (SZ, 309). Moreover, authentication does not stop at the level of ontological structures. Just as anticipation (of death) is not simply an existential structure but an "existentiell potentiality-of-being" (SZ, 309),[9] so too anticipatory resoluteness is not simply existential (i.e., an ontological structure) but also existentiell (i.e., an ontic way of life that a particular Dasein can embrace). As a way of life, anticipatory resoluteness disperses "every fugitive self-covering-over." It leads one to take action "without illusions," for it springs from a "sober understanding" of one's factical possibilities. "Together with the sober *Angst* that brings us before our individualized potentiality-of-being, goes an unshakable joy in this possibility" (SZ, 310).

Hence the orientation with which Dasein inhabits its own disclosedness becomes decisive for Heidegger's conception of truth. Only the readiness and willingness and ability to face Dasein's own finitude and fallibility— not just once, and not simply on occasion, but always again and anew— allows Dasein to be true and, in being true, to let other entities truly be. Dasein's truth can only be true insofar as it is authenticated.

4.1.2   Self-Denial

As I said in the previous chapter, I think Heidegger is right when he refuses to reduce truth to assertoric correctness or to the discoveredness of entities and when he includes the ontological stance of those beings for whom truth itself is always a question. Nevertheless, Heidegger's account of authenticity is problematic in three respects. First, it turns a substantial concept per-taining to actual merits into a formal state of being self-related. Second, it transfigures a historically conditioned and destructive rupture in the fabric of modern society (i.e., "alienation") into an ontological and authenticat-ing encounter with one's own finitude. Third, it turns a mediated process of disclosure into a denial of mediation. Let me take up each problem in turn.

Formal self-relation   In ordinary usage, people describe something as authentic when it proves itself unique, or is particularly trustworthy (e.g., "the real thing"), or meets high expectations (e.g., "genuine"). To use the term in this way, one must already have sufficient dealings with the entity in question, both to detect its characteristic tendencies and to discriminate whether, in comparison with other entities or with other pathways open to this particular entity, its characteristic tendencies are particularly praisewor-thy. Hence, whether in German (*eigentlich*) or English ("authentic"), ordi-nary usage serves the making of substantial judgments about the merits of an entity or of its accomplishments.

Heidegger's account of authenticity exploits the nimbus of discrimi-nation surrounding "authentic," as ordinarily used, to commend what

is little more than a formal state of being self-related.[10] The formality of
this state emerges in the ease with which Heidegger's account equates self-
understanding with *deciding* ("choosing to choose"), *desiring* ("wanting to
have a conscience"), and *adopting* modes of comportment (anticipation
and resoluteness). Moreover, that which distinguishes such authenticity
from inauthenticity is neither available for intersubjective judgment nor
susceptible to "verification" by way of personal self-criticism. At best, the
constituents of resoluteness (i.e., wanting to have a conscience, readiness
for anxiety, and reticence) are predispositional states of consciousness or
states of preconsciousness. As such, they need have no intrinsic connection
with the self's characteristic understandings, dispositions, and linguistic
practices. Presumably one could want to have a conscience, be ready for
anxiety, and be reticent in conversation without characteristically having
a conscience, being anxious, or exercising conversational restraint. Indeed,
the self to which one "relates" in resoluteness is little more than the possibility of a possibility—one relates to the possibility that one's own existence could be impossible. To call such a state of self-relation "authentic"
is to forestall any assessments of the actual merits of that self and of its
accomplishments, whether these assessments occur as self-criticism or as
intersubjective judgment.

   It is so, of course, that Heidegger does not intend his account of authenticity to provide criteria for self-criticism or intersubjective judgment. Yet
his notions of self-understanding, anticipation, choosing to choose, and
keeping silent make little sense apart from the notion of an individualized
self that finds itself (and, according to Heidegger, reclaims itself) among
other selves in a public world. Heidegger admits as much when he describes
anticipatory resoluteness as not only *existential* but also *existentiell*.

   But what does it mean for a self to find itself among other selves in a
public world? Heidegger's own answer turns on the notion of letting others
be themselves by wresting one's own self from falling prey to public talk. He
says: "Resoluteness toward itself first brings Dasein to the possibility of letting the others who are with it 'be' in their ownmost potentiality-of-being,
and also discloses that potentiality in concern which leaps ahead and frees.
… It is from the authentic being a self of resoluteness that authentic being-
with-one-another first arises, not from ambiguous and jealous stipula-
tions and talkative fraternizing in the they and in what [the] they wants
to undertake" (SZ, 298). Accordingly, *inauthentic* existence is characterized

by irresoluteness, by subservience to public understandings and interpretations, by "being at the mercy of the dominant interpretedness of the they.
As the they-self, Dasein is 'lived' by the commonsense ambiguity of publicness in which no one resolves, but which has always already made its decision. Resoluteness means letting oneself be summoned out of one's lostness
in the they" (SZ, 299). For Heidegger, then, to find one's self among other
selves in a public world is to remove one's self from that world and, in
this removal, to endorse a similar removal on the part of others. But this
amounts to *not* finding one's self among others as they are in public but
rather finding others in relation to what one could be in one's own antipublic stance.

The problem, as I see it, is that Heidegger's formalism leaves little room
for the self's authenticity to be either constituted or tested in public. As
a result, it cannot authenticate truth in a public way. Insofar as the self's
authenticity is Heidegger's primary and perhaps exclusive path for authentication, truth itself becomes a privilege of nonpublic existence. It is only
a small step from this position to the even more problematic position that
participation in an exclusive community is the proper path to authenticat-
ing truth.[11] To that extent, Adorno had good reason to attack the "jargon of
authenticity" as a "German ideology."

Michael Zimmerman and other commentators have attempted to ame-
liorate this problem by tracing it back to a "voluntarism" that Heidegger did
not fully embrace in *Being and Time*, and that he later abandoned when he
transposed the notion of authenticity into that of "releasement" (*Gelassenheit*).[12] Such commentators might dismiss my criticisms as overemphasizing
the voluntaristic elements in Heidegger's account of authenticity. But my
criticisms do not revolve around the question of voluntarism. Even if Heideggerian authenticity were construed as a posture of acceptance, of "letting-
be," rather than of resoluteness, of "choosing to choose," the self that either
accepts or resolves would remain a nonpublic or antipublic self. And this
undermines what I shall discuss later as the public authentication of truth.

Transfigured alienation   Another way to say this is to claim that Heidegger's
account of authenticity transfigures alienation. That is the second problem I mentioned earlier. The alienation of which Heidegger speaks occurs
between Dasein and the public world. Discussing conscience as "the call
of care," he writes: "[The caller] is Dasein in its uncanniness, primordially

thrown being-in-the-world, as not-at-home, the naked 'that' in the noth-ingness of the world. The caller is unfamiliar to the everyday they-self, it is something like an *alien* voice. What could be more alien to the they, lost in the manifold 'world' of its heedfulness, than the self individualized to itself in uncanniness thrown into nothingness?" (SZ, 276–277). At the core of authenticity, and voicing itself as Heideggerian conscience, is Dasein's alienation from its own everyday concerns, from the public world in which these concerns have their place, and from the public communications, per-ceptions, and interpretations that give these concerns their shape.[13] To be authentic, Dasein must be triply alienated, alienated from everyday con-cerns, from the public world, and from public interpretations of everyday concerns. For Heidegger, this "must" reflects not a historical condition but an ontological necessity.

Accordingly, when Heidegger elaborates his notion of conscience and contrasts this with other conceptions, he insists on a state of "being-guilty" prior to any responsibility or obligation. His is essentially an amoral con-ception of guilt. Dasein is guilty just by virtue of being Dasein and never gaining "power over one's ownmost being from the ground up" (SZ, 284): "The summons [of conscience] calls back by calling forth: *forth* to the possi-bility of taking over in existence the thrown being that it is, *back* to thrown-ness in order to understand it as the null ground that it has to take up into existence. This calling-back in which conscience calls forth gives Dasein to understand that Dasein itself—as the null ground for its null project, stand-ing in the possibility of its being—must bring itself back to itself from its lostness in the they, and this means that it is *guilty*" (SZ, 287). Hence the call of conscience is neither related to any specific deed nor critical with respect to specific courses of action.

Remarkably, this account seems to turn a sociohistorical problem into an existential virtue. The very notion of an interior self whose authenticity resides in public withdrawal and perennial impotence is itself the philo-sophical expression of a modern cultural tendency whose societal matrix lies in the development of a market economy, privatized family life, and a depoliticized middle class.[14] It would not be difficult to find in Heidegger's characterization of authenticity the forms of alienation identified in Karl Marx's *Economic and Philosophical Manuscripts* and explained in Marx's subsequent writings. What Marx criticizes as societal ruptures—the alien-ation of workers from their labor, products, and fellow workers—Heidegger celebrates as ontological clues to the most primordial truth of Dasein. The result is the picture of a sober and anxious self whose inner authenticity renders it immune from both praise and blame for decisions and actions that are inescapably public. Not only does this self not find itself among others in public, it also secures itself against any challenge they might bring to the truth it claims and to the authentication it supposedly supplies. On a more charitable reading, of course, one could say that Heidegger does not endorse social alienation; he simply characterizes the sort of public nonattachment or self-disentanglement that allows one truly to be true to oneself and to others. Even on that reading, however, it would remain difficult to say either why such truth-to-selfhood requires public nonattachment or how it actually contributes to a public pursuit of truth.

For these reasons I remain skeptical of attempts to find a basis for ethics in Heidegger's account of conscience. In an illuminating paper, Iain Macdonald argues that Heidegger's account offers us "an understanding of normativity rooted in non-identity."[15] The nonidentity lies in the difference between Dasein as it is and Dasein as it can be. Because of this difference, Dasein is always already "guilty." Macdonald interprets such guilt to mean that individual Dasein exists in the gap between what it *is* and what it *ought to be*: "Dasein's self-identity contains an irreducible moment of negativity, of non-identity, in the form of this gap between what Dasein is and what it can or ought to be. The gap is neither bridgeable nor fillable, and the difference it makes essential to existence always remains, no matter how Dasein pursues its projects." Because of this difference, Macdonald thinks Heidegger cannot be accused, à la Adorno, of "undialectically suppressing" nonidentity.[16]

I am not convinced by this attempt to rescue Heidegger, for three reasons. First, Heidegger's self-constituting "difference" does not lie between "is" and "ought" but between "is" and "can be." Nothing in his account of conscience, guilt, and resoluteness would turn a possibility into an obligation. Perhaps Heidegger thinks individual Dasein has an "obligation" to pursue what it can be rather than staying stuck in what it is. But such an "obligation" would be completely formal and open-ended, since my possibilities, while not infinite, are so varied that choosing any one of them, no matter how trivial and misguided, could count as my discharging the "obligation."

In the second place, to the extent that an "ought," an "obligation," surfaces in Heidegger's account, it is completely individual and self-related. Individual Dasein is called—indeed, calls itself—to be what it can be.

Although this may seem to make me "responsible for saying what is or is not right," as Macdonald puts it,[17] it does not make me responsible for *doing* either what *is* right or what *others say* is right. This is a strange sort of "responsibility," for it strips the self of any shared vocation, social ethics, and moral duty. Nor is it clear that an individual has a *responsibility* to pursue what "ought-to-be-for-me."

My third objection concerns the relation between guilt and responsibility. On Macdonald's construal, individual Dasein is responsible by virtue of being guilty, where guilt is understood as the unavoidable condition of the self's never being what it can be. Yet this gets matters precisely backward. If I am not already responsible for who I am and who I am becoming, then the gap between who I am and who I can be would not be a condition of guilt. It would simply be a gap between actuality and possibility, and deciding on one possibility over another would simply be an arbitrary choice. Nor would I be "answerable or accountable"[18] for such a choice, whether to myself or to others, unless I were already responsible, in some sense, for who I am and who I am becoming.

At bottom all three of my objections to Macdonald come to this: Because Heidegger's nonidentity is a purely formal difference between the actual and the possible, it cannot be a source of normativity. In Kantian terms, to make individual Dasein the source of its only genuine norms is to reduce moral obligation to one's pursuing idiosyncratic maxims without asking whether those maxims are right.

Denial of mediation   Yet it is precisely this alienated self, in its predispositional state of formal self-relation, that provides the authentication for truth in Heidegger's account. As I noted earlier, he regards the discoveredness of entities and the disclosedness of Dasein as conditioned by Dasein's authenticity. Only to the extent that Dasein's disclosedness is authentic can Dasein wrest entities from illusion and distortion and reclaim itself from falling prey. This means, however, that Heidegger's "most primordial" truth (SZ, 221) is exactly the opposite of that complex mediation which his own critique of correspondence theories might lead one to expect. The most primordial truth is not a process in which various individuals and communities criticize, correct, and confirm each other's insights and dealings. Nor is it a process in which such insights and dealings are generated, tested, and revised by way of the entities to which they pertain. Rather, the most primordial truth is an anticipatory resoluteness whereby Dasein secures its own "freedom toward death" in disentanglement from the entities, including others, to which Dasein necessarily stands in relation. Hence Heidegger's ontological key to truth is not mediation. Instead, it is Dasein's self-disentanglement from the mediations whereby it is itself constituted. And because the only orientation for such self-disentanglement is the possibility of Dasein's own death, the most primordial truth amounts not only to a denial of all that helps constitute the self but also to a self-denial.

It is because of this displacement from mediation to disentanglement that Heidegger can consider Dasein to be "equiprimordially in truth and untruth" (SZ, 223) and can claim that Dasein's resoluteness "appropriates untruth authentically" (SZ, 299). In both of these formulations, untruth has to do with Dasein's unavoidable entanglement with entities and others that would divert Dasein from its "ownmost possibility." To think of these relations along the lines of entanglement and diversion, however, is to refuse those mediations without which, in my view, no self could be authentic and no truth could occur.

Lest this criticism of Heidegger seem hasty or unfair, let me quote at length from the pages that explain what the authentic appropriation of untruth comes to:

As the they-self, Dasein is "lived" by the commonsense ambiguity of publicness in which no one resolves, but which has always already made its decision. Resoluteness means letting oneself be summoned out of one's lostness in the they. The irresoluteness of the they nevertheless remains in dominance, but it cannot attack resolute existence. ...

For the they, however, [the] situation is essentially closed off. The they knows only the "general situation," loses itself in the nearest "opportunities," and settles its Dasein by calculating the "accidents" which it fails to recognize, deems its own achievement and passes off as such.

Resoluteness brings the being of the there to the existence of its situation. ... The call of conscience does not dangle an empty ideal of existence before us when it summons us to our potentiality-for-being, but calls forth to the situation. (SZ, 299–300)

It might seem at first as if Heidegger here acknowledges the mediations with entities and others that help constitute the self. Yet it is only Dasein as a "they-self," not as a resolute and authentic self, that is so constituted: "Resoluteness means letting oneself be summoned out of one's lostness in the they." Again, it might seem as if such resoluteness is mediated with the public world on which resolutions depend. Yet the content of resoluteness does not arise from the situation on which resolution seizes, but rather from a conscience that calls one forth into the situation and allows Dasein to make its own "factical existence possible for itself" (SZ, 300). The relation between Heidegger's resolute self and the public world is not one of mediation but rather one of self-disentanglement.

Hence I cannot fully endorse Taylor Carman's ingenious attempt to combine the two sides to Heidegger's account of selfhood. Taking a middle road between Guignon's "metaphysically optimistic" and Dreyfus's "pessimistic" construals of Heideggerian selfhood,[19] Carman reads Heidegger as both a "social externalist" (Carman's term) and an "ontological personalist" (my term). On the one hand, Heidegger's account of "the they" or "the one" (*das Man*) makes "anonymous social normativity" constitutive for all of Dasein's hermeneutic practices, including those of authentic self-interpretation. Although Dasein has "a structural tendency … to lapse into banal, inauthentic interpretations of itself," established social practices have a "positive role" to play "in normatively structuring our practices and thereby constituting the intentionality of our everyday understanding."[20] Consequently, according to Carman's interpretation of Heidegger, "existing authentically does not consist simply in freeing oneself from all entanglements with the one, but rather in taking up a new, distinctive relation to the social norms always already governing one's concrete possibilities."[21] On the other hand, Heidegger's nonexpressivist and nonholistic account of authenticity emphasizes both the ontological irreducibility of a first-person perspective and "a profound asymmetry between first-person and second- and third-person modes of interpretation."[22] This first-person emphasis is so strong that Heidegger omits the social character of being a self and neglects the "other-oriented dimension of selfhood, indeed authentic selfhood."[23]

While I agree with the main lines of Carman's double reading, I wonder whether he recognizes sufficiently how the gap between social externalism and ontological personalism vitiates Heidegger's account of authenticity. For the problem is not simply, as Carman puts it, that Heidegger's account remains silent about the hermeneutic conditions for bringing first- and other-person perspectives together "in an overarching interpretation of human beings as selves." The problem is not simply to say how it is possible "to come to understand myself, if only partially, as another" and thereby to engage "in empathy and imagination that is arguably essential to our mundane ethical self-understanding."[24] Rather, the problem is that

Heidegger does not recognize, indeed, he explicitly rejects, the constitutive role that others play in the emergence of a first-person perspective.

As Carman himself correctly observes, Heideggerian conscience "expresses and communicates ... an explicit recognition of the distinction between the everyday self of the one ... and the *proper* self, or one's *own* self, which is an ontological structure formally distinct from any of its own self-interpretations. ... Conscience calls Dasein away from all its ordinary self-interpretations back ... to the bare fact of its existence in all its concrete particularity."[25] But this presupposes, problematically, it seems to me, that there can *be* a "proper self" in its "concrete particularity" that is not always already, in its very "mineness," constituted by the relationships it sustains with other selves. It presupposes that one can have the perspective of "I" without always already having the perspectives of "myself" and "me," perspectives that do not emerge unless the "I" stands in relation to others and internalizes those relationships into its own "I-ness." From a Hegelian perspective, Heideggerian authenticity should be considered "abstract" rather than "concrete": social normativity must always remain *external* to this self and can never play a positive *normative* role in structuring the authentic self's existence. A Heideggerian authentic self can neither learn from social normativity nor contribute to it. This self is fundamentally asocial and therefore also ontologically impossible.

Let me summarize my three criticisms of Heidegger's account of authenticity. I have argued that his account reduces authenticity to a formal state of self-relation, transfigures historical ruptures in modern society into an ontological state of alienation, and turns the truth of Dasein into a denial of mediation. Because of the pivotal role "authenticity" plays in Heidegger's general conception, his idea of truth becomes internally untenable: despite the emphases on interdependence and intersubjectivity in his notions of "being-in-the-world" and "being-with," the most primordial truth of Dasein, whose own disclosedness is itself truth in the most primordial sense, lacks interdependence and intersubjectivity. Or rather, authenticity displays interdependence and intersubjectivity only in a privative way, as that from which Dasein must distance itself in order to be authentic.

In other words, the possibilities opened up by Heidegger's expansive idea of truth as disclosedness get slammed shut by his account of authentication. For if the authentication of truth depends upon Dasein's authenticity, and if Dasein can be authentic only in antipublic self-relation, then truth itself can no longer be attested in public. I would submit that, even on the most comprehensive conception of truth, what cannot be publicly authenticated is not truth at all.

4.2 Emphatic Experience

It should be apparent that my criticisms of Heidegger resemble and in fact draw on Adorno's. Nevertheless, if one asks what account of authentication Adorno himself would offer instead of Heidegger's, one discovers a remarkable point of contact. This connection does not show up in the part of *Negative Dialectics* on Heidegger's ontology (ND, 59–131/67–136).[26] Nor does it surface in the closely related ideology critique titled *The Jargon of Authenticity*. Rather, the point of contact appears at the beginning and end of *Negative Dialectics*, in the introduction and the concluding "Meditations on Metaphysics," where Adorno takes on the issues to which Heidegger's account of authenticity responds. I shall concentrate on a passage from the introduction where Adorno explicates the concept of philosophical experience.[27]

4.2.1 Negative Dialectic

In general, Adorno's negative dialectic is a philosophical attempt to conceptualize the nonconceptual without subsuming the nonconceptual under a system of concepts. As such, negative dialectical philosophy must rely on experience that provides access to the nonconceptual and is neither conceptually prescribed nor incompatible with conceptuality. The experience on which philosophy must rely can be called "emphatic experience." Following J. M. Bernstein, I use the term "emphatic experience" (*Erfahrung*) to refer to something the subject undergoes in relation to a particular object in its nonconceptualized particularity. Emphatic experience is characterized by novelty and by the object's directing the subject's response. It involves "a transformation of the individual [subject] and the emergence of a new object domain."[28] Adorno sees modern societies as having diminished the possibility and authority of such experience. That is why what he calls "philosophical experience" is crucial. Philosophical experience would reconnect rationality with emphatic experience while making palpable its modern demise. Adorno's concept of "philosophical experience" points to the complex ways in which the mediation of conceptualization and the nonconceptual occurs.[29]

Inevitably the question arises whether Adorno's appeal to experience is arbitrary. He takes up this question in the section titled "Privilege of Experience" (ND, 40–42/50–53). The section begins by claiming that "the objectivity of dialectical knowledge" requires more from the epistemic subject rather than less. The standard "positivist" objection to this requirement would be that the requirement is "elitist and undemocratic." It is elitist and undemocratic, says the objector, because the "experience" on which dialectical objectivity supposedly depends is itself the prerogative of individuals who have a particular ability and biography. How can "philosophical experience" be a condition of knowledge if not everyone is capable of such experience?

Adorno immediately concedes that not everyone is capable of philosophical experience. But he says the standard objection ignores a fundamental reason for this incapacity, namely, how "the administered world" intellectually cripples the inhabitants of its iron cage. Only those who resist the pressure to fit in can challenge such a society, and their numbers are limited. In fact, the "privilege" of having experiences from which to critique an undemocratic society is created by that very society: "Critique of privilege has become a privilege: that is how dialectical the course of the world is" (ND, 41/51, tm). Conversely, to expect that everyone in this society could understand everything worth noticing would be to orient knowledge to "pathological traits" of people whose capacity to have experience (*Erfahrungen zu machen*) has been destroyed "by the law of perpetual identity [*Immergleichheit*]" (ND, 41/51, tm). Although seemingly democratic, this expectation of public intelligibility would actually undermine the critique needed to counter antidemocratic tendencies.

The privilege of experience is not really elitist, Adorno suggests, because it comes with a moral obligation. Those who, despite the constraints of prevailing norms, are capable of experience that gives rise to social critique have a moral obligation to express what most people cannot see. Expressing this is a "representative" (*stellvertretend*) effort in which some speak on behalf of many. Nor would "elitist pride" befit philosophical experience, since the capacity for such experience is largely an accident of history and results from the way class-based society is structured (ND, 42/52).

Still, one could ask whether philosophical experience suffices. Should not the critique to which philosophical experience gives rise be subject to public discussion? And what about the experience itself? Should not it be subject to intersubjective testing? Adorno suggests two responses to this line of questioning. The first is simply to say, Do not confuse truth with public intelligibility: "The criterion of what is true is not its direct communicability to everyone. … Truth is objective and not plausible" (ND, 41/51–52, tm). Adorno's second response is that truth mediated through experience loses its supposedly privileged character by becoming publicly discussable. This occurs when philosophical truth claims do not make special pleas for the experiences that give rise to them, but instead enter "configurations and contexts of justification [*Begründungszusammenhänge*]" that either bear them out or establish their inadequacies (ND, 42/52, tm). So philosophical experience gives rise to claims whose truth can be debated, even though what makes them true is not their public intelligibility.

Yet Adorno glosses "philosophical experience" in a way that raises the worry of elitism he has just tried to allay. He writes: "Within philosophical experience chances that the universal randomly grants individuals turn against the universal that sabotages the universality of such experience. Were this universality achieved [*hergestellt*], the experience of all individuals would change accordingly and would lose much of the contingency that meanwhile continues fatally to disfigure their experience" (ND, 42/52, tm). In other words, thanks to the way society is structured, certain individuals are capable of an experience that challenges this structure and its distorting of other people's experience. To the extent that other people's experience is distorted, not accidentally, but necessarily by virtue of society's structure, it would appear that the experience that challenges this structure is itself immune from intersubjective testing. Would not intersubjective testing itself be suspect, Adorno seems to ask, insofar as this occurs under distorting societal conditions?

4.2.2 Unintelligible Truth

This looks to me like a reverse image of Heidegger's account of authenticity, including its attendant problems. Like authenticity in Heidegger's ontology, emphatic experience is supposed to authenticate truth in Adorno's negative dialectic. But just as Heidegger's concept of authenticity renders truth immune from public authentication, so Adorno's idea of truth cordons truth-authenticating experience off from intersubjective testing. Each of the three problems already noted in Heidegger's account of authenticity has a reverse image in Adorno's account of philosophical experience.

Whereas Heidegger turns a substantial concept into a formal state of self-relation, Adorno derives a substantial experience of the nonconceptual from a formal concept of societal structure. Whereas Heidegger transfigures sociohistorical ruptures into an ontological structure, Adorno transforms particular experiences of such ruptures into universal sources of critical insight. Whereas Heidegger turns a mediated process of disclosure into a denial of the self's mediation, Adorno turns an affirmation of the self's mediation into a restriction on the process of disclosure. Let me indicate how each of these problematic reverse images shows up in Adorno's text.

Universal abstraction   The first problem in Adorno's account of philosophical experience pertains to the relation between societal structure and substantial experience. Adorno regards the structure of late capitalism as highly abstract and as one that operates through universal abstraction. In permeating everyday life, such abstraction "sabotages the universality" of experience. Yet at the same time this very same structure "randomly grants individuals" chances that "turn against" universal abstraction. And from this random bestowal, an experience somehow emerges that resists universal abstraction. Adorno considers this experience sufficiently substantial to secure access to the nonconceptual that must be conceptualized but not systematized.

I find Adorno's own account of this relation highly abstract, quite unlike the very specific comments he makes about the ideological positioning of Heidegger's "jargon of authenticity." Adorno refrains from identifying the sociological roles and cultural traits that would be prerequisites for having philosophical experience. Although he waves his hands at the class structure that remains in effect, he makes no effort to acknowledge the differential insights various class positions could afford. The transition from universal societal structure to particular experience has a nearly magical quality. His claim that the experience of certain unnamed individuals is an exception—an exception made possible by the universal rule of abstraction—threatens to become a mere assertion.

Self-authentication   Nevertheless, Adorno repeatedly claims that philosophical experience, of which many people have been made incapable, is a crucial source of critical insight into the society that incapacitates them. Not only is it a crucial source, it is also a universal source, in two respects. First, it puts the one who has philosophical experience in a position to speak on behalf of all others. It entitles, indeed, morally obligates the critical theorist to make this "representative" effort. Second, philosophical experience comes with the presumption that the insight it generates is universally true. In fact, there would likely be no moral obligation to express what most people cannot see if philosophical experience were not presumed to generate universally true insight.

Unfortunately, to turn particular experiences of sociohistorical ruptures into universal sources of critical insight is to cordon these experiences off from intersubjective testing. The problem is that Adorno has made emphatic experience self-authenticating such that the experience being articulated cannot be challenged. The "elitist" element in Adorno's account of philosophical experience is not that it puts some people in a position to speak on behalf of everyone else. The elitist element is that the representative is both self-nominated and self-elected. This is not simply a matter of careless formulation on Adorno's part. By describing others as incapacitated by the societal system, he has effectively disqualified them as participants in the critical process. Or, rather, he has acceded to the disqualification purportedly carried out by society itself. Such disqualification comes back to haunt the position that declares others disqualified. For if *they* are disqualified, then the "representative" effort also loses its point, and the quality of the critical theorist's experience no longer matters. Experience that is self-authenticating in this way cannot be a universal source of critical insight.

Esoteric index   Compared with Heidegger's account of authenticity, Adorno's account of philosophical experience has the advantage that it affirms rather than denies the objective mediation of the self. Adorno rightly criticizes Heidegger's account for ignoring such mediation. According to Adorno, it is because society mediates the self that truth requires subjective mediation. When he develops this emphasis on the self's mediation in his account of philosophical experience, however, he does so at the expense of truth's public intelligibility. A dramatic instance occurs when Adorno declares: "Today every step toward communication sells out the truth and makes it false" (ND, 41/51–52, tm). One wonders how this rather jaundiced view of public intelligibility jibes with Adorno's subsequent acknowledgment that truth claims arising from philosophical experience need to be justified. Presumably the "contexts of justification" are ones where public

intelligibility is required. Yet Adorno makes it seem that the public intelligibility of a philosophical truth claim has no direct bearing on the truth
of the claim or on the truth of the experience from which the claim arises.

To the extent that this is indeed Adorno's position, his idea of truth
becomes untenable. It is made untenable by his regarding self-authenticating experience as the way to authenticate truth. Adorno tries to forestall
this consequence by saying that the interwoven texture (*Geflecht*) of truth is
"the index of itself" (ND, 42/52, tm). In saying this he subscribes to a holistic idea of truth, as Heidegger does with his insistence on disclosedness.
But just as Heidegger undermines his ontological idea of truth by seeking
authentication in antipublic resoluteness, so Adorno weakens his negative
dialectical idea of truth by seeking authentication in publicly unintelligible
experience. For if the strands that supposedly make up the texture of truth
cannot be contributed or checked by those on behalf of whom the dialectical thinker weaves or unfolds this texture, then truth will be an index
that few will consult. We shall be left with what Habermas and Albrecht
Wellmer describe as an esoteric idea of truth.

The problem with an esoteric idea of truth is not simply that it is "elitist and undemocratic," charges that people too easily trot out when they
understand a critique but wish to ignore it. Rather, the problem is that an
esoteric idea of truth cannot do justice to truth itself as a mediated process
in which everyone has a stake and outside which no one in contemporary
society can flourish. Nor can truth be authenticated by publicly unintelligible experience that an abstract societal structure randomly grants, even
though this experience is claimed to be a universal source of critical insight.
While correcting Heidegger's account of authenticity, Adorno shares his
failure to provide for the public authentication of truth.

4.3   Public Authentication

Earlier I distinguished truth from the authentication of truth. But that distinction is not transparent. Although one can speak of truth that has not
been authenticated, it is difficult to imagine authentication that does not
already claim to be true. So the distinction between truth and authentication cannot assign equal weight to each side. Rather, authentication must
be regarded as an extension of truth. Although the unfolding of truth relies
on this extension, the direction of truth's unfolding does not derive from

authentication. Hence, to work out a viable conception of authentication, one must begin with a sufficiently comprehensive idea of truth.

In the previous chapter I characterized truth as an indissoluble and dynamic correlation between human fidelity and societal disclosure, and I qualified the disclosure of society as "life-giving disclosure." By this I mean a societal process in which human beings and other creatures come to flourish in their interconnections. I also specified human fidelity as faithfulness to societal principles such as justice and solidarity that commonly hold for people and that people hold in common. The correlation between disclosure and fidelity is indissoluble: creaturely flourishing depends in part on how human beings pursue fidelity to the commonly holding/held, and the telos of their fidelity is to promote the interconnected flourishing of human beings and other creatures. The correlation is also dynamic: it is a continually unfolding process, not a static structure. So too, the societal principles in question are historical horizons, not timeless absolutes: they emerge from social struggles in which such principles are always already at stake.

Regarded in this way, truth can be authenticated if cultural practices and social institutions enable people to bear witness to a correlation between societal disclosure and their fidelity to societal principles. But what people attest cannot simply be the general process of correlation. It must be specific correlations that occur as people engage in cultural practices and participate in social institutions. In that sense, as Heidegger claimed about authenticity, authentication is both existential and existentiell. Because authentication is supported by cultural practices and social institutions, however, and because it occurs through involvement with these practices and institutions, authentication is intrinsically intersubjective, unlike Heideggerian authenticity. At the same time, one must recognize that society as a whole can be so distorted that specific correlations between societal disclosure and principial fidelity are the exception rather than the rule. In that sense, Adorno's appeal to "emphatic experience" is not misplaced. Yet, because the possibility and occurrence of these correlations depends upon practices and institutions sustained by that same society, the "exceptions" cannot be attributed to a "privilege of experience." They are made possible by the very principles and disclosive process that a distorted society occludes. In other words, authentication depends on truth. As both Heidegger and Adorno acknowledge, truth cannot be exceptional.[30]

What does it mean to bear witness to correlations between disclosure and fidelity? It does not mean simply to articulate concerns in language and to raise and defend certain validity claims, even though linguistic and discursive practices are indispensable ingredients. Rather, to bear witness is to participate in such correlations in a manner that invites both oneself and others to do the same. If, for example, the correlation of contemporary justice and human flourishing requires the elimination of systemic racism, one bears witness to this correlation by doing what one can, with others, to transform the racist practices and institutions to which one belongs, whether through gestures, policies, or public protests. To bear witness to the truth means to do what truth requires in a social context and with respect to others who co-inhabit that context. Bearing witness involves the full range of human activities, not only linguistic and discursive but also aesthetic, ethical, political, economic, and the like.

Whereas truth is the processual correlation between fidelity to principles and life-giving disclosure, the authentication of truth is an invitational enactment of specific correlations in particular circumstances. It is the invitational quality of this enactment that makes authentication public and not privileged. For an invitation always welcomes a response from those invited, including the one who invites. And to be an open invitation rather than a demand or statement or idiosyncratic gesture, it must invite uncoerced acceptance or rejection or inattention.

Describing authentication in this manner casts a different hue on those modes of authentication that Western philosophy has valorized. I think here of a standard emphasis on discursive justification and verification. Earlier I claimed that justification and verification are inescapable elements of authentication to which authentication cannot be reduced. Now I wish to add that, as elements of authentication, justification and verification themselves are at bottom invitational enactments of correlations in context. What distinguishes them from other modes of authentication is their peculiar structure, which singles out the purported universality and necessity of enacted correlations. Such discursive practices try to bear out the purported universality of the validity claims raised in other practices. They try to do this with an appeal to their own inherent validity. Their inherent validity is not a matter of other societal principles such as solidarity and justice but rather a matter of logic and rhetoric. Hence the appearance arises that justification and verification are not modes of authentication and that what gets justified or verified has little to do with the comprehensive idea of truth. Moreover, given a pervasive "logical prejudice" (Dahlstrom) in Western philosophy, which both Heidegger and Adorno challenge, it also appears that the comprehensive idea of truth has little to do with truth "properly speaking"—that is, with truth as assertoric correctness or propositional accuracy.

Such appearances turn truth upside down. What drives discursive practices and makes them important is their role within multidimensional processes of authentication. Part of invitationally enacting correlations of fidelity and disclosure is to test the reach of the principles at stake and to establish the extent of the circumstances in which correlations are enacted. It makes a difference for the enactment itself whether justice is only for "just us" or also for "others," whether the flourishing of some comes at the expense of others. It also matters that we have discursive practices and discursively attuned institutions within which deliberation about such differences can occur. For this, neither prelinguistic intuitions nor postdiscursive decisions suffice.

Yet it would be a mistake to think that discursive practices have the final word or that they transcend the contexts of authentication. Discursive practices occur within multidimensional processes of authentication; other modes of authentication provide their context. This implies that conflicts can occur between discursive and nondiscursive modes of authentication, and that such conflicts cannot always be resolved in a discursive fashion. What is logically true can be contextually false: a "good argument" can support unjust and destructive arrangements. Conversely, what is "true in practice" may receive articulations and defenses that are logically invalid.

Nevertheless, the normative role of justification and verification as modes of authentication is to test the universality of societal principles and the necessity of specific correlations between principial fidelity and societal disclosure. Is the contemporary principle of justice such that systemic racism must be eliminated? And are particular gestures, policies, or protests necessary in that regard? Although one does not need well-articulated answers to such questions in order to challenge systemic racism, resistance would falter if the questions never arose.

The structurally peculiar focus on validity, combined with Western philosophy's logical prejudice, has led many philosophers to link the public character of authentication with the "rationality" of discursive practices.

Both Heidegger and Adorno question that linkage. They do so, however, at the expense of authentication's public character. I have proposed, in a preliminary fashion, to retain their concern for the authentication of truth without either surrendering the public character of authentication or reducing authentication to discursive practices.[31] Truth as such may not be democratic, but its invitational enactment must be public. A public invitation will be open to free recognition and acceptance or refusal on the part of those invited. To that extent, and to the extent that public freedom, recognition, and participation are the hallmarks of democracy, the authentication of truth must be not only public but democratic. Truth calls for public authentication. It calls for democratic truth-telling, both verbal and nonverbal, that does not avoid public presentation and response.

It is precisely because Heidegger and Adorno emphasize nondiscursive authentication that their contributions are important and their hidden point of contact deserves further attention. Both Heidegger and Adorno recognize that philosophical conceptions of truth have far-reaching implications for the kind of society we inhabit and the sorts of people we become. They make compelling cases for the claim that traditional Western conceptions of truth, whether classical and metaphysical or modern and epistemological, have supported destructive tendencies in society, while also opening up potentially fruitful paths. Neither one thinks "truth" can be left to the logicians and the technicians of philosophy. Each has attempted in his own way to reconnect the idea of truth with the cultural issues and social crises from which overly professionalized and hyperspecialized philosophies take distance. Their assessments may be dramatically opposed, but together Heidegger and Adorno have placed such matters at the center of philosophical attention.

The concern Heidegger and Adorno share for the authentication of truth needs to be understood in this societal context. Both of them recognize that truth is not simply a theoretical concern, that truth must be borne out in contemporary lives and practices and institutions. Both of them claim that the historical trajectory of modern Western society makes this requirement increasingly difficult to sustain. Both of them seek a site from which that trajectory can be resisted and perhaps redirected, whether the site be the authenticity of Dasein or the occurrence of emphatic experience.

But these sites are oppositional rather than transformative, and their access is restricted rather than open to a broader public. As I have tried to suggest, oppositional and restricted sites of authentication are inadequate for the comprehensive process of truth that both Heidegger and Adorno endorse. Their philosophies leave us with an exceptional challenge: to discover how truth can be borne out in ways that are authentic, emphatic, and thoroughly democratic. In such modes of public authentication, and in a society that sustains them, the dialectical extremes of Heidegger and Adorno would not only touch but be true. No longer restricting the ranges of experience that can authenticate the truth of its conceptual reflection, philosophy itself would be transformed.[32]

5   Truth and Justification: Jürgen Habermas

Although truth cannot be reduced to ... justified assertibility, there has to be an internal relation between truth and justification.

—Jürgen Habermas[1]

A sufficiently comprehensive account of the relation between truth and authentication, as initially sketched in the previous chapter, would need to encompass the relation between propositional truth and discursive justification, as discussed in recent Anglo-American debates about alethic realism. These debates are significant for how we think about truth; questions about the relation between propositional truth and discursive justification lie at their heart.

In 1982, for example, Alvin Plantinga delivered a presidential address titled "How to Be an Anti-Realist" at the annual meeting of the Western Division (now the Central Division) of the American Philosophical Association (APA).[2] He proposed to mediate a dispute about realism encapsulated in addresses given by three previous APA divisional presidents, with Hilary Putnam and Richard Rorty on the antirealist side and William Alston on the realist side. Plantinga argued that contemporary antirealism is "wholly unacceptable" and Platonist "unbridled realism" is "unlovely."[3] The right way to be an antirealist, he said, is to be a theist in the manner of Thomas Aquinas.

Plantinga characterizes Putnam and Rorty as "creative" antirealists concerning propositional truth. He says that, following a line of thought that supposedly began with Kant, Putnam and Rorty think if human minds "can't settle the question whether a proposition is true, then there's no truth there to be known."[4] In other words, the truth of a proposition depends on whether the proposition can be humanly justified. Plantinga raises two objections to this apparent reduction of truth to justification. First, Putnam and Rorty tend toward "self-referential incoherence": if truth is as they say it is, then their construals are not true.[5] Second, their antirealist views, which "begin by taking fundamental disagreement seriously," end up "denying its possibility."[6]

Nevertheless, Plantinga does acknowledge that truths and propositions can hardly be "totally independent of minds or persons." He is not attracted to "Platonist" realism, by which he means the position that the existence of truths and propositions is completely independent "of minds and their noetic activity."[7] Accordingly, he splits the difference and proposes theistic antirealism in the style of Aquinas as an alternative to both Platonism and creative antirealism. On a theistic antirealist construal, truth must be independent of *human* noetic activity but cannot be independent of *God's* noetic activity. Propositions exist because God thinks them, and they are true if and only if God believes them.[8]

Undoubtedly this is a bold set of claims to make, especially in a presidential address to the largest professional association of philosophers in North America. Yet whether Plantinga avoids the two problems he attributes to Putnam and Rorty is an open question. Although I agree that what he calls "creative anti-realism" is deeply problematic, I find Plantinga's epistemological reversion to medieval theism no more acceptable than Plantinga considered the positions of Putnam and Rorty to be.[9]

To find a better resolution to this dispute, I plan to discuss the theory of truth put forward by German social philosopher Jürgen Habermas. Habermas has moved from an antirealist to a quasi-realist conception of propositional truth, and this trajectory points in a promising direction. Moreover, he has taken this path in response to Putnam and Rorty. First I describe the development of Habermas's theory of truth and examine a recent version in greater detail. Then I propose an alternative account of propositional truth, one that critically appropriates Habermas's insights with an aim to resolving the realism–antirealism dispute. In the background to my account lie the more comprehensive conceptions of truth and authentication introduced in the previous chapters.

Before I discuss Habermas, however, let me explain two sets of terms: *alethic realism* and *antirealism*, and *nonepistemic* and *epistemic* conceptions of propositional truth. These two sets overlap to a large extent, and I use them somewhat interchangeably: alethic realism is usually nonepistemic, and alethic antirealism is usually epistemic. Taking a cue from Michael Lynch, by alethic realism I mean the position that propositional truth "hinges not on us but on the world." Whether a proposition is true depends on whether "things in the world are as that proposition says they are."[10] Many correspondence theories of truth, which define truth as correspondence between propositions and facts or states of affairs, are good examples of alethic realism. Alethic antirealism is the position that propositional truth does not hinge on whether things in the world are as propositions say they are. Instead, it hinges on other factors, such as how well the proposition coheres with other propositions (coherence theories) or what consequences follow from employing the proposition in inquiry or action (pragmatic theories). Plantinga's position straddles these alternatives, since he argues that it is not the world's existence but God's noetic activity that makes propositions true.

The distinction between nonepistemic and epistemic conceptions of truth pertains primarily to the relation between the truth of propositions and justifications of their truth. A nonepistemic conception claims that "whether a proposition is true does not depend on whether anyone is justified in believing the proposition."[11] In that sense, propositional truth is "mind-independent," as Plantinga holds with respect to human minds but not with respect to God's mind. An epistemic conception, by contrast, claims that whether a proposition is true does depend to some significant degree on whether someone is justified in believing it.[12] In principle, one could subscribe to alethic antirealism without having an epistemic conception of truth, but usually the two go together,[13] as in Habermas's earliest formulations of a truth theory.

5.1 Habermas's Conception of Truth

Habermas's conception of truth arises from his lifelong attempt to spell out a critical theory of contemporary society that accords with deeply democratic politics. His development of this conception has gone through three stages, which I label "consensus theory," "formal pragmatics," and "pragmatic realism."[14] For more than two decades, Habermas developed an epistemic and antirealist conception of truth. In the 1990s, however, he began to change his mind, and his current pragmatic realist conception incorporates some elements of alethic realism.

5.1.1   Consensus Theory and Formal Pragmatics

Consensus theory   Habermas's consensus theory of truth emerged in the early 1970s.[15] Like Rorty during that decade, Habermas proposed an epistemic conception of truth: he tried to explicate the concept of truth by saying how truth claims can be justified. His central claim is that truth primarily has to do not with a supposed correspondence between propositions and facts but with the discursive redemption or vindication (*Einlösung*) of the validity claims that we unavoidably raise when we use language to reach understanding with one another. There are three such validity claims—claims to truth, to rightness, and to truthfulness or sincerity (*Wahrhaftigkeit*)—and our various speech acts raise all three either explicitly or implicitly.[16] The claim to truth arises most explicitly in constative speech acts: in assertions, explanations, descriptions, and the like.

To illustrate, imagine you and I are talking and I tell you, "Alumni Hall is in the Victoria College building at the University of Toronto." When I make this assertion, I unavoidably and simultaneously claim that the proposition asserted—that Alumni Hall is in the Victoria College building, and so on—is true. If you are puzzled by my assertion or question its veracity, then I owe it to you to back up my truth claim. Such questioning and backing of claims typically occurs through argumentation, according to Habermas. Argumentation and potential agreement concerning validity claims are what he has in view when he writes about their discursive vindication. On a consensus theory, he says, "The truth condition of propositions is the potential assent of *all* others. ... The universal-pragmatic meaning of truth, therefore, is determined in terms of the demand of reaching a rational consensus."[17] In this way, Habermas indexes the truth of propositions to the quality of their justification.

Formal pragmatics   Habermas modifies and deepens his account of discursive justification in his two-volume *The Theory of Communicative Action*, published in German in 1981.[18] There he begins to distinguish more clearly between truth and justification by linking justification with *meaning* rather than with *truth* per se. In place of a consensus theory of truth, he proposes a formal pragmatic theory of meaning.[19]

Habermas's most important move in this context is to embed *linguistic* meaning—the meaning of sentences—within *communicative* meaning—the meaning of human interactions that employ sentences to reach mutual understanding. To understand linguistic meaning, he says, we need to understand how people use language to communicate. At bottom, linguistically mediated interaction serves three pragmatic functions: to represent states of affairs, to establish and renew interpersonal relations, and to present one's own experiences. The first function is cognitive; the second, regulative; and the third, expressive. Just as truth-conditional semantic theories stemming from Gottlob Frege argue that we understand the meaning of a sentence when we know under what conditions the sentence is (or would be) true, so Habermas argues that we understand the meaning of a linguistically mediated interaction when we know the conditions under which it is (or would be) acceptable. Given the differentiation of language functions, however, and the correlated differentiation of validity claims, Habermas says one must expand these acceptability conditions "beyond the truth of propositions" and no longer identify them "on the semantic level of sentences but on the pragmatic level of utterances" or speech acts.[20]

The acceptability conditions for *assertoric* speech acts are assertibility conditions. According to Habermas, to understand the meaning of my asserting "Alumni Hall is in the Victoria College building," you need to know more than the truth conditions for the proposition asserted. You also need to know when I, as the speaker making the assertion, have "good grounds to undertake a warrant that the conditions for the truth of the asserted sentence are satisfied."[21] In other words, you need to know what would authorize me to claim that the asserted proposition is true and what would correlatively motivate you to accept my claim. So, a hearer understands the meaning of a speaker's assertoric speech act if the hearer knows two sets of conditions: first, the conditions that would make the asserted proposition true (e.g., what must be the case in order for the proposition "Alumni Hall is in the Victoria College building" to be true); and second, the conditions under which the asserter would have convincing reasons to claim that the proposition is true (e.g., what sorts of additional information I would have to provide to support my claim that the asserted proposition about Alumni Hall is true).

Despite the distinction between truth conditions and assertibility conditions, however, Habermas has not really provided a theory of propositional truth. Instead, he has offered a theory of discursive justification. Essentially, *truth* means "justified" or "warranted" assertibility. As Barbara Fultner pointed out in 1996, however, there is "a patent tension between truth and warranted assertibility."[22] For, as Putnam indicated in 1981, truth is supposed to be a feature "that cannot be lost, whereas justification can be lost."[23]

5.1.2   Pragmatic Realism

Habermas responds to such concerns in a 1996 essay titled "Richard Rorty's Pragmatic Turn." Emphasizing both the distinction between truth and justification and their internal relation, he argues that "truth cannot be reduced to ... justified assertibility."[24] This argument relies heavily on two claims. The first claim concerns human behavior: "as interacting and intervening subjects, we are always already in contact with things about which we can make statements"—not *despite* language but precisely *in virtue of* the linguistically mediated character of human action. The second claim concerns the presuppositions of communication: participants in communicative action cannot reach understanding with each other unless we "refer to a single objective world" and suppose this world to be "independent of our descriptions." Whereas Rorty tends to deny both claims, Habermas thinks that linguistically mediated behavioral contact with things and the supposition of an independent objective world are necessary if everyday practices are not to "come apart at the seams."[25]

Accordingly, in *Truth and Justification* Habermas presents what he calls a "Janus-faced" concept of truth.[26] The current version of his theory is (roughly) realist with respect to truth and antirealist with respect to justification. Habermas's own description suggests the label "linguistic-pragmatic epistemological realism" or, more simply, "pragmatic realism."

A Janus-faced concept   Habermas formulates his Janus-faced concept of truth in response to two questions. First, if all forms of human life emerge contingently from natural evolution, how can we account for our unavoidably raising truth claims that transcend the contexts in which we raise them? Second, how can we reconcile the claim that any human access to so-called reality is linguistically mediated with the intuitively plausible realist assumption that "there is a world existing independently of our descriptions of it and that is the same for all observers" (TJ, 2/8)? If Habermas cannot give satisfactory answers, then he will need to adopt Richard Rorty's epistemic, antirealist, and radical contextualism with respect to propositional truth. Habermas responds by introducing several pairs of distinctions: between communication and representation, between life-world and objective world, between meaning and reference, and, most significantly for present purposes, between justification and truth. Let me summarize these distinctions.

To begin with, Habermas insists that representation and communication are equiprimordial functions of language usage. In our speech acts, we communicate with others by referring to "the world and its objects," and vice versa: "As representation and as communicative act, a linguistic utterance points in both directions at once: toward the world and toward the addressee" (TJ, 3/9). Both representation and communication are made possible by "deep-seated structures of … the lifeworld" (TJ, 11/20), and they pragmatically presuppose a shared objective world. The *lifeworld* encompasses all types of rule-governed action, both linguistic and nonlinguistic and both communicative and strategic or instrumental. The notion of an *objective world*, by contrast, pertains to the subset of rule-governed actions that aim "instrumentally to intervene in or strategically to influence the course of events" (TJ, 15/23). This "performatively established relation to objects," in turn, has links to "the semantic relation to objects that interlocutors establish in asserting facts about them" (TJ, 15/24). Agents and language users pragmatically presuppose "a shared objective world as the totality of objects to be dealt with and judged" and "as existing independently and as the same for everyone" (TJ, 16/24–25). This pragmatic presupposition underlies our truth claims.

Habermas links successful reference and propositional truth to "the normativity of successful coping" (TJ, 15/24). To explain this link, he introduces a firm distinction between meaning and reference.[27] The distinction relies on two claims. First, linguistic practices enable us to "refer to language-independent objects about which we assert something." Second, any language user, regardless of his or her context, can "refer to a common system of possible referents" and can "identify independently existing objects." Accordingly, "reference to the *same* object must remain constant even under *different* descriptions" (TJ, 33/44–45).[28] This is possible because the purposive contact we have with objects funds the "semantic relations" we "explicitly establish" when we make assertions (TJ, 35/47). So, for example, our assertion that "this is water, not oil" is rooted in our nonlinguistic actions of drinking water, swimming in it, using it to cultivate crops, and the like. If we were not able, on the basis of ordinary practices, to keep the reference of "water" constant, then we could not use the term successfully in multiple situations.

Yet the constancy of reference does not explain the truth of statements or propositions, which "can be justified only by means of other statements" and not by a direct appeal to practical experience (TJ, 35/47). To that extent, Rorty's contextualism is not off base. Nevertheless, Habermas points to three factors that cannot be reconciled with radical contextualism, namely, the assumption of "epistemological realism" in ordinary practices, the "power of learning processes" to revise the contexts in which they occur, and the tendency of truth claims to have "universalist import" that transcends the context in which we raise them (TJ, 36/48). In everyday life, when we assert "This is water, not oil," we assume the statement to be true with respect to the liquid we experience; we can use such a statement to learn something new about our environment; and we consider the statement to be true not just here and now and for ourselves, but also at any relevant time and place and for anyone who could respond to it.

Action and discourse   Habermas's pragmatically realist conception of truth aims to account for action and discourse. He does not give up his emphasis on rational discourse as the privileged mode for sorting out truth claims.[29] Instead, he says the fact that, epistemologically, we must connect truth and justification should not mislead us into thinking that truth is simply an idealization of justification. According to Habermas, a nonepistemic concept of truth shows up in everyday action. Ordinarily, in the course of action, we do not doubt the truth of our beliefs. We rely on "certainties of action" in our "practical dealings with an objective world" and naively take the beliefs that guide our actions "to be true absolutely." As Habermas puts it, "We don't walk onto any bridge whose stability we doubt." Implicit in such "realism of everyday practice" is "a concept of unconditional truth." As soon as our practices fail and contradictions arise, however, we begin to see the truth of the relevant beliefs "as merely 'presumed truths,' that is, as fundamentally problematic truth *claims*." Moreover, if someone else challenges the truth of what we assert, then our only recourse is to try to justify "the now thematized truth of controversial propositions" (TJ, 39/52).

In other words, the concept of truth plays a different role in the domain of *action* than it does in justificatory *discourse*. In action, we implicitly hold our beliefs to be undoubtedly true and implicitly make truth claims about them when we communicate. At this level we assert facts that concern "objects *themselves*" (TJ, 39/53). In discourse, by contrast, our claims to truth are always and unavoidably provisional. The only way to vindicate such claims is via "the convincing power of good reasons," and even the best reasons remain "under the proviso of fallibility" (TJ, 40/53). A discursive agreement authorizes us to accept only the justified claim that a proposition is true, not the truth of the proposition as such.

Habermas thinks the nonepistemic concept of truth presupposed in action provides a "justification-transcendent standard for orienting ourselves by context-independent truth claims." This in turn sheds a pragmatic light on the concepts of objectivity, facts, and states of affairs that figure prominently in more robustly realist conceptions of truth. According to Habermas, the concept of objectivity arises from our failures to cope with the world, when we "experience in practice that the world revokes its readiness to cooperate." Such failures force us to recognize that "the world is not up to us" but exists independently of our language usage and actions. Moreover, the concept of an objective world enables us to "refer to things that can be identified as the same under different descriptions" and so to regard the world as "the *same* for all of us" (TJ, 254–255/293–294). Such pragmatically recognized objectivity sustains the robustly realist claim that true assertions refer to facts about the world or to states of affairs that obtain, a claim that calls attention to "a connection between … the truth of statements [*Aussagen*] and the 'objectivity' of that about which something is stated" (TJ, 254/293). Accordingly, truth cannot be a merely epistemic notion.

Two questions   Compared with his earlier consensus theory of truth and his formal pragmatics of meaning, Habermas's Janus-faced pragmatic realism goes some distance to answer objections like the ones Plantinga poses for Putnam and Rorty. Yet it also raises two new questions that need to be addressed. One concerns the relation between propositions and what we experience as an "objective world." In what way, if any, does this relation make propositions true? The other concerns the relation between propositional truth and discursive justification. Does argumentation aim only to establish the acceptability of truth claims? Or does it also seek to affirm the truth of propositions as such? I do not believe Habermas has a satisfactory answer to either question.[30] To address them, I wish to propose an alternative conception that, reworking Habermas's insights, promises a post-Plantingian resolution to the debate between realists and antirealists in Anglo-American philosophy.

5.2   Truth, Facts, and Justification

My overarching conception of truth is much broader than a concept of propositional truth, and my conception of the authentication of truth is considerably more expansive than a concept of discursive justification.[31] I assume, for example, that propositional truth is neither the only nor the privileged mode of truth. I also assume that discursive justification is only one manner of authentication and that it regularly supports and receives direction from other ways of authentication. With those qualifications in mind, let me discuss the concept of propositional truth in relation first to empirical facts and then to discursive justification.

5.2.1   Propositional Truth and Empirical Facts

In the analytic literature on truth, disagreements about the relation between propositional truth and empirical facts have to do with "truth bearers," "truth makers," and the connection between the two. Although Habermas rejects alethic realism as a general position, he wishes to retain aspects of the connection realism posits between truth bearers and truth makers. Specifically, he is interested in the realist intuition that the truth of propositions is indexed to the existence of facts or states of affairs. Yet Habermas does not follow the empiricist path of positing facts as experienced objects. Facts are related to what we experience in our practical engagements with the world, he says, but we do not experience them as such. Rather, they are formulated when we assert propositions or, more broadly, when our speech acts employ sentences that have propositional content.

If, contrary to standard versions of alethic realism, the facts that make assertions and propositions true do not "exist" in the "real world," then Habermas needs to account for how facts relate to the things with which we are "in contact" as "interacting and intervening subjects"[32]—what I call *practical objects*. Habermas's view of this relationship is not very clear. But let me posit a two-way process of decontextualization and recontextualization to make sense of how he views the fact–object relation.

In the ordinary course of action, I experience a liquid that looks, smells, tastes, and feels a certain way, and I say to you, "This is water." I have no reason to doubt the liquid is water, and so I take the belief I have formulated to be straightforwardly true. In this context, *true* seems to mean that the belief in question is reliable in practice and that my assertion is a reliable articulation of my belief. If you challenge my assertion, you question the reliability of my belief and of what I have said. Such questioning *decontextualizes* the practical belief and the content of what I have said: "Is it really water?" Only under such conditions of decontextualization does the fact that "this is water" emerge, when the content of what I have said becomes a topic for disagreement and potential agreement. What is reliably believed in practice is decontextualized into what is questionable in fact.

Recontextualizing occurs when sufficient agreement is reached for both interlocutors to rely on the belief whose content was questioned. For example, we could end our discussion by both deciding not to imbibe the mysterious liquid. Alternatively, I could offer you a cup of cold water. At this point, whether the liquid is water no longer functions as a fact to be disputed but as the reliable content of what both of us believe in practice.

Reliability and interdependence   I find much to commend this proposed reworking of Habermas's approach. Yet there is something missing. What is it about practical objects that allows us to acquire true beliefs about them— that is, practically reliable beliefs—in the first place? And what is it about practical objects that allows us to make truth-claiming assertions about them? Habermas has no answer to these questions. Moreover, I suspect that the linguistic-pragmatic underpinnings to his truth theory would not support his venturing an answer. This is one bridge he is not ready to cross. I, by contrast, think an answer is necessary if we want to give full credence to the correct intuitions of alethic realism.

It is not enough, in my view, to presuppose an independent objective world that is the same for everyone. We also need to presuppose, in both action and discourse, that practical objects lend themselves to our actions and interactions, and do so in ways that are not solely of our own making or choosing. In other words, we need to presuppose an *interdependent* world, one where the "readiness to hand" or "handiness" (Heidegger: *Zuhandenheit*) of practical objects sustains our projects in ways that supervene on the particular uses to which we put such objects in specific contexts. We can have reliable beliefs about water, for example, because water really does quench our thirst and we can rely on it to do so.

We can talk about practical objects, which is one way they lend themselves to our actions and interactions. We can refer to them and make predications. I call something "water" and tell you it is cold. If we speak the same language, you probably understand what I mean. To explain how this is possible requires more than theories of reference and predication and more than accounts of speech acts and their propositional content. It also requires acknowledging how practical objects let us talk about them.

If, in addition, we want to explain how our talking about practical objects can be reliable and how our assertions about them can be true, then we need to account for the specific ways practical objects support reliable talk and true assertions. In previous chapters I identify this feature of practical objects as *predicative availability*. The predicative availability of practical objects is the way they allow us to assert something about them. To do so, we must be able to refer to practical objects with language. We can establish their identity through referring expressions and referential language without allowing this referential identity to be the entirety of what they are. Predicative availability is the face that practical objects turn toward us when we call their names— that is, when we successfully refer to them using language.

There is more to predicative availability than linguistic referability, however. To lend itself to reliable talk and true assertions about it, a practical object must also allow its linguistically established identity to be linguistically specified. "The water is cold," we say, or "Alumni Hall is in the Victoria College building," and the water lets itself be specified with respect to temperature, while Alumni Hall lets itself be specified with respect to location. Predication is the linguistically embedded specification of linguistically identified objects, and it is a normal part of everyday language usage. Predicative availability is how practical objects let us refer to them with specificity in language.

Facts as predicative self-disclosure   Reliable talk and true assertions with respect to practical objects require more than reference, predication, and predicative availability. The way a practical object shows itself to us must line up with some other relevant way in which it is available. If I say to you, "The water is too cold," for example, that which allows me to refer to it as "water" and to speak of it as "too cold" must also allow me to relate this predicate to the water's *non*predicative availability for, say, swimming. This capacity on the part of practical objects is what I call *predicative* *self-disclosure.* Predicative self-disclosure is what the object under reference allows us to specify in relation to at least one other way in which the object is available to us.

Here the concept of a *fact* becomes significant. A fact is simply the predicative self-disclosure of an object or of a range of objects on the occasion of language usage in which reference and predication occur with respect to these objects. A fact is not either real or linguistic—it is both. It is a way in which objects relate to human practices, insofar as these practices include linguistic ones of reference and predication.

To this extent, facts are relevant for all reliable talk, and not only for constative speech acts in general or assertoric speech acts in particular. Habermas casts facts too narrowly when he portrays them as what we assert and what makes statements or propositions true. Although he is right to warn us against equating facts with practical objects as such, he fails to see that facts are a mode in which practical objects disclose themselves.

Correctness and accuracy But how should we understand the relation between assertions and propositions on the one hand, and facts on the other? I agree with Habermas that assertions are speech acts that raise a truth claim and that facts make propositions true. I also agree that propositions are the content of our assertions and that, via analysis, we can assign a propositional content to any speech act, whether assertoric or not. Yet I find implausible his early claim, which he seems not to have given up, that truth "is not a property of assertions" and is rather only something we claim concerning the propositions or statements (*Aussagen*) we assert.[33] For in everyday communication we are just as concerned that someone's asserting something is true as we are concerned about the truth of the proposition asserted. If you are not convinced of the water's temperature when I assert, "The water is too cold," you could exclaim, "That's not so!" But you could also ask, "Are you sure about that?" A question or exclamation of the first sort pertains to the truth claimed for the proposition—that it is true that the water is too cold. A question of the second sort pertains to the truth of my asserting this.

If my description is right, then the concept of truth appears to have a double role when we assert propositions. In one role it pertains to the *correctness* of the practice of making assertions. In the other role it pertains to the *accuracy* of the result of engaging in this practice, namely, the accuracy of the content of what one asserts—the accuracy of the proposition.[34] How, then, do facts relate to both the truth of asserting (i.e., correctness) and the truth of propositions (i.e., accuracy)? From the preceding analysis of facts, it appears that asserting is true (i.e., correct) just in case the practical object about which we make an assertion self-discloses in the manner asserted. My asserting "The water is too cold" is a correct speech act on a specific occasion if, for example, the water shows itself to be insufficiently warm for us to swim in it.

The truth of propositions, by contrast, involves a further decontextualization from this underlying assertoric relation. The propositional content of an assertion takes the form "that something is the case," for example, "that the water is too cold." Typically, we use this form to take up assertions in discourse. We argue about the content of what someone asserts and seek agreement about whether this or that is the case. Facts also undergo decontextualization in relationship to propositions. They are no longer simply a way in which practical objects self-disclose for linguistic practices. Now they are "states of affairs" that must "obtain" in order for the proposition to be accurate. Owing to double decontextualization, the proposition is available for anyone to discuss, and the state of affairs is projected beyond a particular object to encompass any practical objects that would be similar in a relevant way.

According to the proposed analysis, the relation that sustains the truth—that is, accuracy—of propositions is not a correspondence between propositions and facts or states of affairs. Rather, it is one of decontextualized disclosure. In this relation, the proposition helps to identify the asserted object as an abiding topic for potential discussion and debate, and the fact as a state of affairs presents the asserted object as nothing other than how it has been asserted to be. A proposition about a practical object is true (i.e., accurate) just in case the asserted object presents itself as nothing other than how it has been asserted to be. Propositions are decontextualized statements of decontextualized predicative identity.

Insofar as contemporary truth theories restrict truth to propositional truth, and insofar as propositional truth involves decontextualization, we can understand why theorists such as Putnam claim that propositional truth "cannot be lost." Apart from its role in assertoric practices and its underpinnings in action, interaction, and their practical objects, however, propositional truth would never be gained. Although Habermas's

Janus-faced concept of truth in both action and discourse points in this direction, I hope to have offered a better explanation for the relation between propositional truth and empirical facts. I suggest that we must distinguish three facets of truth—practical reliability, assertoric correctness, and propositional accuracy—and not simply subsume all three under an undifferentiated notion of propositional truth.

5.2.2 Propositional Truth and Discursive Justification

Habermas's pragmatic realism also raises questions about the relation between propositional truth and discursive justification. Although he has revised his conception of truth, the main lines of his account of justification remain the same: discursive justification is a process of argumentation that aims to establish the validity of the claims that are raised with speech acts. The claims it aims to establish are ones whose validity would transcend the context in which a claim arises.

Truth claims   What do we attempt to justify discursively when propositional truth is at issue? According to Habermas, we do not try to justify the truth of the proposition as such. Rather, we try to justify our *claim* to propositional truth—the claim to truth that is raised with our speech act. We do not argue for or against the truth of the proposition as such, but we exchange reasons for accepting or rejecting the claim that an asserted proposition is true. Our readiness to back up our claims with convincing reasons sustains our assertoric interactions.

Here, however, an issue arises that Habermas has not successfully addressed. Does the truth or falsity of a proposition make any difference to the outcome of discourse about truth claims? Intuitively, one wants to say yes, it does make a difference. It appears that even the most convincing reasons I can give would not be good reasons to claim that my asserted proposition is true if it is untrue. Habermas, however, is hesitant to say this. In his account, what makes for better and worse justifications is not so much the content of the reasons we give as the manner in which we give them. What matters most for him is the degree to which justification approximates a genuinely democratic process.

Hence Habermas's account of justification poses a challenge for someone who shares his democratic, procedural emphasis but sees a more substantial link between propositional truth and discursive justification and does not endorse a correspondence theory of truth. To explain this link, I view the argumentative justification of assertoric truth claims as a discursive mode of authenticating propositional truth. As I indicated in chapter 4, authentication in general encompasses all the ways we bear witness to truth, and truth in general requires authentication in order to unfold.[35] Accordingly, the argumentative justification of assertoric truth claims is how we bear witness to propositional truth and how propositional truth unfolds. This implies that, although propositional truth "cannot be lost," it also cannot be static—propositional truth is not eternal or immutable. It also implies that discursive justification is normatively indexed to propositional truth and not simply to procedural norms of argumentation.

Disclosive insight and logical validity   Let me elaborate. The proposition one asserts, if it is true, discloses a fact—itself a mode of self-disclosure—in a decontextualized way. When I assert a proposition, I simultaneously claim that the proposition is true in the sense that it is accurate. The accuracy of a proposition is its ability simultaneously to decontextualize and to disclose a practical object's predicative self-disclosure. I raise a truth claim not simply to elicit your agreement but also to affirm the insight that the proposition affords. I am not simply saying, in effect, "This is true, don't you agree?" I am also saying, "This is a reliable insight, correctly asserted, that anyone should be able to share." Although it is so that discourse unavoidably "fallibilizes" both my claim and the purported insight, such fallibilism can only make sense if we simultaneously expect propositions to be genuinely insightful, albeit in a decontextualized way. Good arguments connect a proposed insight with other insights that are relevant for understanding the matter about which the original assertion was made.

Moreover, such connecting of insights occurs in a manner that is distinctive to argumentation. It occurs with reference to the societal principle of logical validity. Although this principle is only one among many that guide human action and interaction, and although in nondiscursive contexts it is rarely the primary principle offering guidance, the pursuit of logical validity plays a leading role in discourse. Argumentation is the best way to justify problematized truth claims because it allows us to disclose propositions within the horizon of logical validity, and thereby to discover just how far their purported insight reaches—that is, whether they have the universality and necessity we claim for them.

On this account, the aim of argumentation is not simply to vindicate the truth claims raised for an asserted proposition, but also to bear witness to the truth—that is, accuracy—of the proposition itself. We raise truth claims and argue about them because we presuppose, when we assert a proposition, that it offers genuine insight and because we want to discover whether this is so. We assume that the insight offered is one anyone, not merely the person or community or organization that asserts the proposition, can understand and accept. We also assume that argumentation itself, when carried out well, either discloses the insight in question or shows it not to be a genuine insight—by linking it with other insights, by opening it to consideration by other people, and by testing its implications. In other words, discursive justification serves to authenticate propositional truth.

By enriching the concepts of discourse and propositional truth, I suggest that the concept of truth in everyday practice is not as "unconditional" or "absolute" as Habermas claims it to be, nor is the discursive vindication of truth claims as fallibilistic as he suggests. For in action and discourse our assertions orient us to the predicative self-disclosure of practical objects and the propositional disclosure of such disclosure. We ordinarily understand that not every purported insight is genuine—otherwise we might not bother to make assertions. But we also understand that the claims we raise with our assertions and about which we argue would hardly be worth raising if none of their propositional content were accurate. Nor do we need to presuppose ideal justificatory conditions in order to engage in discourse. The principle of logical validity, which is always already in effect in a society such as ours, is sufficient to orient our attempts to give good reasons and better arguments.

5.3   Beyond Anti/Realism

If my critical appropriation of Habermas is on the right track, then the framework of the Anglo-American debate about realism is misconceived. The fundamental question about propositional truth is not whether it exists *independently* of our knowing it. Rather, it concerns the *interdependence* between linguistically competent, intersubjectively connected human agents and the events and entities these agents act and interact with and make predicative reference to. Plantinga is right to suggest that Kant's Copernican revolution disturbs our understanding of this relationship. Yet he is wrong, in my judgment, to propose that locating true propositions in the mind of God will undo the revolution, for Plantinga's proposal presupposes the problem it is meant to solve. We need to begin instead with the *interdependence* of "mind" and "object"—with our "being-in-the-world," as Heidegger puts it—and with the *corporeal multidimensionality* of both human knowers and that about which they acquire knowledge.

Habermas's linguistic-pragmatic conception of truth is a postmetaphysical attempt to retain truth's context-transcending quality in the face of contextualism such as Rorty's that would deny this quality. Plantinga also wishes to preserve this context-transcending quality, but by reverting to a metaphysical paradigm. And, like Habermas, he ends up with a compromise between realism and antirealism. To my way of thinking, such compromises indicate problems rather than solutions. I believe the only way to solve these problems is to go beyond the contemporary framework of realism versus antirealism. What I have proposed could be called *post-anti/realism* with respect to propositional truth. The key to my proposal is to replace questions of independence with questions of interdependence. Questions of interdependence with respect to propositional truth assume continuity between human agents and whatever they take up in their actions and interactions. For a post-anti/realist, it does not make sense to locate propositions on one side of a mind–object gap and then argue about whether what makes them true is independent of the assertions that raise a claim to truth. Rather, it makes sense to recognize how propositions and truth claims arise within an interrelation between human practices and practical objects that is always already in effect. We also need to acknowledge that the discursive justification of problematized truth claims is unavoidably indexed both to this interrelation and to a societal principle of logical validity that is also always already in effect.

How, then, should one *not* be an antirealist? I have suggested three ways. One should not be a radical contextualist à la Rorty, for this forces one to give up a substantial concept of propositional truth. One should not be a radically theist antirealist à la Plantinga, for this compels one to remove the concept of propositional truth from contexts of discursive justification. And one should not be a Janus-faced pragmatic realist à la Habermas, for this reinscribes the gap between propositional truth and discursive justification that his consensus theory and formal pragmatics sought to remove.

Instead, one should subsume the insights of contemporary antirealism into a differentiated and post-anti/realist conception of propositional truth. If we follow this path, then we can also recontextualize the concepts of propositional truth and discursive justification within a broader conception of truth and authentication. By sorting out the many matters of truth that go beyond propositions and argumentation, such a conception would also demonstrate why truth matters.[36]

III Truth and Objectivity

6 Synthetic Evidence and Objective Truth: Husserl Revisited

Our right to a more expansive interpretation of these concepts [of being and truth] is unassailable.

—Edmund Husserl[1]

A post-anti/realist conception of propositional truth, as proposed in the previous chapter, can call additional attention to the contemporary significance of the early Husserl's conception of truth, with which this book began.[2] Now, however, his conception can be seen not only to resist some of the post-Heideggerian criticisms discussed in chapter 2 but also to point beyond certain impasses within recent Anglo-American truth theory. Yet to see this one needs to extricate the early Husserl's conception of truth from frameworks of interpretation that assume rather than challenge the analytic realism–antirealism debate. The current chapter aims at such extrication, by revisiting early Husserl's notions of evidence and objective identity.

Debates about whether Edmund Husserl has an epistemic conception of truth have decisively shaped Anglo-American interpretations of his *Logical Investigations*. These debates revolve around the following question: Does Husserl think the truth of a proposition depends on whether someone is or could be justified in believing or asserting the proposition? Philosophers who affirm that propositional truth depends on discursive justification to some significant degree have what is called an *epistemic conception* of truth. Philosophers who deny this have a *nonepistemic conception*. This question is especially prominent in discussions of how early Husserl's theory of evidence relates to his conception of truth.

Such discussions presuppose a more comprehensive divide among those who interpret Husserl as an epistemologically motivated idealist, those who read him as a realist, and those who argue that he moved from the realism (whether Platonic or not) of his early *Logical Investigations* (1900–1901) to the idealism of his later *Ideas I* (1913), *Cartesian Meditations* (1931), and other writings. A survey of Anglo-American Husserl scholarship of the past fifty years would show how deeply this divide over realism versus idealism has channeled the reception of Husserl's discussion of "truth" in the *Logical Investigations*. Louis Dupré (1964), for example, reads Husserl as a lifelong idealist: "If by idealism one understands an epistemological position in which truth is entirely immanent [to consciousness], then the *Logical Investigations* are as idealistic as his later works."[3] Dallas Willard (1984), by contrast, reads Husserl's *Logical Investigations* as realist, even though Willard thinks Husserl's quest for a rigorously scientific philosophy, which motivates such realism, was bound to fail: "If there are minds with true assumptions or beliefs about the objects of 'experience,' then those objects must exist, and insofar there is of necessity a 'world.' The world's existence is therefore relative to *truth*, but not to minds; and ... truth itself is for Husserl independent of minds."[4] More recently, Lee Hardy (2013) has argued that, both in the *Logical Investigations* and in later writings, Husserl's philosophy of the physical sciences was realist with respect to theories and theoretical entities—and with respect to truth—even though he was an instrumentalist with respect to scientific laws and their objects: "Husserl was indeed an instrumentalist, but ... his instrumentalism is restricted to an interpretation of scientific laws, not theories. His phenomenology is in fact consistent with a realistic construal of scientific theories."[5]

Such interpretations help indicate the potential relevance of Husserl's work for contemporary debates in Anglo-American truth theory. Yet they also occlude the challenges his work raises to the framework of these debates. These challenges make up the deeper significance of his work—as I aim to show, focusing once more on Husserl's *Logical Investigations*. First I comment on Hardy's interpretation and preview the Husserlian concept of truth as objective identity (sections 6.1–6.2). Next I reconstruct early Husserl's conception of evidence and truth in connection with his account of intuitive fulfillment (sections 6.3–6.4). Then I propose a different framework for understanding Husserl's conception (section 6.5), emphasizing not the relation between propositional truth and the discursive justification of beliefs but instead the relation between synthetic knowledge and objective identity.

6.1   Propositional Truth

Lee Hardy begins by pointing to a necessary correlation between truth and *existence* in Husserl's conception of truth: "If a proposition is true, then the corresponding state of affairs obtains; if a state of affairs obtains, then the corresponding proposition is true."[6] Yet Husserl also posits a close connection between truth and *evidence*, leading some commentators to argue, in effect, that Husserl has an epistemic conception of propositional truth. Specifically, such commentators, whom Hardy opposes, argue that for Husserl a proposition is true if and only if it is evident, in the sense that the corresponding state of affairs is perceptually given.[7] On this epistemic construal, propositional truth hinges on the *perceptual givenness* of a state of affairs, not on its *existence*. Moreover, Hardy argues, this construal "commits Husserl to a form of idealism" understood as "the claim that the existence of things is somehow dependent upon states of consciousness" such as conscious perception.[8]

Hardy's alternative reading, which allows Husserl to maintain a nonepistemic conception of truth, is to regard evidence as the necessary and sufficient condition for *justified belief* and not for *truth* as such: "Evidence does not make a proposition true. But it does make us justified in believing it is true."[9] This reading allows Husserl to be a realist concerning theoretical entities, which can exist even though they cannot be perceptually given.[10]

To develop this interpretation, and to reject epistemic construals of Husserl's conception of truth, Hardy makes three crucial moves. First, he distinguishes between "monothetic" and "synthetic" concepts of evidence in Husserl's work and claims that the synthetic concept is "a nonstarter."[11] Whereas monothetic evidence pertains to a single act "whereby an object or state of affairs is intuitively given"[12]—for example, an act of sensuous perception—synthetic evidence pertains to a coinciding between two qualitatively distinct acts whereby an intuitively empty signitive intention is intuitively fulfilled. Next, focusing on the monothetic concept, Hardy argues that Husserl posits a correlation not between the truth of propositions and actual or occurrent cases of evidence but rather between propositional truth and "the ideal possibility of evidence," where ideal possibility means that "the actual occurrence of evidence" is ideally possible "in some possible consciousness."[13] Then Hardy claims that, on "Husserl's mature theory of evidence" (presumably in writings subsequent to the *Logical Investigations*), "all occurrent cases of evidence are fallible" and hence incapable of guaranteeing propositional truth: "Given that every occurrent case of evidence is necessarily inadequate, it is not true that if p is evident, p is true." At most, occurrent cases of evidence make us "justified in believing" that the corresponding propositions are true.[14]

With these moves, Hardy clarifies the issues at stake in the *Logical Investigations* with respect to evidence and truth. Contrary to Hardy's interpretation, however, I regard the synthetic concept of evidence as central to early Husserl's conception of truth, and I do not consider it a "nonstarter." Moreover, Hardy's proposed idealization of actual evidence undermines the clear sense in which Husserl regards truth as more than simply propositional. Although I share Hardy's view that the early Husserl does not have an epistemic conception of truth, I believe the conception proposed in the *Logical Investigations* points beyond the epistemic–nonepistemic polarity in contemporary truth theory. A first step toward explaining this belief, as well as my reservations about Hardy's interpretation, is to consider the concept of truth as objective identity in Husserl's Sixth Investigation.

6.2 Truth as Objective Identity

Like Hardy and Elisabeth Ströker, I agree that "Husserl is not proposing a theory of truth *simpliciter*; rather, he is conducting a phenomenological clarification of the *sense* of truth." Yet "the question of the sense of truth" is not simply, as Hardy puts it, "the question of how, in the course of experience, a proposition comes to acquire the status of being true *for us*."[15] Certainly the truth of propositions for us is part of the question. But it is only part, and three of the four concepts of truth laid out in Investigation Six are not about the truth of propositions per se. Indeed, as Ströker points out, the decisive concept there is not the truth of propositions but the truth of objective being. Moreover, this concept "differs essentially from the usual concept of truth in the sense of the old theory of adequation, which defines the truth of propositions, a more precise form of which today dominates the discussion of truth in the analytic theory of science. As Husserl understands it, 'true' is not a predicate of judgment, but a predicate of the state of affairs."[16]

The concept of truth Ströker has in view here is the first of four that Husserl describes, all of which he accepts, namely, truth as the objective correlate to the synthetic act of "evidence." As was explained in chapter 2, I label this the concept of truth as (1) objective *identity*, to distinguish it from the other three closely related concepts of truth as (2) inter-active *coincidence* (i.e., what Husserl means by evidence in the strict sense), (3) intuitive *fullness*, and (4) signitive *correctness*. Only the fourth of these maps onto standard notions of propositional truth, although its extension is wider than such notions.

When he calls truth as identity the "objective correlate" of evidence—that is, of evidence in its *"epistemologically precise sense"* as "the act of [the] most perfect synthesis of fulfillment" (LU II.2, 651; LI 2, 263, tm)—Husserl, as I read him, does not make any claims about whether evidence either justifies true belief (Hardy) or guarantees propositional truth (epistemic construals). Husserl's claim is that truth as objective identity is the state of being to which an objectifying act of knowledge must be adequate. Depending on the nature of the act, it must be adequate either to the "state of affairs" (*Sachverhalt*) the act signitively identifies or to the objective "identity" (*Identität*) the act synthetically posits. Whereas a state of affairs is the objective correlate to signitive acts in which we assert propositions—what I shall call "signitive identifications"—an objective identity is the correlate to an act of synthetic identification in which signitive and intuitive acts coincide. In such synthetic acts, when they are completely adequate, we "experience" truth as objective identity, he says.

Leaving aside truth as a state of affairs for now, we can ask what it means to experience truth as objective identity. Such experience does not necessarily mean that we propositionally grasp this truth when we synthetically posit identity, for such positing need not be propositional. This is an obvious implication of the reservation Husserl had expressed earlier in the addendum to §8 in Investigation Six (LU II.2, 569–570; LI 2, 208) and mentions once again when he presents the concept of truth as objective identity (LU II.2, 652; LI 2, 263). In what Husserl calls a *nominal* act one can correctly name or refer to a perceived object (e.g., "This house") and thereby experience the identity between the object as perceived and the object as signified—that is, experience truth as objective identity—without one's engaging in a *relational* act—an *"act of relational identification"* (LU II.2, 569; LI 2, 208)—that, typically, would be propositional (e.g., "This is a house"). Because the act of "evidence" need not be relational or propositional, to call truth as identity the "objective correlate" of evidence is not to make or imply a claim about what justifies or guarantees propositional truth, for truth as objective identity can be experienced, in an act of evidence, in a prepropositional way.[17]

To explicate this relation between synthetic evidence and truth as objective identity, one needs to reconstruct pertinent elements in the phenomenology of knowledge that Husserl develops before he discusses the concepts of evidence and truth. Only after analyzing intentional experiences and their "contents" in Investigation Five, and distinguishing intuitive acts from merely signitive acts in Investigation Six, does Husserl land on his account of evidence and truth (chapter 5 in the Sixth Investigation). Then he enriches this account in a section on "Sense and Understanding," where he lays out his theory of categorial intuition. Let me review some of the preparatory moves Husserl makes in Investigations Five and Six, focusing on his accounts of meaning-fulfillment and intuitive fullness as constituents of cognitive synthesis.[18]

6.3   Cognitive Synthesis

According to Husserl, to assert a proposition requires the use of linguistic expressions that have meaning. Already in Investigation One he had explained what such linguistic meaning involves. It involves someone's intentionally employing linguistic expressions to say something about the objects to which one refers. By itself, however, such use of linguistic expressions does not give us full cognitive access to the intended objects. The linguistically expressed meaning needs to be fulfilled through acts of perception or imagination or both.

6.3.1   Meaning and Fulfillment

To account for this relationship between meaning and fulfillment, Husserl introduces a fundamental distinction between two sorts of objectifying acts: signitive acts and intuitive acts. The constant theme of early Husserl's epistemology is the distinction between signitive and intuitive acts and their coincidence in synthetic acts of fulfillment (and frustration) that provide "the synthesis of knowing [*Synthesis des Erkennens*]." All signitive and intuitive acts aim at a "unity of fulfillment," whether as a "unity of identification" or, more narrowly, as a "unity of knowledge" to which "objective identity corresponds as the intentional correlate" (LU II.2, 582–586; LI 2,

216–218, tm).[19] So knowledge is the overriding goal of objectifying acts. Given Husserl's concept of truth as objective identity, we can also say that, in principle, objectifying acts aim at truth.

As we saw in chapter 2, Husserl's "phenomenological elucidation of knowledge" in the Sixth Investigation begins with the example of a relational act, namely, a judgment of perception (*Wahrnehmungsurteil*). He concludes from this example that the expressed meaning (*Bedeutung*) lies not in the act of perception but in the expressive act of making the judgment. Yet, to yield knowledge, the two acts must mutually coincide in "the unity of fulfillment" (LU II.2, 556; LI 2, 199). A similar pattern obtains for nominal expressions and meaning-intentions. First Husserl considers examples of a "static unity" between signitive and intuitive acts, such as the use of the word "inkpot" to name a directly perceptible object (LU II.2, 558–565; LI 2, 201–206). Then he turns to a "dynamic unity" between the act of pure meaning (*der Akt des puren Bedeutens*) and the act of rendering something intuitive (*der veranschaulichende Akt*). Dynamic unity occurs when a nominal expression first functions symbolically or signitively[20] and then a corresponding perception or imagination comes to accompany it.

In such cases of dynamic unity, the phenomenology of fulfillment becomes completely apparent: by itself, the signitive act is an act of meaning-intention; only in conjunction with the corresponding intuitive act, in which the object is given, does the signitively intended meaning get fulfilled. From the standpoint of the intended object, we can speak of a (potential) knowledge of the object. From the phenomenologically preferable standpoint of the two coinciding acts, we can speak of a fulfillment of the meaning-intention (LU II.2, 566–567; LI 2, 206–207). On the object side, there is a more or less complete objective identity. On the act side, there is a more or less complete fulfillment that is simultaneously an experience of identity, an act of identification (LU II.2, 567–569; LI 2, 207–208). The same relationships, albeit with a higher degree of complexity, are in effect for relational and propositional acts such as judgments and assertions.

These relationships are not additive, however, as if the object as synthetically intended were added to the object as intuited and to the object as signified. No, objective identity is "there from the start as ... unexpressed, unconceptualized experience" and is not dragged in later "through comparative, cogitatively mediated reflection." Nevertheless, the act of identification or fulfillment is a distinct act, not to be equated with either the act of signification or the act of intuition. This is so because the objective identity, more or less complete, "corresponds to the act of fulfillment," and not to either the signitive or the intuitive act (LU II.2, 568; LI 2, 207–208, tm).

Like signitive acts, perceptual acts also seek fulfillment, through what Husserl calls "the synthesis of thingly identity [*sachliche Identität*]." Although every single perception of a particular object will be "a mixture of fulfilled and unfulfilled intentions," he says, all perceptual syntheses of ful-fillment aim to be "identifications"—to identify "self-appearances [*Selbst-erscheinungen*] of an object with self-appearances of the same object" (LU II.2, 590–591; LI 2, 221, tm).

A similar dynamic between partial adumbrations and an ideal synthesis characterizes acts of imagination, which typically employ images (*Bilder*) that must, in some important way, resemble the appearance of the object imagined.[21] In this way, acts of perception and imagination have a "mutual affinity" (*Zusammengehörigkeit*) both to one another and to the object itself (*Sache selbst*), and such affinity distinguishes intuitive acts from acts that have a signitive intention, where sign and signified "'have nothing to do with one another'" (LU II.2, 591; LI 2, 221–222).

6.3.2 Intuitive Fullness

As was noted in chapter 2, acts of fulfillment display different degrees of fullness, just as correlative acts of knowledge display different degrees of perfection (*Vollkommenheit*). We cannot explain differences in degrees of fulfillment via either the quality or the matter of acts: these differences can occur between two or more acts that have the very same quality and matter and aim at the same object. Rather, we must trace differences in the degree of fulfillment—and in degrees of epistemic perfection—back to the relative "fullness" (*Fülle*) of the intuitive act. Because only intu-itions can have fullness, we can say of signitive intentions that they are "in themselves 'empty.'" They merely point to (*hinweisen*) the object, and "they 'are in need of fullness.'" They receive such fullness only insofar as they are rendered intuitive within acts of identification and fulfillment (LU II.2, 607, LI 2, 233, tm). Accordingly, we must regard fullness as a new and third "moment" of the *intuitive* act, in addition to the act's quality and matter, although as a completion (*Ergänzung*) of the act's matter (LU II.2, 600–601, LI 2, 229).[22]

There is an important difference, however, in the types of fullness achieved by acts of imagination and perception, respectively. Whereas the fullness of an imaginative presentation—an analogical representation (*analogische Repräsentation*), in Husserl's technical vocabulary—depends on how many of the presented object's features (*Merkmale*) it *accommodates* and how closely it *resembles* them, the fullness of a perceptual presentation—*Präsentation*, in Husserl's technical vocabulary—depends on the extent to which it *grasps* the thing itself (*Selbsterfassung*) and *presents* the thing's objective moments (*Selbstdarstellung*) (LU II.2, 608; LI 2, 234). Nevertheless, whether as imaginatively or perceptually apprehended, the purely intuitive contents of intuitive acts "point unambiguously" to the object's "definitely corresponding contents," presenting (*darstellende*) these intuitive contents "in imaginative or perceptual adumbrations [*Abschattungen*]." Husserl calls such intuitively apprehended intuitive contents the "*intuitive substance (Gehalt) of the act*," to the exclusion of all signitive components (LU II.2, 609–610; LI 2, 235, tm).

Yet even the intuitive substance of a pure perception is not identical with the object itself. It may still be a "mere" perception: "it need not attain the ideal of adequation, where the presenting [*darstellende*] content is simultaneously the presented [*dargestellte*] content." Thus, like pure imagination, pure perception admits of "differing degrees of fullness" with respect to the same intentional object: there can be potentially more to be perceived or more exactness to be achieved (LU II.2, 613–614; LI 2, 237–238, tm).

The differing degrees of fullness pertain to an intuition's *extent or richness* (the relative completeness with which the content of the object gets presented or represented), its *liveliness* (how closely the presentation or representation approximates [*Annäherung*] the object's corresponding moments of content), and its *substantial reality* or *substantiality* (*Realitätsgehalt*) (the relative number of the presenting or representing contents). Ideally, perception would have maximal richness, liveliness, and substantiality—it would be "the self-apprehension [*Selbsterfassung*] of the full and whole object" (LU II.2, 614; LI 2, 238, tm), in conjunction with synthetic acts of identification within which signitive intentions can find fulfillment. Relative fullness accrues to intuitive contents within their role in a possible fulfillment-synthesis.[23]

What, then, is the relationship between the fullness of intuitive contents, on the one hand, and what Husserl describes as the "matter" (*die Materie*) of objectifying acts? An act's *matter* is what makes the act intend "exactly this object in exactly this manner, i.e., in exactly these articulations and forms and with special reference to exactly these features [*Bestimmtheiten*] or relationships" (LU II.2, 617; LI 2, 240, tm). Matter is what allows qualitatively different acts, such as signitive and intuitive acts, intend the same with respect to the object. Whether, for example, one believes that the tree is green or simply asserts this without believing it or simply perceives the tree as green without either believing or asserting it, the intended greenness of the tree is a matter that all of these acts have in common. Hence, in the context of a wholly unified act of identification, matter is what serves in the coinciding acts "as the basis for identification [*als Fundament der Identifizierung*]" (LU II.2, 618; LI 2, 241, tm). The *fullness* of intuitive contents, by contrast, is the degree to which the matter of an intuition is *adequate* to the content of the object that an intuition presents or represents. Moreover, intuitive fullness is what allows signitive acts not simply to intend an object and have this signitive intention fulfilled but to have this fulfillment be more or less *adequate* to the object.[24]

From an epistemic perspective, then, we can distinguish between adequate and inadequate intuitions (*Anschauungen*) of an object, as well as between complete (*vollständig*) and defective (*lückenhaft*) intuitions in the context of fulfillment.[25] Similarly, an object meant in a signitive act can be rendered intuitive (*Veranschaulichung*) in either an adequate or an inadequate fashion. In the case of adequately intuitioned (signitive) meanings that are complex, either all of the meaning's parts receive fulfillment "through corresponding parts of the fulfilling intuition" or the fulfilling intuition itself, in all of its corresponding parts, is intrinsically adequate to the object. If we have both, then our intuitional rendering is "objectively complete" LU II.2, 627–630; LI 2, 246–248, tm).[26]

To summarize: Early Husserl's accounts of truth as objective identity and of evidence as a synthetic act presuppose a phenomenology of fulfillment and fullness that refuses to divorce propositional truth from a more comprehensive cognitive synthesis. This cognitive synthesis involves both unity between qualitatively distinct objectifying acts—that is, between signitive and intuitive acts—and gradations in the adequacy with which an intuitive act presents or represents the object of cognition. One needs to keep his account of cognitive synthesis in mind in order to make sense of the relation early Husserl posits between synthetic evidence and objective truth.

6.4 Evidence and Truth

The background we have canvassed, culminating in the notion of intuitive adequacy, lays extensive groundwork for the Sixth Investigation's relatively brief chapter on evidence and truth (chapter 5). Husserl regards adequation, properly understood, as the ideal of knowledge, which itself arises in intentional experience that involves signitive and intuitive objectifying acts.

6.4.1 Adequation and Evidence

We need to distinguish between two types of adequation as an ideal, however. First there is the (ideal of) adequation between the act of intuition and an object that is imagined, perceived, or both imagined and perceived. In the strict sense, only intuitive acts can have fullness, to a greater or lesser degree, depending on the completeness, precision, and number of their adumbrations—that is, depending on the richness, liveliness, and substantiality of their intuitive contents. Moreover, only a perception can be completely adequate to the intended object: whereas the images of imagination make the object indirectly present (*Vergegenwärtigen*), only perception can make it directly present (*Gegenwärtigen, Präsentieren*). This is so even though our perceptions, for the most part, are mere perceptions.[27] The content of perception, even when it offers an appearance, counts for us as being identical with the thing itself, thanks to the perception's relative fullness and the directness with which it presents the object. The ideal of adequation for the fullness of perceptual adumbrations is the object's "absolute self ... for every presented element of the object" (LU II.2, 647; LI 2, 260).

The second type of adequation pertains to acts of fulfillment where intuitive and signitive intentions coincide. Such acts achieve adequation "when the signified objectivity [*die bedeutete Gegenständlichkeit*] is in the strict sense *given* in the intuition, and is given exactly as what it is thought and meant." Every intellectual (*gedankliche*) intention finds its "final fulfillment" (*letzte Erfüllung*) when the intuition in its fulfilling function no long implies any "unsatisfied intentions" (LU II.2, 648; LI 2, 261, tm). Further, this second type of adequation depends on the first: only the intuition's adequation offers the final (*letzte*) fulfillment of the intention that terminates in it, for only it does not need any further fulfillment.

Accordingly, the ideal of adequation would be completely met when fulfillment increases to the point that "the complete and entire intention has reached … an ultimate and final fulfillment." In such a fulfillment, the intuitive substance (*Gehalt*) is "the absolute sum of possible fullness; the intuitive representative is the object itself, just as [*so wie*] it is in itself."[28] When this occurs, "the objective element [*das Gegenständliche*] is actually 'present' ['*gegenwärtig*'] or 'given' ['*gegeben*'] exactly as what it is intended; no partial intention is further implied that would lack fulfillment" (LU II.2, 647; LI 2, 260–261, tm).[29]

This account of adequation provides the basis for Husserl's notion of evidence (*Evidenz*), which he regards as the ideal synthetic act of identification. In a loose sense, he says, we can use the term "evidence" to refer to any such act of identification where a positing intention, especially an affirmation or declaration (*Behauptung*), receives confirmation (*Bestätigung*) through a perception that corresponds to it and is completely adapted to it (*vollangepasste Wahrnehmung*). In the strict sense, however—in "the epistemologically precise sense"—evidence concerns "the ideal of adequate perception, of the complete self-appearance of the object" *within an act of fulfillment*. Evidence in this strict sense concerns the act of "the most complete [*vollkommensten*] fulfillment-synthesis, which gives the intention, e.g. the intention of judgment, the absolute fullness of content, that of the object itself. The object is not merely meant, but rather it is in the strictest sense *given*, given just as it is meant and made one with the meaning [*in eins gesetzt mit dem Meinen*]." As the objectifying, identifying, and most complete synthesis of coincidence (*Deckungssynthesis*), evidence has its objective correlate in "being [*Sein*] in the sense of truth" or, more simply, "truth"—in at least one sense of the term (LU II.2, 651; LI 2, 263, tm).

Before we (re)turn to this concept of truth as objective identity, it is important to elaborate what Husserl means by evidence in the strict sense, to which truth as objective identity is the "objective correlate." As I read him, Husserl here proposes a synthetic concept of evidence as an ideal guiding all acts of knowing. He does not have in view either occurrent cases of evidence or the mere possibility of evidence. Nor does he regard evidence primarily as the basis for discursively justifying beliefs. Evidence in its strict sense is the operative ideal of complete adequation that obtains both within and for synthetic acts of identification and fulfillment. As we have seen, such adequation is intuitive in a double sense: it involves both the relative fullness of intuition with respect to the intended object and the degree to which a signitive intention is intuitively fulfilled. Such adequation is not *simply* actual, insofar as it cannot be equated with the occurrence of particular synthetic acts that aim to be adequate. Nor is it *merely* possible, for it provides the sense for all acts that aim at knowledge.

Moreover, although we can loosely speak of perceptual acts or previous perceptions that confirm propositional claims as "evidence" or "evident," evidence in this loose (monothetic) sense is itself governed by evidence in the strict (synthetic) sense. For the cognitive sense of both perceptual acts and propositional claims is anchored in synthetic acts whose operative ideal is evidence in the strict sense. Accordingly, evidence in the strict sense is not to be regarded primarily as a basis for justifying propositional truth claims. Nor, for that matter, can truth as objective identity be reduced to evidence. Instead, as Husserl asserts, evidence as ideal synthesis and truth as objective identity are correlative. In other words, they are simultaneously in effect as the twinned ideal of adequation that governs synthetic knowledge, such that we cannot make sense of one without making sense of the other.

6.4.2   Four Concepts

By the same token, Husserl's concept of truth as objective identity is not a concept of propositional truth. As I mentioned earlier, Husserl distinguishes among four concepts of truth: as objective *identity*, as inter-active *coincidence*, as intuitive *fullness*, and as signitive *correctness*. The first and third pertain to what I label the "object side" of intentional acts of objectification.[30] The other two pertain to what I label the "subject side" of such intentional acts. His account moves back and forth between object side and subject side.

The first concept—objective identity—concerns the objective correlate to acts of identification and fulfillment. Truth in this sense is either the state of affairs (*Sachverhalt*) that correlates with a signitive identification or the objective identity (*Identität*) that correlates with a coinciding synthetic identification (*Korrelate einer deckenden Identifizierung*). Objective identity would be the complete agreement (*Übereinstimmung*) between the signitively meant object and the intuitively given object. When we perform a synthetic and fulfilled identification, we can experience this objective agreement in the act of synthetic evidence (LU II.2, 651–652; LI 2, 263).

Importantly, as Husserl immediately indicates, such experience can occur in a prereflective manner: we can intentionally experience the truth as correlated objective identity without signitively objectifying the identity we have experienced. "Prereflective" here does not mean preconscious or unintentional or presignitive. Plainly, the experience of objective identity is conscious and intentional, and it involves a signitive dimension. Rather, prereflective means that the identity presents itself directly to the synthetic act and does not need to present itself as a "state of affairs" about which one makes a propositional claim. As Husserl puts it, this synthetic act, this act of evidence, in which truth as objective identity is experienced, need not be the perception (*Wahrnehmung*) or adequate perception *of* truth as objective identity, taking perception in a broad sense that includes what he later discusses as "categorial intuition." To perceive the objective agreement between the signitively meant and perceptually given object would require its own act of objectifying interpretation (*Auffassung*) (LU II.2, 652; LI 2, 263–264).

Perhaps the following example illustrates what Husserl means. Let's say I judge a house to be green on the basis of perceiving it as a green house, and my judging and perceiving completely coincide. In this case I can experience the objective agreement between the house as judged and the house as perceived—I can signitively-intuitively and truly know "This house is green," without needing to assert successfully "It is true that this house is green." If I successfully say concerning a perceived object "This house is green," I experience the house's indeed being green, just as I said—I experience truth as objective identity. If you then ask me what I just experienced, I might reply "that this house is green, just as I said." In this second experience—the experience in which I make a reply—the original objective identity presents itself as a state of affairs about which propositional claims can be made. I am no longer directly intending *the object* but intending something *about* the object as originally intended. According to Husserl, I can experience the truth as objective identity—the house's being green, as I said—without necessarily experiencing this truth as a state of affairs—that the house as meant is identical with the house as perceived.

The second concept of truth, a subject-sided concept, concerns a unity of coincidence (*Deckungseinheit*) between qualitatively different acts that must occur when we experience truth as objective identity. This unity is what Husserl means by evidence in the strict sense, and it is what I have labeled "inter-active coincidence." The agreement here occurs not between the object as signitively meant and the object as intuitively given but between the epistemic essence of the signitive act and the epistemic essence of the intuitive act. Because this agreement is not between the concrete acts but between their epistemic essences, Husserl describes this concept of truth as "the idea that belongs to the act-form" of evidence: this concept has to do with "the ideal relationship ... between the epistemic essences of the coinciding acts." Thus, for example, my act of synthetic identification with respect to the house's being green would be true in this sense if the semantic-epistemic essence of my signifying with words "This house is green" coincided with the intuitive-epistemic essence of my act of perceiving the house as being green. Although, when I perform this synthetic act, the coinciding of the actual signitive and intuitive acts is contingent, their coinciding has an "ideal essence," namely, "the Idea of absolute adequation as such" (LU II.2, 652; LI 2, 264, tm). In other words, the contingent act of evidence is governed by the idea of (subject-sided) truth. Evidence in the strict sense is nothing other than truth as ideal inter-active coincidence.

Returning to the object side, Husserl introduces a third concept of truth, one that concerns the fullness of the intuited object in which the synthetic act finds fulfillment. Here we can say the object itself is true, insofar as it is indeed given intuitively just as it is signitively meant. Hence, for example, if I find complete fulfillment for my intentional act of identifying the house as green, then the perceived object, insofar as it provides "ideal fullness" for this intention, is true (LU II.2, 652; LI 2, 264).

This third concept, a concept of truth on the object side, points in turn to a fourth concept, another subject-sided concept, namely, the truth of a signitive intention. As a terminological marker for this specific sense of truth on the subject side, Husserl introduces the term "Richtigkeit"—"rightness," in Findlay's translation, and "correctness," in my own rendering. Our signitive intention can be true—that is, correct—with respect to the identified object. It can be adequate to its true object. Again, we are dealing with the idea of truth, namely, as "the correctness of the intention's epistemic essence *in specie*" (LU II.2, 653; LI 2, 264, tm). This fourth concept of truth is particularly relevant for understanding traditional conceptions of propositional truth, such as Aristotle's formulation "to say of what is that it is, and of what is not that it is not, is true."[31] According to Husserl, an asserted proposition is true—correct (*richtig*)—if it "'directs' itself to [*richtet sich nach*] the thing itself, it says that it is so, and it really is so." All such propositions are governed by the "ideal possibility" that a proposition having a certain content (*ein Satz solcher Materie*) can find complete fulfillment, can find "the most rigorous adequation" to the true object (LU II.2, 653; LI 2, 264).

Hence, as I noted more briefly in chapter 2, Husserl identifies four interrelated concepts of truth as the ideal of adequation. In my own terms, those related to the object side (the first and third concepts), which have to do with so-called truth makers, pertain to epistemic object functions: states of affairs, objective identity between the signitively meant and the intuitively given, and the fullness with which the object is intuitively given when signitively meant. The concepts related to the subject side (the second and fourth concepts), which pertain more or less to the truth of so-called truth bearers, single out what I would call epistemic subject functions: the ideal coinciding between signitive and intuitive acts, and the correctness of a signitive intention with respect to the intended object (i.e., the object identified). In other words, Husserl's conception of truth distinguishes four sites of adequacy: adequacy between object functions (identity), adequacy between subject functions (coincidence), adequacy of the object as given for the intention (fullness), and adequacy of the intention for the given object (correctness).

6.4.3   Objective Identity and Propositional Truth

The relation between Husserl's first and fourth concepts is especially important in light of contemporary debates about whether Husserl has an epistemic conception of truth. Husserl himself explores this relation in some detail, first to secure his distinction between truth as objective identity and truth as propositional correctness, and then to show how his approach can accommodate standard conceptions that restrict truth to propositional correctness.

Husserl secures his distinction from two interrelated angles, namely, from the object side and from the subject side. He begins from the object side, insisting that we should not confuse objective identity with what I would term predicative identity—something's predicatively identified being such and such. In Husserl's own language, we should not confuse "being" in the "first, objective sense of truth" with "the being of the copula of the 'affirmative' categorical assertion [*Aussage*]" (LU II.2, 653; LI 2, 264, tm)—for example, the being indicated by "is" in the assertion "This house is green." Whereas, in synthetic acts of identification, identity pertains to the complete coincidence (*totale Deckung*) between the object functions in question—between the meant object and the object intuited—the "is" of an assertion usually indicates only a partial identity: the assertion usually picks out and means only one feature or one set of features (greenness, for example), and, to count as knowledge, it requires intuitive fulfillment that the assertoric act cannot itself provide. Even if "is" were to indicate a total identification—if, for example, an assertion about the house mentioned all of the relevant features—predicative identity would not be the same as the synthetically intended identity of the object. Even in such cases, being as objective identity is "experienced but not expressed," and it "never coincides with the being meant and experienced in the 'is' of the assertion" (LU II.2, 653; LI 2, 264, tm).

This distinction between objective identity and predicative identity is reinforced when one considers the subject side of truth—truth as inter-active coincidence between signitive and intuitive acts. The assertoric "is" expresses a predicative identity. It expresses an agreement (*Übereinstimmung*) between the subject and predicate of the assertion itself. But the assertoric "is" does not, in and of itself, express the coincidence between a signitive (specifically assertoric) act and an intuitive (specifically perceptual) act that nevertheless is required in order for the act of assertion to achieve interactively coincident truth. Such subject-sided, inter-active coincidence "is plainly not asserted," and, unlike predicative identity, it "does not belong objectively [*gegenständlich*] to the asserted state of affairs [*zum beurteilten Sachverhalt*]." We can, of course, successfully make an assertion *about* the subjective coincidence required for a particular assertion to be true. But then this new assertion about subjective coincidence as a state of affairs will itself require an act of truth whose coinciding acts are not (yet) objectified. At each step, Husserl says, we must distinguish between "the objectified and the not-objectified state of affairs" (LU II.2, 653–654; LI 2, 264–265, tm). In other words, we must distinguish between what is asserted and what allows the act of assertion to be true, which latter always necessarily includes a nonassertoric, intuitive act as well as a coincidence between assertoric and intuitive acts. Or, to make the same point from the object side, one-dimensional predicative identity is not the same as multidimensional objective identity.

Nevertheless, Husserl's approach can accommodate narrower conceptions of truth. The standard narrower accounts restrict truth to judgments (*Urteile*) and propositions (*Sätze*) or to "their objective correlates, to states of affairs [*Sachverhalte*]." Claiming an "unassailable right" to a more expansive (*allgemeinere*) account, Husserl says that "the very nature of the case demands that the concepts of truth and falsehood should, in the first instance at least, be cast so widely as to encompass the whole sphere of objectifying acts" (LU II.2, 654–655; LI 2, 265, tm). In other words, the concept of truth should encompass, at a minimum, signitive and intuitive acts, acts of identification and fulfillment, and the objective correlates to these acts.

Hence, for example, both acts of naming and acts of asserting can be true, and not only states of affairs but also other intended objects can be true. Even if we agree to limit "truth" (*Wahrheit*) to objectifying acts themselves and reserve the term "being" (*Sein*) or "being-true"/"truly-being" (*Wahrhaft-sein*) for their objective correlates (LU II.2, 655; LI 2, 265–266), truth would still encompass more than propositional correctness, and being would encompass more than asserted states of affairs. Propositional correctness is a narrower concept of truth. It pertains to typically relational acts—as distinct, for example, from nonrelational acts of naming—that are among many possible acts of signification. Propositional correctness primarily pertains to acts of judging, asserting, and the like—to constative acts, to borrow a term from speech act theory. Similarly, states of affairs need not be the same as the intuited object that is meant in an act of assertion, nor are they to be equated with the fullness of the intuited object in which the synthetic act of identification finds fulfillment. When the object is a sensuously perceived object, such fullness is not a state of affairs, for states of affairs are objective correlates to assertoric acts and not to acts of sensuous perception.[32]

Even the narrower concept of truth that Husserl proposes, once he has phenomenologically secured his wider conception, goes beyond the common understanding of truth as the correspondence between propositions and facts or states of affairs. His narrower concept identifies truth as "the ideal adequation of a relational act to the corresponding adequate perception of a state of affairs [*an die zugehörige adequate Sachverhaltwahrnehmung*]" (LU II.2, 655; LI 2, 266, tm). In other words, truth and falsity pertain not simply to propositions or beliefs but to the entire range of objectifying relational acts that have signitive meaning. Moreover, that to which such an act must be adequate is not an empirical fact. It is instead the perception of a state of affairs. This perception, strictly speaking, cannot occur sensuously but only via categorial intuition, which itself must be adequate—that is, it must attain the requisite degree of (categorially) intuitive fullness. The understanding of truth as a proposition–fact correspondence is too narrow to do justice to the phenomenology of propositional correctness, and it leaves out the objective identity and subjective coincidence that provide the wider context within which correct propositions can contribute to true knowledge.[33]

6.5   Early Husserl's Significance

The phenomenology of evidence and truth in Husserl's *Logical Investigations* places in question the framework of debates about whether or not he has an epistemic conception of truth. For his early work does not regard evidence in the strict sense as what justifies belief, and it does not restrict truth to propositions. Indeed, on my reading, the productive potential of early Husserl's conception of truth is to provide an alternative to contemporary frameworks in truth theory. Unlike contemporary epistemic conceptions of truth, he gives full weight to "truth makers" (i.e., perceptible objects, objective identity, and states of affairs) that have their own being. Yet, unlike contemporary nonepistemic conceptions, he also insists both on the intentional givenness of such truth makers and on the phenomenological complexity of the intentional experience within which propositional truth claims arise. For Husserl, the truth (correctness) of propositions cannot be divorced from relations between intentional acts and intentional objects, as some nonepistemic conceptions seem to hold. Neither, however, can it be reduced to the justifiability or warranted assertibility of propositional claims, as occurs in various epistemic conceptions of truth. Early Husserl's conception challenges the framework of debates in which one must have either an epistemic or a nonepistemic conception of truth.

Hence, despite my admiration for Lee Hardy's illuminating reconstruction of Husserl's philosophy of the physical sciences, I do not find it fruitful to regard Husserl's early conception of truth as nonepistemic. In questioning such a reading, however, I also find it unfruitful to regard it as an epistemic conception. Hardy's nonepistemic interpretation of Husserl rejects the synthetic concept of evidence in the *Logical Investigations*. To support his rejection, Hardy appeals to Ernst Tugendhat's claim that a "difficulty" in the synthetic concept led Husserl to abandon it in favor of a monothetic

concept in *Ideas I* and later writings. On the monothetic concept, "the signitive act passes over into the intuitive act," such that these two acts do not
need first to be "distinguished and then identified," as purportedly would
occur in a synthetic act of evidence.[34] According to Tugendhat, the "normal
act of evidence" does not involve such a reflective awareness of two distinct
acts and their agreement. That's why Tugendhat appears to attribute greater
plausibility to the later monothetic concept, on which the act of evidence
is simply "the fulfilled, intuitive act itself."[35]

Yet the purported difficulty with the synthetic concept of evidence stems
not from Husserl's account but from his interpreters' confusing different
levels of analysis. Certainly, to *account for* what occurs in evidence as an
act of synthetic identification, Husserl needs to distinguish between two
acts (signitive and intuitive) and postulate their agreement within an act
of fulfillment. This does not mean, however, that someone who *carries out*
a synthetic act of evidence must, while carrying it out, consciously distinguish and relate these acts. They all happen simultaneously as part of the
same intentional whole, such that one directly experiences truth as objective identity without reflecting on the components of this experience or
on the components of the objective identity experienced. I simultaneously
perceive this house as green and say it is green, for example, and my acts of
perception and signification coincide, without my having to say to myself,
"Now I am not only perceiving this house but also saying it is green, and
my distinct acts of perception and signification synthetically coincide."
Further, the objective identity I experience on this occasion is more like a
Gestalt than a state of affairs: all at once the object presents itself as green,
just as I say. Of course, if you claim the house is not green, then I might
wonder whether I had misperceived or misspoken, and in such wondering
I could begin to distinguish my act of perception from my act of signification, which indeed are distinct. In the initial experience, however, I would
not need to be consciously aware of this distinction. As Husserl says in
his explication of meaning-fulfillment, the relationships between perception and signification in this initial experience are not additive. Rather,
the objective identity presents itself in an "unexpressed, unconceptualized
experience" and is not dragged in later "through comparative, cogitatively
mediated reflection" (LU II.2, 568; LI 2, 207, tm).

Moreover, while it is so, as Hardy says, that the synthetic act of evidence will never present "the truth" or "the verifying state of affairs" for

a "particular proposition under explicit consideration," the reason for this is not that the act presents "the truth of a more complex, unexpressed proposition."[36] Rather, the reason is that the synthetic act of evidence is prereflective and holistic. It *can* be analyzed and *can* be rendered explicit in propositional language, but it *need not be thematized in this way* in order to be an experience of truth as objective identity. The role of synthetic evidence with respect to propositional correctness is not to verify the truth of a proposition but both to make it possible for a correct proposition to contribute to true knowledge and to allow the truth of the intuited object—the truth of *die Sache*, as Tugendhat puts it—to have a purchase on the proposition. The concept of synthetic evidence is not a wrongheaded account of monothetic evidence but a phenomenological description of what makes monothetic evidence possible.

My defense of the early Husserl on this topic assumes, as he does, that truth includes more than propositional truth, that it has both a subject side and an object side, and that, in his words, it requires the synthesis of fulfillment between signitive and intuitive acts whose ideal is synthetic evidence. To count as a case of evidence, the monothetic "passing over" (*übergehen*, in Tugendhat's formulation) of the signifying act into the intuitive act, when a particular proposition "directs itself" to an intuitively given object, must be guided by the ideal of synthetic evidence.

Further, the experience of truth need not be propositional, although it often is. Husserl specifically points to nominal acts, such as are expressed in the use of names and definite descriptions, as signitive acts that are not propositional but can be intuitively fulfilled or disappointed. We can use the right name or the wrong name or a name that is not quite right but not entirely wrong. Moreover, we can do this without necessarily making a propositional truth claim. As Tugendhat points out, Husserl emphasized the possible truth of nominal acts because that allowed him to attach truth to "the complete grasp [*Erfassung*] of the object" rather than to the confirmation or verification (*Bestätigung*) of propositional claims. In this way Husserl could incorporate intuitive fulfillment and object-sided truth (*Wahrheit der Sache*) into the problematic of truth (*Wahrheitsproblematik*).[37]

Tugendhat is of two minds about Husserl's assigning truth capacity to nominal acts. On the one hand, Tugendhat applauds it for expanding the conception of truth beyond the truth of propositions toward object-sided truth or the truth of the matter (*Wahrheit der Sache*). Concern about the truth of the matter is normal "in life as in science," he says, when, for example, we ask historically about the truth of an event, about what truly happened (*die Wahrheit eines Geschehens*). On the other hand, Tugendhat faults Husserl for not distinguishing sufficiently between the truth of nominal acts and the truth of propositional acts. Only propositional acts, because they raise a claim to truth, can prove to be false. An act of naming or of assigning a definite description does not raise a truth claim, even though it might suggest one. According to Tugendhat, Husserl fails to account for the absence of a concept of falsity in the case of nominal acts. Thereby Husserl also fails to distinguish sufficiently between the truth of propositions (*die Wahrheit vorgegebener Setzungen*) and the truth of the matter (*die Wahrheit der Sache*).[38]

Be that as it may, Tugendhat's main point, which I endorse, is that the significance of early Husserl's conception of truth lies in the possibilities it opens up rather than in the results it delivers.[39] One possibility is to give greater weight to the nonpropositional elements in what Husserl calls "the experience of truth" and to consider how propositional truth arises within and from such experience. A second possibility is to work out a more dynamic account of the relations between subject-sided and object-sided truth, between what Husserl calls "synthetic acts of fulfillment" and "true being" or "objective identity" or what Tugendhat calls "the truth of the matter." In such a dynamic account, the two sides would be correlates, as Husserl says, but their correlation could involve mutually imbricated processes of discovery and disclosure that go beyond merely intuitive fulfillment. A third possibility, which I have indicated from the outset, is to point contemporary truth theory beyond the polarity between either epistemic or nonepistemic conceptions of truth. The deeper significance of early Husserl's conception lies in its potential to unsettle the framework of contemporary debates by resituating propositional truth within a broader and more dynamic conception of truth, a topic to which I return in the next chapter.[40]

7 Transforming Truth: Heidegger and Horkheimer in Dialectical Disclosure

Everything turns on grasping and expressing the True, not only as *Substance*, but equally as *Subject*.

—G. W. F. Hegel[1]

Early Husserl's conception of truth marks a starting point, not a destination, for my project of critical retrieval. Previous chapters have explored the relevance of his conception for both post-Heideggerian thought and contemporary analytic philosophy. They have also examined the potential of Heidegger and Adorno for comprehensive conceptions of truth and authentication as well as Habermas's more recent contributions to a post-anti/realist understanding of propositional truth and discursive justification. To help tie these explorations together, it is time to dialectically reconstruct definitive reflections on the idea of truth by two central figures in the post-Husserlian traditions this book considers.

Critical theory and Heideggerian thinking are the conflicted offspring of Husserlian phenomenology. Their lineage goes through Husserl to the phenomenology of Hegel. This mixed ancestry, whether acknowledged or suppressed, is especially evident in two path-breaking essays from the 1930s on the topic of truth. One, by Martin Heidegger, carries the title "On the Essence of Truth" (1930). The other, by Max Horkheimer, is titled "On the Problem of Truth" (1935). A single word sets the English titles apart: where Heidegger considers the "essence" (*Wesen*) of truth, Horkheimer discusses a "problem" (*Problem*).[2] In that difference echo many others stemming from conflicts in their appropriations of Husserl and Hegel.

Indeed, on a first reading, the essays by Heidegger and Horkheimer seem to be worlds apart, even though they were written within five years of each other in a German context.[3] If we place these essays in relation to phenomenology, however, not only dramatic differences but also deep similarities emerge between them. Both Heidegger and Horkheimer connect truth with history and freedom, and they do so in ways that recall Hegelian rather than Husserlian phenomenology. They part company over precisely the same topics. According to Hegel, the true must be grasped as both substance and subject. Whereas Heidegger wants more substance and less subject, Horkheimer wants more subject and less substance.

Lest this comparison seem facile, I shall demonstrate what it means. A first step is to ask which alternatives each author wishes to avoid. In Horkheimer's case, the answer is obvious: neither relativism nor absolutism suffices as a position concerning truth, he says; both positions play an ideological role in capitalist society. What is the equivalent polarity for Heidegger's essay? Although he does not name it as such, Heidegger wishes more than anything to avoid the polarity of logicism versus nihilism. His early efforts to reconceptualize truth aimed at avoiding the "logical prejudice" in Western philosophy, to use Dahlstrom's term,[4] and Heidegger increasingly recognized the danger of jumping from the logicist frying pan into the Nietzschean fire. His essay seeks to give an account of truth where meaning in human existence does not depend on propositional correctness and where relativizing such correctness does not eliminate normativity and purpose. Heidegger's concern is whether and how a postmetaphysical philosophy can disclose rather than conceal the meaning of Being. Horkheimer's worry, by contrast, is whether and how a critical social theory can contribute to human liberation and societal transformation. Neither one wants to abandon propositional truth, and neither one dismisses entirely a correspondence theory of propositional truth. Yet each attempts to reconnect propositional truth with larger issues of life and society.

Precisely such reconnections make their essays important today. In the past century many philosophical theories of truth have restricted their scope to beliefs, statements, propositions, and the like—in short, to propositional truth bearers. Correspondence theories (e.g., those of Bertrand Russell and J. L. Austin) characterize truth as consisting in a congruence or correlation between propositional truth bearers and states of affairs that obtain; coherence theories (e.g., Brand Blanshard) regard truth as the coherence among propositional truth bearers in a larger system of knowledge; and pragmatist theories (e.g., William James and John Dewey) consider truth to be something that occurs to propositional truth bearers when they are put to appropriate use. Some theories (primarily correspondence theories) have also tried to explain the "truth" of what makes beliefs and the like true—the truth of the "truth makers," to use a common term. Even then, however, the account of truth makers such as facts or objects subserves an account of propositional truth bearers.

As we shall see, both Heidegger and Horkheimer challenge this focus on propositional truth bearers. In challenging it, they raise crucial questions about connections between propositional correctness[5] and more comprehensive truth. This chapter explores such questions in four sections. First I summarize and comment on Heidegger's essay. Then I do the same for Horkheimer's. The third section develops a dialectical critique of both essays. Employing this critique, and building on previous chapters, in the final section I offer an alternative sketch of how propositional correctness relates to comprehensive truth.

7.1 Heidegger's Ontological Excavation

Martin Heidegger's "On the Essence of Truth" (1930) excavates the ground where the usual concept of truth lies, the concept of a correspondence between proposition and fact. After digging through the layers below the usual concept, Heidegger will conclude that asking about the essence of truth is essential to philosophy itself, in two respects. First, this question reveals what philosophy is in truth—what is, we could say, philosophy's true vocation. Second, asking about the essence of truth shows that philosophy always already participates in "the disclosure of the 'meaning' of what we call Being" (ET, 153/200)—that this, we could say, is philosophy's true preoccupation.

What sort of excavation is this? It is not epistemological. Neither, strictly speaking, is it transcendental à la Kant or the later Husserl. Nor is it historical à la Hegel, Marx, or Nietzsche. I would characterize Heidegger's project as "critical metaphenomenology." Taking as his phenomenon the conceptually (mis)articulated (non)essence of "truth," Heidegger sets out to disclose conceptually, within the phenomenon, the more-than-conceptual structures and process that make this (mis)articulated (non)essence possible. If successful, his uncovering of the essence of truth would also change the conceptually (mis)articulated (non)truth of essence, insofar as the usual concept of truth feeds like a parasite on the fatal and historical reduction of

Being to beings, a reduction that surfaces in the conceptually (mis)articulated phenomenon of essence.

7.1.1 Truth as Correctness (§§1–2)

According to §1 of Heidegger's essay, the usual concept of truth construes it as a double-sided accord between a statement (*Aussage*) or proposition (*Satz*) and an entity (*das Seiende*) or a matter of fact (*Sache*). Truth on this conception amounts to "correctness" (*Richtigkeit*). Historically the conception presupposed that the two sides (proposition and fact) line up correctly because of their placement within either the order of creation (*Schöpfungsordnung*) or a less theologically conceived world order (*Weltordnung*). What remains from this history is the common presupposition that correctness is the essence of truth, and that defining truth requires no account of either "the Being of all beings" or "the essence of [humanity]." That, and the untested presumption of bivalence,[6] whereby "it is considered equally obvious that truth has an opposite, and that there is untruth"—untruth being either the "incorrectness" of propositions or the "non-genuineness" of entities, and in either case being "conceived as a non-accord" (ET, 139/181–182). So Heidegger will examine the notions of "accordance" (*Übereinstimmung*) (§2) and "correctness" (§3) in order to uncover the essence of truth (§§4–5) and of untruth (§§6–7). Then he will pursue the implications of this essence for philosophy (§8) and, in a note (§9), link the essence of truth with the truth of essence.

Let us pause here to consider how and why Heidegger interrogates the notions of accordance and correctness. He aims to find the "inner possibility" (*innere Möglichkeit*) of accordance (ET, 140/182) and "the ground of the possibility of correctness" (ET, 142/185). In German this last phrase is "der Grund der Ermöglichung einer Richtigkeit." It could be more accurately but awkwardly translated as "the ground of making a correctness possible." Heidegger's aim is to excavate the ground that *dynamically makes* truth-as-correctness *possible*, not simply the ground for a static possibility of correctness.

The usual concept of truth characterizes the accordance between statement and thing as "correspondence" (*Angleichung*—a term that suggests similarity). Heidegger immediately raises a standard objection to robust correspondence theories of truth, namely, that statements cannot be like things and still be statements: "Correspondence here cannot signify a thing-like approximation between dissimilar kinds of things" (ET, 141/183). He does not stop there, however, nor does he simply switch to a coherence or pragmatist theory. Rather, he explicates the relation between statement and thing as one where the statement pre-sents (*vor-stellt*) a pre-disposed thing (*wie es bestellt sei*), and the thing stands up to (*entgegensteht als Gegenstand*) the statement and dis-plays itself (*erscheint im Durchmessen eines Entgegen*) within "a domain of relatedness [*Bezugsreich*]" (ET, 141/183–184).[7]

What makes this relation possible is a human comportment that "stands open to beings," together with the fact that "beings present themselves" in a certain way (ET, 141/184).[8] Hence statements and propositions can no longer be "the sole essential locus of truth." They must give way to suitably open human comportment that makes the correctness of statements possible. Two characteristics stand out in such open comportment. First, it takes over a "pregiven standard" according to which the statement must "conform to the object" (ET, 142/185).[9] Second, it neither constitutes the object nor simply receives it. Rather, "standing in the open region, it ... adheres to something opened up *as such*" (ET, 141/184).

7.1.2 Letting Beings Be (§§3–4)

When §3 poses Heidegger's question about the ground that makes truth-as-correctness possible, he is really asking what makes possible such a normative and disclosive comportment, with its "pregiven" and "binding" directedness (ET, 142/185–186). What makes it possible, he answers, is a certain kind of freedom: the freedom to enter into "an open region for something opened up that prevails there and that binds every presenting. To free oneself for a binding directedness is possible only by *being free* for what is opened up in an open region. ... *The essence of truth, as the correctness of a statement, is freedom*" (ET, 142/185–186).[10]

Heidegger recognizes that the usual concept of freedom seemingly has little to do with what makes truth possible. Indeed, placing the essence of truth-as-correctness in freedom appears to make truth arbitrary. It appears "to submit truth to human caprice," to drive truth "back to the subjectivity of the human subject" (ET, 143/187). But this appearance arises, he says, owing to a preconception of freedom as a human property. When Heidegger says freedom is the essence of truth, he aims to challenge that preconception.

What, then, is the essence of freedom? According to §4, the essence of freedom lies in receptivity and acceptance, not in initiative and control. That is why Heidegger says the essence of freedom, which makes possible truth-as-correctness, itself derives "from the more originary essence of the uniquely essential truth" (ET, 144/187)—the topic of §5. Heidegger describes the essence of freedom as "letting beings be" (*das Seinlassen von Seienden*). To let beings be (*Sein-lassen*) is not to distance oneself from them, however, but to engage (*Sicheinlassen*) with them: "Sein-lassen ist das Sicheinlassen auf das Seiende."[11] And this engagement is not simply with the beings themselves but "with the open region and its openness into which every being comes to stand" (ET, 144/188). Accordingly, truth-as-correctness derives from truth-as-unconcealment (*Unverborgenheit*), from the process whereby beings in their disclosedness (*Entborgenheit*) undergo disclosure (*Entbergung*). For correct statements or propositions to occur, one must engage with beings in such a way that they "might reveal themselves [*sich offenbare*] with respect to what and how they are" (ET, 144/189). The comportment required is one of self-transcending[12] "exposure to the disclosedness of beings" (ET, 145/189).

From this account of freedom flow both a conception of history and a preliminary characterization of untruth. Heidegger claims that history begins when, on the basis of being-there (*Da-sein*), human beings question "the unconcealment of beings by asking: what are beings?" and thereby experience unconcealment "for the first time" (ET, 145/189). This implies, in turn, that freedom is not a human possession; rather, "freedom, ek-sistent, disclosive Da-sein, possesses the human being—so originarily that only *it* secures for humanity that distinctive relatedness to beings as a whole as such which first founds all history" (ET, 145–146/190). Moreover, truth and history are neither separate nor opposed. Instead, history at bottom is an unfolding of truth: "The rare and simple decisions of history arise from the way the originary essence of truth essentially unfolds." Untruth can unfold too, insofar as human beings do "*not* let beings be the beings which they are and as they are" and beings become "covered up and distorted." Untruth does not derive from human failure, however: "untruth must derive from the essence of truth" (ET, 146/191). Hence the purported bivalence of truth is not so obvious as the common concept of truth supposes, nor can we equate untruth with propositional incorrectness—a topic to which Heidegger returns in §§6–7.

7.1.3   Truth and Untruth (§§5–7)

Section 5, titled "The Essence of Truth," lies midway through an essay whose compositional structure resembles an inverted arch. After §5 Heidegger returns layer by layer to where his excavations began. He examines what the essence of truth means for untruth (§§6–7) as the context for correctness (§3) and accordance (§2). Then he presents true philosophy (§8) as the antidote to untrue common sense (§1) and balances the essay's opening paragraphs on "actual truths" with a note summarizing why the question concerning the essence of truth is essential (§9).

Section 5 brings to the surface three streams that have run beneath previous sections: attunement, holism, and concealment. Now we discover that attunement (*Stimmung*) makes possible the accordance (*Übereinstimmung*) said to prevail between proposition and fact: "As engagement [*Eingelassenheit*] in the disclosure of beings as a whole as such, freedom has already attuned all comportment to beings as a whole" (ET, 147/192). This attunement is not so much an experience or feeling as it is the process or ongoing event (what Heidegger later calls *Ereignis*) that makes possible experience or feeling or other modes of comportment. Nor should we regard the "whole" to which all human comportment is attuned as the sum total of what we already understand. Rather, this whole exceeds what is familiar. Indeed, the more that science and technology flatten "the openedness of beings as a whole," the less essentially can this openedness prevail, even though science and technology would not be possible without attunement. Because of such flattening, also in "everyday calculations and preoccupations" (ET, 147/193), the "as a whole" becomes indefinite (*das Unbestimmte*) and indeterminable (*Unbestimmbare*), even as it "ceaselessly brings everything into definite accord [*ständig alles stimmend*]." This "according" or "attuning" simultaneously "conceals [*verbirgt*] beings as a whole. Letting-be is intrinsically at the same time a concealing [*Verbergen*]" (ET, 147–148/193). As we shall see in greater detail, because attunement and holism are essential to truth, untruth is too.

Heidegger discusses untruth in two registers, as "concealment" (*Verbergung*) (§6) and as errancy (*die Irre*) (§7). The first is "un-truth proper." As the "proper non-essence of truth," concealment is "the mystery" (ET, 148/194). It has to do with the concealment of beings as a whole. The second register—errancy—is not so much a nonessence (*Un-wesen*) as a counteressence (*Gegenwesen*). It is "the essential counteressence to the originary essence of truth," Heidegger writes. Errancy is not the mystery as such but a direction in which human beings respond to mystery, namely, in "flight from the mystery toward what is readily available." In this register, untruth has to do with the way in which human beings are "always astray" (ET, 150/196–197).

Heidegger says that untruth as concealment is older than any particular being's "openedness," and older than "letting-be itself." Concealment holds sway as mystery "throughout the Da-sein of human beings" (ET, 148/193–194). Concealment conceals itself, and self-transcending or eksistent Da-sein conserves this double concealment. Even though, as letting beings be, all comportment is directed toward the disclosure of beings, this predisposal toward disclosure (*Entbergung*) conceals concealment (*Verbergung*) and lets the mystery be forgotten. Taking our bearings from the openedness of particular beings, we "cling to what is readily available and controllable even where ultimate matters are concerned" (ET, 149/195). We push to the margins "the concealment of beings as a whole." We forget the mystery, and the mystery leaves us to our own resources. So we pursue our own plans according to our own standards, and thereby "go wrong as regards the essential genuineness [*Wesens-Echtheit*] of [our] standards" (ET, 149/196)—presumably also the genuineness of the common standards for truth. Thus our forgetfulness deepens, secured by a bearing (*Verhältnis*) of not only ek-sisting but also in-sisting on what beings offer us, "as if they were open of and in themselves" (ET, 150/196) and not open within the openedness of beings as a whole.

In both insisting on "the most readily available beings" and self-transcending or ek-sisting toward them as a standard, human beings pass the mystery by. They go astray. This going astray or "errancy" (*die Irre*) is not incidental or occasional. It "belongs to the inner constitution" of our Dasein, and it makes possible various modes of erring, including incorrect judgment, which Heidegger regards as the "most superficial" mode of erring (ET, 150–151/196–197). Yet at the same time errancy allows human beings to catch themselves, to "*not* let themselves be led astray." Even more prominent, however, is the indigence of Da-sein, the simultaneous subjection of human beings to both "the rule of the mystery" and "the oppression of errancy" (ET, 151/197). Just as freedom is the essence of truth-as-correctness, then, so necessity originates in untruth-as-errancy.

Nevertheless, as Heidegger summarizes in the last paragraph of §7, truth and untruth are not binary opposites. The disclosure of particular beings *is* their concealment as a whole. Conversely, both concealment and errancy "belong to the originary essence of truth." Freedom can be the essence of truth-as-correctness because freedom itself stems from truth's originary essence, from "the rule of the mystery in errancy." We can recognize this complex interrelation, Heidegger suggests, because from time to time—presumably also in Heidegger's time and in this essay—a question arises about beings as such as a whole, affording a glimpse out of errancy into the mystery. This amounts to "the question of the Being of beings," Heidegger's leading question, and one he considers decisive for philosophy as a whole (ET, 151–152/198).

7.1.4 Thinking of Being (§§8–9)

In §8 Heidegger assigns to philosophy a world-historical task. Or, rather, he displays the world-historical vocation to which truth assigns philosophy. His display illuminates four areas. First, he claims that "the thinking of Being" articulates the history-grounding liberation (*die geschichtegründende Befreiung*) of human beings for self-transcendence or ek-sistence (ET 152/198–199). Second, he defines philosophy as a discordant questioning into the full essence/nonessence of truth. It is characterized both by "gentle releasement [*Gelassenheit*] that does not renounce the concealment of beings as a whole" and by "stern and resolute openness [*Ent-schlossenheit*]" that entreats the concealing's unbroken essence "into the open region of understanding and thus into its own truth" (ET, 152/199). Third, quoting Kant, Heidegger identifies two ways in which philosophy's "letting beings as such be as a whole" is properly distinct from common sense: philosophical questioning "does not cling solely to beings," and it cannot allow an "externally imposed decree." If freed from modern subjectivism such as one finds in Kant's thought, philosophy could find its proper autonomy in being appointed "by the truth of that to which [philosophy's] laws … pertain" (ET, 152–153/200). Fourth, Heidegger indicates that his inquiry into the essence of truth raises a question about the truth of essence, a question in which "philosophy thinks Being." Hence the essence of truth occupies a unique role "in the unremitting history of the disclosure of the 'meaning' of what we call Being"—which, for Heidegger, is not identical with beings as a whole (ET, 153/200).

In retrospect, then, we can say that §8 takes philosophy's world-historical vocation to be thinking Being, in gentle releasement and stern resoluteness toward the concealment of beings, and as appointed by truth itself. The note that follows in §9 strengthens these world-historical overtones: "Truth signifies sheltering that clears [*lichtendes Bergen*] as the fundamental trait of Being." This clearing-sheltering "lets essentially unfold" the "accordance

[*Übereinstimmung*] between knowledge and beings." With implicit reference to his own work, Heidegger then writes: "The answer to the question of the essence of truth is the saying of a turning [*die Sage einer Kehre*] within the history of Beyng." That is why, although his thinking still seems to follow the path of metaphysics, "in its decisive steps ..., it accomplishes a change in the questioning that belongs to the overcoming of metaphysics." His essay not only leaves behind all human subjectivity to seek the truth of Being "as the ground of a transformed historical position" but also "sets out to think from this other ground (Da-sein)." His thinking in this essay "experiences and tests itself as a transformation of its relatedness to Being" (ET, 153–154/201–202).

7.2 Horkheimer's Dialectical Critique

Max Horkheimer's "On the Problem of Truth" (1935) proposes an alternative to relativism and absolutism as two positions that characterize much of modern Western philosophy and whose contemporary polarity expresses an underlying contradiction in capitalist society. The polarity between relativism and absolutism and that polarity's pervasiveness make up what Horkheimer calls "the problem of truth." His addressing this problem has significance not only for philosophy but also for the society to which philosophy belongs. It has special significance for the development of a historical-materialist "dialectical logic," Horkheimer's central project in the 1930s.[13]

By "relativism" Horkheimer means the position that knowledge (*Erkenntnis*) "never has more than limited validity [*Gültigkeit*]" (PT, 177/321). Appealing to historical variability and human finitude, relativists regard truth as relative to both time and person. "Absolutism," by contrast, is the tendency toward "blind faith," toward "absolute submission." Describing this tendency as "characteristic of the cultural situation today," Horkheimer obliquely associates it with Heidegger and other successors to Husserl (PT, 178/322). Horkheimer does not actually say what the absolutist position claims. Instead, he portrays it as a response to how, within the dynamic of capitalist society as a whole, "liberal, democratic, and progressive tendencies" hollow out their own normative content. In this milieu a few rigid views come to dominate public culture, and absolutism becomes attractive (PT, 178/322).

Although Horkheimer does not overtly divide his essay into sections, there are at least six. The first reviews the intellectual and social history of the relativism–absolutism dialectic in "the bourgeois era," beginning with Descartes and Kant (PT, 178–183/322–327). The second section examines Hegel's dialectical method (PT, 183–189/327–334). Section 3 frees this method from idealist trappings in order to sketch an alternative conception of truth (PT, 189–194/334–339). Then the fourth section takes up the topic of corroboration (*Bewährung*), with special reference to pragmatism (PT, 194–203/339–349), so that the fifth section can fill in Horkheimer's sketch of a materialist dialectical conception of truth (PT, 203–211/349–358). He concludes with a coda on religion (PT, 211–215/358–363). Let me ignore sections 1 and 6, and move directly to the appropriation of Hegel in section 2.

7.2.1 Hegel's Dogmatism (§2)

Horkheimer regards Hegel's dialectical method as the "most ambitious attempt" on the part of "bourgeois thought" to transcend the antinomy between relativism and absolutism (PT, 183/328). While recognizing that particular truth claims have limited validity, Hegel's dialectic incorporates them into a more encompassing system of truth, so that the process of "continuous delimitation and correction" becomes their proper concept as the "knowledge [*Wissen*] of limited insights in their limits and connection" (PT, 184/328). This process of "determinate negation" allows "every negated insight" to be "preserved [*aufbewahrt*] as a moment of truth" in the progression of knowledge (*Fortgang der Erkenntnis*) and to undergo further determination and transformation "with every new step" (PT, 184/328–329). Unlike relativism, then, the dialectical method takes variable and finite matters (*das Bedingte*) seriously. And, unlike absolutism, the dialectical method does not seek some mysterious absolute "behind the scenes" that "only the initiate knows." Rather, "what presents itself as absolute and eternal" is found "in development and flux" (PT, 185/329).

Unfortunately, Hegel also retains the worst features of relativism and absolutism: relativism's indifference to particular truth claims, and absolutism's inability to historicize its own thought. The latter inability—Hegel's dogmatism—is of special concern to Horkheimer. Although Hegel does not essentialize an abstract concept into a history-transcending Being (*Sein*), he does "hypostatize" his own system. Nor is Hegel's "dogmatic narrow-mindedness" merely incidental: it informs every dialectical move. Despite

Hegel's emphasis on experience (*Erfahrung*), his systematic self-reflection overlooks the significant role played by "temporally conditioned interest" in his own "dialectical presentation" (*Darstellung*),[14] and it covers up how his practical stance (*Parteistellung zu den Fragen des Lebens*) helped constitute his philosophy (PT, 186–187/331). In this way Hegel's thought becomes ideological. It takes on a "transfiguring function," giving oppression and misery a "higher" and "eternal" meaning, rather than exposing their societal origins (PT, 187/332).

Relativism sits quite comfortably in this absolutist pew, Horkheimer says. To assert dogmatically that all-embracing thought transcends every particular and opposing view is to tolerate all points of view, no matter how reactionary some might be. Hegel's dogmatism keeps him from recognizing and affirming the progressive interests expressed in his own "science of experience," to borrow a phrase from the original title for *Phenomenology of Spirit*. It is only a small step from this to a post-Hegelian relativism that discredits progressive ideas as mere rationalizations no better than any other historically conditioned idea. The dogmatism concealed in such "impartial relativism" is its endorsing the status quo (PT, 188–189/333).

7.2.2 Materialist Dialectic (§3)

With this criticism, Horkheimer arrives at a "dialectical proposition" that "takes relativism beyond itself," namely, the claim that impartiality is a form of partisanship, that "indiscriminate objectivity represent[s] a subjective [stance]" (PT, 189/334). Accordingly, the next pages in his essay (PT, 189–194/334–339) present a materialist version of the dialectical method and begin to sketch an alternative conception of truth. Here it becomes apparent that "critical theory," as Horkheimer labeled his project in a famous essay published two years later,[15] is a metacritical phenomenology. The phenomena in question are not noetic à la Husserl, nor are they conceptually articulated essences à la Heidegger. Rather, they are historically informed, sociocultural tendencies à la Hegel and Marx. Horkheimer's approach to these tendencies is metacritical in a twofold sense. First, like Marx, he develops his theoretical understanding of the phenomena by criticizing ideological distortions. Second, he continues Hegel's line of dialectical critique, but takes it in a materialist direction.

Horkheimer distinguishes his materialist dialectic from Hegel's idealist version in three respects: (1) it is an open process rather than a closed system; (2) its test of truth lies in ongoing praxis rather than in theoretical completion; and (3) it takes seriously the historical mediation between sociohistorical reality and theoretical thought. Let me discuss each characteristic in turn.

(1)   According to Horkheimer, Hegel's dialectic is a closed system because it presupposes "that concept and being are in truth the same." Materialism rejects this idealist presupposition. "Objective reality" and human thought are not identical, nor can they merge. For example, to conceive of a defect does not overcome it, even though concepts and theories contribute to its removal and form prerequisites for corrigible and right action (*Handeln*) (PT, 189/334). Such materialist openness jibes with the traditional definition of truth as the correspondence (*Übereinstimmung*) of knowledge (*Erkenntnis*) with its object (*Gegenstand*), provided we do not construe correspondence as either a simple given or an intellectual occurrence. Instead, "real events and human activity" always *establish* this correspondence, and they do so within a definite societal period (PT, 190/334–335).[16]

(2)   That is why the test of truth lies in ongoing praxis and not in theoretical completion. Action (*Handeln*) is no mere afterthought; it is intrinsic to theory itself. Conversely, thought never achieves unity with the object of thought (*die Sache*). The meaning and value of any specific knowledge (*Wissen*) depends both on the concrete situation and on the condition of society as a whole (PT, 191/336). This does not mean, however, that an open-ended dialectic loses "the stamp of truth" (PT, 191/337). Because the identity of concept and object is not presupposed, the experiences (*Erfahrungen*) gained in "perception and inference," in "methodical inquiry and historical events," and in "daily work and political struggle" either do or do not measure up to "the available means of cognition" (*den verfügbaren Erkenntnismitteln standhalten*). When these experiences do measure up, they are "the truth" (PT, 192/337). Moreover, even when criticisms are internally justified, materialists will remain alert to their own errors and flexible in their thinking. It does not make sense to call such knowledge "relative" if one no longer has a God's-eye concept of truth (PT, 192/337).

In other words, truth is historical but not relative: changes in interest and circumstance can make "correct" theories disappear, yet later corrections do not mean former truths were untrue earlier. Truth advances not because history takes care of this but because human beings who have the truth "stand by it ..., apply it and carry it [out], act according to it, and bring it to power against the resistance of reactionary, narrow, one-sided points of view" (PT 192–3/338). So truth is practical, not just theoretical, and the process whereby we attain truth—what Horkheimer calls the "process of knowledge" (*der Prozess der Erkenntnis*)—includes "real historical will and action" (*Wollen und Handeln*) just as much as it contains experience and conceptualization (*Erfahren und Begreifen*) (PT, 193/338).

(3) Accordingly, the way to surpass the relativism–absolutism antithesis is to take seriously the historical mediation between sociohistorical reality and theoretical thought. Recognizing this mediation, a materialist dialectic neither denies its own relativity nor abandons the claim to comprehensive truth. It considers its own insights to be universally valid in the whole context to which they refer, and it views "the opposing theory" as wrong (PT, 193/338). The opposing theory, in this context, would be one that denies the historical mediation of concept and object—a denial common to much of Western philosophy. Yet, like the predominant correspondence theory of truth, a materialist dialectic regards truth as valid for those who deny or ignore it. The relation of thought (*Vorstellungen*) to reality is decisive for truth, not an individual's beliefs, and not "the [epistemic] subject in itself" (PT, 194/339). Consequently, "only that theory [of society] is true which can grasp the historical process [*Geschehen*] so deeply that it is possible to develop from it [i.e., from the theory] the closest approximation to the structure and tendency of social life in the various spheres of culture." What makes this theory true is not its political standpoint but its insight, the truth of which even those who reject the theory will one day experience (PT, 194/339).

7.2.3   Pragmatism and Corroboration (§4)

Horkheimer's emphasis on openness, praxis, and mediation makes his approach sound like a pragmatist theory of truth. Accordingly, section 4 (PT, 194–203/339–349) distinguishes his conception of corroboration (*Bewährung*) from a pragmatist conception. Citing William James and John Dewey, Horkheimer says pragmatists hold that the truth-value (*Wahrheitswert*) of theories is decided "by what one accomplishes with them" (PT, 195/340). The pragmatist criterion of truth is a theory's "power to produce desired effects" for human well-being, to promote human flourishing. This makes the practical corroboration of thoughts "identical with their truth" (PT, 195/341).

The main problem with this view, according to Horkheimer, is its unwarranted social optimism, which gives ideological support to a capitalist economy (PT, 196/341–342). Pragmatism fails to distinguish sufficiently between the theoretical verification (*Verifikation*) of truth[17] and truth's practical meaning or significance (*Bedeutung*). In this way, pragmatist accounts of corroboration support the liberal illusion that scientific and human progress run in tandem. But the pragmatist's claim that truth promotes life might not itself be true if pragmatist epistemology "does not belong to a whole in which the tendencies working towards a better, life-promoting [condition] really find expression" (PT, 197/343).

Materialism also employs a concept of corroboration, as a weapon against elitism and mysticism and on behalf of truth that is publicly accessible. Yet Horkheimer insists on a dialectical relation between theory and practice, in contrast to pragmatism's preestablished harmony (PT, 198/343–344). Although human activity draws on theoretical insight, other factors and obstacles play a role as well. Horkheimer gives the example of how Marxian historiography relates to emancipatory praxis. The course of history has borne out Marx's theory of history, he says, and if it had not, the theory would not serve emancipatory praxis. But one needs to distinguish two closely related lines of verification (*Verifikation*): the corroboration (*Bewährung*) of hope for liberation, and the confirmation (*Bestätigung*) of tendencies predicted by the theory. Their mediation lies in "the actual struggle, the solution of concrete historical problems based on [a] theory substantiated by experience." Similarly, theoretical progress depends just as much on "unswerving loyalty [*Treue*] to what is recognized as true" as on "openness to new tasks and situations" (PT, 199/344–345).

On the flip side, Horkheimer suggests that premature claims, incorrect diagnoses, and temporary defeats need not disconfirm an emancipatory theory. Even the descent of humanity into barbarism does not destroy the true insights of those who fight for liberation. In other words, corroboration is not a simple criterion of truth. Truth is a moment of correct praxis, but truth is not the same as success. To equate truth and success would be to ignore history and to endorse the status quo (PT, 200/345).

Whereas pragmatism equates corroboration and truth, then, Horkheimer keeps them distinct. On his account, corroboration—the evidence

(*Nachweis*) that thought and objective reality correspond—is "a historical occurrence that can be obstructed and interrupted." When something
blocks corroboration, when "a given constellation of the world" prevents
an idea from being realized, this need not mean that the idea is untrue. A
"more rational form of human association" than the current social order
is demonstrably possible, for example, and the continuing prevalence of
misery and terror is no proof to the contrary (PT, 200/346).[18]

7.2.4 Emancipatory Theory (§5)

What, then, is the upshot to reappropriating Hegel and criticizing pragmatism for Horkheimer's conception of truth? It appears that Horkheimer
combines the holism of coherence theories with the partial realism of some
correspondence theories and the practical orientation of pragmatism, but
in combining them transforms all three. His holism has two aspects: (1) the
corroboration of truth claims depends on open-ended historical processes
(PT, 203/349), and (2) social categories historically change their function
as "aspects [*Momente*] of the whole body of knowledge at a given time"
(PT, 204/350). Because of his partial realism, however, Horkheimer insists
that historically developed knowledge as a whole "is never identical with
reality," which also unfolds historically. Rather, dialectical thought tries
to model (*nachbilden*) reality (*Wirklichkeit*) with utmost precision and to
correspond (*übereinstimmen*) as far as possible with the principles (*Form-
prinzipien*) of actual events (*Verläufe*) (PT, 204/350). Yet, unlike many correspondence theorists, Horkheimer sees both sides—both the dialectic in
thought and the actuality it models—as processual rather than static, and
as interconnected rather than as consisting primarily of discrete concepts
and objects. The nonidentity between dialectical thought and historical
actuality is what allows theory to have a practical orientation, without theory's either dictating praxis or simply succumbing to the test of "success."
Progress in both theory and praxis requires the pursuit of a definite theory
at the highest contemporary level; yet applying this theory has reciprocal
impact on the theory's shape and meaning (PT, 203/349–350).

Materialist dialectical thought, then, is the continual attempt, based
on ongoing experience (*auf Grund fortschreitender Erfahrung*), to relativize
every exclusive determination (*jedes ausschliessende Bestimmungsurteil*), and
to do so with reference to changes on the part of the subject, the object,
and their relationship. Dialectical thought analyzes purportedly universal

properties, brings out their contradiction with particular objects, and shows that, to be grasped correctly, such properties must be related to "the whole system of knowledge" (PT, 204/350). Hence Horkheimer's holism—"every insight is to be regarded as true only in connection with the whole body of theory" (PT, 204/350)—does not become full-blown coherentism—dialectical thought must not only interconnect the concepts it reconstructs from social science but also use them to reconstruct reality (*Wirklichkeit*). Indeed, all the characteristics of dialectical thought "correspond" (*entsprechen*) to the form of reality, which is complex (*verschlungen*) and "constantly changing in all its details" (PT, 204/351).

This means that concepts such as "commodity" and "value" and categories such as "money" and "capital" must always be understood in their interrelationships and in their historical setting. Yet materialists do not expect their own dialectical reconstructions of concepts and categories to bring an end to the "contradictions and tensions" of history. For this requires historical struggle: theoretically informed struggle, to be sure, but not merely theoretical—in fact, a struggle whose outcome no theory can predict. The outcome depends on "human beings interacting with one another and with nature, who enter into new relationships and structures and thereby change themselves. The resolution of contradictions in subjective thought and the overcoming of objective antagonisms can be closely intertwined, but they are in no way identical" (PT, 209–210/356–357). Accordingly, Horkheimer says, the proper stance for dialectical social critics is not only to criticize the "great truths" but also to remain committed to truth—to uphold the truth by remaining "firm in its application even if it may sometime pass away" (PT, 211/357–358).

7.3 Dialectical Disclosure

I said earlier that both Heidegger and Horkheimer challenge the traditional focus on propositional truth bearers. Both of them suggest that truth is more comprehensive than what propositionally inflected accounts can notice, that the primary reasons for wondering about propositional truth escape the purview of propositionally inflected accounts. Whereas Heidegger thinks the narrowing of attention to propositional matters manifests a Western forgetfulness of Being, Horkheimer considers it an expression of bourgeois ideology and its acceptance of the status quo.

Both of them are right, in my view, even though each would direct his own charge toward the other.

Why would they raise such charges against each other? Apart from sociopolitical differences, which were thoroughgoing and became even deeper once Adorno entered the fray—or rather, *within* these sociopolitical differences, Heidegger and Horkheimer have different visions of freedom and history. They reconstruct propositional correctness in line with their social visions. One seeks meaning; the other, liberation. One enacts an intellectual turn (*Kehre*) within the history of Being; the other pursues a material transformation (*Umschlag*) in the structure of society. For one, truth is an ontological disclosure; for the other, it is a dialectical achievement. For both of them truth is historical, and for neither is history the truth; but what history comes to differs from one to the other.

Upon closer examination, however, Heidegger and Horkheimer's positions prove to be complementary in their mutual opposition. Let me trace this implicit dialectic by comparing and questioning their essays on four topics: (1) propositional correctness, (2) freedom, (3) history, and (4) bivalence. I shall argue that neither Heidegger nor Horkheimer provides a convincing account of how propositional correctness and comprehensive truth, although distinct, go together.

7.3.1 Propositional Correctness

Heidegger sees more clearly than Horkheimer does, it seems to me, that propositional correctness would hardly matter if there were not nonpropositional matters about which and in relation to which human knowledge can be more or less correct. Nor can these matters simply be constituted or constructed by human knowledge. Rather, they must offer themselves within a field of relations to other matters. They must display what I have labeled "predicative availability." Heidegger also recognizes correctly that for such connections to occur between propositions and nonpropositional matters—or better, between predicative activities and matters that are both predicatively and nonpredicatively available—both human openness and "objective" self-presentation or self-disclosure are required. His account becomes problematic, however, when he extrapolates from such "correspondence" a notion of freedom as "letting beings be." I shall return to this problem shortly.

Horkheimer, by contrast, understands more adequately than Heidegger that, when the nonpropositional matters at stake are societal and cultural, their connection with predicative activities must be dialectical.[19] The attempt to achieve correct knowledge with respect to sociocultural matters requires more than human openness and "objective" self-presentation. The matters to be understood cannot be taken at face value; correct insights must be wrested from incorrect understandings; and whether an insight is correct needs to be tested, in both theory and praxis, with reference both to a larger nexus of concepts and claims and to the historical context to which the subject matter belongs. As Horkheimer puts it, the so-called correspondence between knowledge and object needs to be established amid historical struggles both theoretical and practical. It would appear, however, that Horkheimer locates the key to this process in a critical social theory. This presupposes a confidence in dialectical thought that I find problematic, for reasons I give later.

7.3.2 Freedom

Heidegger, for one, does not share this confidence. By grounding truth-as-correctness in "letting beings be," he introduces a notion of freedom that runs counter to the struggle and striving intrinsic to dialectical thought. To let beings be is neither to correct incorrect understandings nor to test the correctness of an insight. It is rather to let oneself be admitted (*Sicheinlassen*) into the open region where beings can reveal what and how they are. Hence the initiative, if we may continue to speak of initiative, does not lie with human thought or action. Rather, it rests with a process of disclosure (*Entbergung*) that sustains beings in their disclosedness (*Entborgenheit*), including human beings in their ecstatic Da-sein. This implies that freedom or "letting beings be" is itself made possible by a transsubjective and transobjective process, such that correctness becomes a gift to be received rather than a goal to be achieved.

Heidegger's account of freedom instructively reorients truth theory in a normative direction, pointing it past the nexus of subject and object and of theory and praxis toward fundamental questions of orientation and direction. At the same time, however, his account distorts the meaning of freedom. To let beings be in the manner he describes is to assume that they, or the process of disclosure in which they stand, would be worth accepting "as is." But much about which we seek correct understanding is already caught up in historical struggles over what is better and what is worse: cultural conflicts, scientific debates, political battles, economic strife. In such settings, simply to let beings be would require a surrender of responsibility, obligation, agency, and, yes, power—without which human beings can hardly promote the interconnected flourishing of all creatures. Such flourishing, I submit, is the central meaning of freedom, rather than either Heideggerian acceptance of disclosure or the model of mastery he rightly challenges. To flourish, and to seek the flourishing of fellow human beings as well as of other creatures, we cannot ignore or deny "how and what" human beings themselves are. Their freedom might not be a matter of Kantian autonomy, but it is certainly not the same as ontological *Gelassenheit*.

Horkheimer, who wrote his own materialist critique of Kantian morality,[20] never abandoned the central intuition that "getting things right" in theory is tied to "getting them right" in practice. To attain propositional correctness is to engage in historical struggles over what is better and what is worse in society. These *are* matters of effort and achievement, he suggests. In propositional correctness, then, for Horkheimer as for Heidegger, human freedom is at stake. But the freedom Horkheimer has in mind is not to let beings be. Rather, it is to liberate the suffering and needy from their societally secured oppression. Without liberation there would be neither justice nor solidarity, and without a striving for liberation any talk of "freedom" would ring hollow—would in fact ideologically occlude the unfreedom in contemporary society.

I have a great deal of sympathy for Horkheimer's approach to freedom. Yet it presupposes a prior orientation toward human flourishing over which he remains inarticulate. He assumes from the beginning and all along that dialectical thought has the best interests of humankind at heart, and that these interests will prevail. This assumption seems scarcely less "absolutist" than Hegel's all-embracing thought. If it is not absolutist, then at least it displays too little of the critical self-reflection that Horkheimer finds lacking in Hegel. To fill in the content of human flourishing, and to indicate how dialectical thought has this content at heart, Horkheimer would need to sketch more substantial notions of the good than his materialist dialectical commitments permit. Instead, he pushes such content into the future, as something to be revealed when it is achieved, rather than as societal principles that are already in effect, in however distorted a fashion, and that are already available as points of orientation.[21] Whereas Heidegger construes freedom as an originary process to be received, Horkheimer portrays it as a future goal yet to be achieved. Neither construal is adequate.

7.3.3 History

This difference over freedom permeates their conceptions of truth and history. According to Heidegger, the "correspondence" between proposition and fact arises from the "attunement" of human comportment to beings as a whole. Such attunement is secured by freedom, he says: freedom as something that possesses human beings and secures for them a "distinctive relatedness to beings as a whole" (ET, 145–146/189). Attunement also conceals beings as a whole, however, and freedom secures such concealment too. Accordingly, history begins when freedom—letting beings be—simultaneously secures both human attunement and the concealment of that to which human beings are attuned. History in its origins is an unfolding of untruth together with truth. Albeit with some exceptions and temporary reversals, history is the tale of our forgetting the mystery of Being and passing it by.

In this way, Heidegger acknowledges, in opposition to modern thought, that human beings are not the masters of their fate. Nor can they simply "revalue all values" once they notice, as Nietzsche did, the admixture of power in Enlightenment ideals of freedom and truth. Yet the *Kehre* Heidegger seeks would amount to a myth of enlightenment. That is to say, he assigns to an ontological fate the task of unconcealing, and thereby concealing, what beings, including human beings, mean—what their purposes and destinations are. Heidegger continues to hope for enlightenment. If he did not, his attempt to reconceptualize truth would lose its point. But his hope lies in what is essentially a mystery, in a process that few mere mortals—Heidegger among them, I suppose—can understand or effect. This myth of enlightenment occupies an absolutist position, even though Heidegger himself rejects the story of rational enlightenment that Hegel tells and enacts.

Horkheimer, by contrast, embraces a story of rational enlightenment even as he rejects Hegel's purported absolutism. For Horkheimer, and contra Heidegger, history is not the fateful unfolding of truth as un/concealment. Rather, it is the ongoing struggle of human beings to achieve liberation in society. The key to their struggle lies in a mediation between sociohistorical reality and theoretical thought. Horkheimer singles out three aspects of this mediation. First, any "correspondence" between the one and the other needs to be established by "real events and human activity" (PT, 190/334–335). Second, any theoretical understanding of real events and human activity will arise from them and must be borne out by them. Third, the truth of such theoretical understanding depends upon its grasp of the entire historical process informing the structure and tendencies of contemporary society. The theory that has a better grasp will also be borne out by real events and human activity, and will in fact play a leading role in helping to establish the "correspondence" between sociohistorical reality and theoretical thought.

Whereas Heidegger places his hope for enlightenment in the mystery of Being, then, Horkheimer places his hope for liberation in the praxis of theory. By the phrase "praxis of theory" I mean two things: first, the double claim that theory arises from praxis and must be borne out by praxis, and, second, the claim that true theory can and must play a leading role in the transformation of society. In other words, theory is a form of praxis, and true theory is crucial for true praxis. Correlatively, not only is truth historical, but also theoretical truth is crucial for history's becoming true. In these respects, Horkheimer retains more transparently than Heidegger does the connections between propositional correctness and human flourishing, both in theory and in praxis.

Yet Horkheimer's emphasis on the praxis of theory relies on a petitio principii that may itself conceal a troublesome commitment. The petitio principii concerns his appeal to praxis as both the touchstone and the beneficiary of theoretical truth. On the one hand, praxis is the touchstone—as both origin and test—for theoretical truth: theoretical truth originates in praxis and receives corroboration in praxis. On the other hand, not just any praxis can serve as this touchstone. The proper praxis must accord with true theory, and be guided by it, if theory is to play a leading role in societal transformation. Horkheimer is not unaware of the pitfalls here. He certainly does not want to collapse the validity of theoretical claims into either their genesis or their consequences. He distinguishes very clearly between a theory's insights and its social functions, just as he distinguishes between theory-internal confirmation and theory-external corroboration—important distinctions, in my view, and advances beyond both pragmatism and Karl Marx's "Theses on Feuerbach."

Despite the potential fruitfulness of Horkheimer's approach, however, it simply begs the question whether praxis can serve as a touchstone for theoretical truth if praxis is not already the beneficiary of true theory. How can true theoretical insights into the historical process emerge from struggles to change society if these struggles are not already guided by such insights? But if the insights were already available in the struggle, why would true theory need to offer guidance? And if the insights were not already available in the struggle, how could true theory connect with the struggle and offer guidance? Horkheimer repeatedly dances around the places where such questions would arise, either avoiding the questions or not recognizing the need to address them.

Horkheimer's dance may signal a troublesome commitment to the position that theory is the final authority for right praxis, a position Adorno forthrightly articulates three decades later.[22] Horkheimer never straightforwardly says this—nor should he say this, given his critique of Hegel for hypostatizing his own system. Yet a subtle absolutizing of theory may lurk behind the screen of Horkheimer's insistence on the open-endedness of history. When he says that decisions about particular truth claims depend on uncompleted processes, and when he claims that the function of social-theoretical categories changes over time, he assumes that no matter how these processes and changes go, true theories about them will always be possible, and that the truth of the matter can always be theoretically determined. This assumption secretly orients his claim that progress in both theory and praxis requires the pursuit and application of a definite theory at the highest contemporary level. To make such metatheoretical claims, Horkheimer's own philosophy must assume for itself a historical positioning that allows it even now, amid the ongoing historical process, to make true claims about how history and truth intersect. Although no comprehensive truth theory can avoid taking this sort of stance, it matters whether the stance simply occurs in an unexamined way or whether the theorist states it and invites dialogical reflection about it. When the stance occurs as an unexamined assumption, dogmatism is not far away.

7.3.4 Bivalence
Indeed, from Heidegger's perspective, Horkheimer's materialist dialectic would fall prey to both logicism and nihilism, the two alternatives Heidegger himself wishes to avoid. It falls prey to logicism insofar as Horkheimer

locates the key to truth in the praxis of theory, which cannot avoid taking propositional form. It simultaneously suffers from nihilism, however, because Horkheimer attributes the source and test of truth to a will to power—a will to liberating power, no doubt, and a commitment to societal transformation, but a will to power nonetheless. Heidegger will have none of this: to privilege theory is to forget the mystery of Being, and to strive for liberation is to pursue our own plans amid "the most readily available beings." Both tendencies lead us astray, reinforcing that "errancy" which is truth's "counteressence." It is precisely to challenge such tendencies, and to recall the forgotten mystery, that Heidegger questions the bivalence of truth. Untruth, he says, is essential to truth. In questioning the bivalence of truth, philosophy carries out its world-historical vocation to question the full essence/nonessence of truth and to let "beings as such be as a whole."

Important though this questioning might be as a challenge to the praxis of theory, Heidegger cannot avoid relativism, the flip side of absolutism, according to Horkheimer. It is so, of course, that Heidegger successfully extricates truth theory from the epistemic and ethical subjectivism that informs most modern relativism, as well as the logicism and nihilism Heidegger opposes. Heidegger does not say that historical variability and human finitude make truth relative to both time and person. If anything, he says that truth makes times and persons relative to Being. Yet his account of such ontological relativity, of the relatedness of all beings to their being as a whole, eliminates the basis on which specific matters, whether propositional or not, can be, and can be found to be, either true or false. Like relativism of a more subjectivist cast, Heidegger's ontological conception of truth as un/concealment fosters indifference to particular truth claims and permits any number of destructive views. Since all participate in the forgetfulness of Being, and since none can avoid an errancy that "belongs to the inner constitution" of human Da-sein, none can simply be rejected as untrue.

Wishing to avoid logicism and nihilism, then, Heidegger falls into both relativism and absolutism—not of the sorts that characterize epistemic subjectivism, to be sure, but of an ontomythological sort. Abandoning the bivalence of truth, his critical metaphenomenology becomes uncritical. In comparison, Horkheimer, who aims to avoid relativism and absolutism, falls into both logicism and nihilism—not of the sort that bedevils "bourgeois philosophy" from Descartes through Nietzsche, but of a theory-praxeological sort. Not accounting sufficiently for the normative character of truth, his metacritical phenomenology becomes hypercritical. Neither Heidegger nor Horkheimer succeeds in addressing Hegel's challenge, namely, to grasp the true as both substance and subject. From Heidegger we receive too much substance and not enough subject; from Horkheimer, too much subject and not enough substance.

7.4 Transforming Truth

Yet the dialectic between Heidegger and Horkheimer, as reconstructed from their two essays, points beyond them and does not simply return us to Hegel. It points toward connections between propositional correctness and comprehensive truth that are substantial but not antisubjective. Let me briefly articulate these connections, reversing the order of topics from the previous section. I begin with the topic of bivalence.

7.4.1 Bivalence and Normativity

Heidegger challenges the assumption of bivalence because he does not want logic to have the final word. As Horkheimer recognizes, however, to give up the bivalence of truth is to lose the basis in theory for distinguishing between better and worse patterns and trends in society and culture. Accordingly, the primary reason to retain a notion of bivalence is not the traditional one given by propositionally inflected truth theories. The primary reason is not simply that to call a proposition true—that is, correct—is to distinguish it from one that is false—that is, incorrect. Rather, the primary reason is that bivalence is intrinsic to normative considerations in general, including alethic considerations. To find certain practices or institutions or societal structures just, for example, is to contrast them with ones that are or would be unjust. Even when our judgments in these matters acknowledge degrees of justice and injustice, as they usually do, their underlying assumption is a contrast between just and unjust.

Does this mean that normative considerations either follow from or presuppose propositional correctness? That would seem in the end to be Horkheimer's position, despite his emphasizing the *praxis* of theory. But this position reverses the flow of normativity. Propositional correctness does not make nonpropositional normativity possible. Instead, propositional correctness is arrayed alongside other types of normativity, both supporting them and receiving direction from them. One of the ways in which propositional correctness lends support is by highlighting the bivalence intrinsic to all normative considerations, including considerations of propositional correctness.

7.4.2 Historical Unfolding

That implies in turn a different way to regard history as an unfolding of truth. For Heidegger this process is one in which the forgotten mystery simultaneously unconceals and conceals what it means to be. For Horkheimer it is one in which, guided by the praxis of theory, human beings struggle for liberation in society. My alternative is to say that truth enfolds us. Because truth enfolds us, we can help truth unfold. And to help truth unfold is to engage in an ongoing struggle for societal transformation. The telos of transformation would not simply be human liberation, however. It would encompass human liberation within a life-giving disclosure of society in which nonhuman creatures also come to flourish.

Moreover, the guidance for this struggle would come from neither a forgotten mystery nor a critical theory. Rather, it would come via full-fledged fidelity, both practical and theoretical, both propositional and nonpropositional, to societal principles such as solidarity and justice. This fidelity would resemble Heidegger's "gentle releasement" and "resolute openness," but it would not be restricted to philosophy that is directed to "beings as a whole" (ET, 152/199). It would also resemble Horkheimer's "strength to live with the sober truth," but its spread would not be delayed "until the causes of untruth are removed" (PT, 215/363).

7.4.3 Freedom as Flourishing

So too, although freedom and truth would have an intimate connection, freedom would be neither receptive releasement à la Heidegger nor active liberation à la Horkheimer. Instead, as I suggested earlier, freedom would be the interconnected flourishing of all creatures and the human effort to further such flourishing. The content of interconnected flourishing would stem from societal principles such as solidarity and justice that are always already in effect. By societal principles I mean normative horizons that emerge in human history and take shape in cultural practices and social institutions. Societal principles not only commonly hold for people; they also hold people in common. They are not closed horizons, however, but ever open to a future that continually breaks through, often in surprising ways. At the same time, they are at the center of societal struggles over suffering and oppression. No person or community, and certainly no philosophy or social theory, has the final word on what these principles mean and what they require. Yet all of us are caught up in the challenge to interpret, shape, and enact them.

Truth, then, in its most comprehensive sense, is not simply a propositional matter. But neither is it a mysterious fate beyond our control. Truth is a historical process that unfolds as a dynamic correlation between human fidelity to societal principles, on the one hand, and a life-giving disclosure of society, on the other. Moreover, these correlates are indissoluble: creaturely flourishing is the point of human fidelity to societal principles, and such fidelity is a prerequisite for societal disclosure. In that sense, as Horkheimer suggests, human beings need always and again to "establish" a "correspondence" between their knowledge and sociohistorical reality. In my account, however, this "correspondence" is a dynamic correlation, and the correlates are not simply knowledge and the known but rather a practical, institutional, and structural fidelity to societal principles and an ongoing disclosure of society in which all creatures come to flourish.

7.4.4 Correctness in Context

This dynamic and comprehensive correlation is the context in which propositional correctness matters. Propositional correctness matters for three reasons. First, it matters as a way in which human fidelity and societal disclosure occur. The logical validity of propositional truth claims is one of the societal principles that have emerged historically as normative horizons for cultural practices and social institutions. One cannot participate in contemporary practices and institutions without raising and responding to propositional claims. And one cannot raise and respond to propositional claims if one completely ignores or rejects the principle of logical validity. More important still is the societal implication of propositional correctness. For propositional correctness permits the predicative self-disclosure of that about which we make propositional claims. As Heidegger partially indicates, when we "get things right" in our predicative activities we allow nonpropositional matters to offer themselves for correct interpretation and in accord with other ways in which they are available for our engagement. Repeatedly "getting things wrong" has the cumulative effect of covering up what their interconnected flourishing would mean. Hence, for example, if social scientists and policy makers repeatedly misunderstand the sources, experience, and consequences of poverty, we will not have sufficient access to the suffering that comes with poverty and to the prospects for its removal.

In the second place, propositional correctness matters because of the support it provides for fidelity to other societal principles. For example, if we could not say with some accuracy and consistency what justice requires, or if we did not care to pursue logical validity with respect to such questions, it would become very difficult to articulate instances and patterns of injustice and to understand how they should be addressed. That, in turn, would impede a life-giving disclosure of society.

Propositional correctness also matters, in the third place, because it receives context and support from other modes of truth. Both Heidegger and Horkheimer point to this, each in his own way—Heidegger by anchoring correctness in freedom as letting beings be, and Horkheimer by tying correctness to liberation from oppression. In my own terms, propositional correctness matters because the pursuit of other societal principles such as solidarity and justice gives added purpose and significance to our pursuing the societal principle of logical validity. Without such additional context and support, propositional correctness becomes a thin and increasingly irrelevant affair, the preserve, perhaps, of isolated expertise, but not something that truly matters.

Perhaps the ratification of isolated expertise secretly drives contemporary deflationary theories of truth. And perhaps what I propose, in a dialectical revision of both Heidegger and Horkheimer, could be called an antideflationary theory. To be self-consistent and thereby faithful to the principle of logical validity, an antideflationary theory cannot be imprecise. Nor, if it is to contribute in some small way to more comprehensive truth, can it be a merely technical account of propositional "truth." The challenge, as Hegel saw, is to think these matters together. The challenge is to articulate truth as both substance and subject, avoiding both logicism and nihilism, but also moving beyond both absolutism and relativism. If my proposals have a measure of truth, then perhaps they take us a few steps in that direction.[23]

8   Conclusion: Truth and Goodness Intersect

The truth of statements is linked in the last analysis to the intention of the good and true life.

—Jürgen Habermas[1]

In the introduction I pointed to three issues of contemporary concern that orient my critical retrieval of insights about truth in German continental philosophy. They have to do with the relations between propositional truth and existential truth, discursive justification, and objective knowledge, respectively. As subsequent chapters explored these issues, it has become apparent that the insights uncovered require us to reframe each issue. We need to recast the relation *between* propositional and existential truth as a differentiation *within* truth in its most comprehensive sense. We must resituate the relation between propositional truth and discursive justification as *one* manifestation of an encompassing dynamic between comprehensive truth and equally comprehensive authentication. And we should redescribe the relation of propositional truth to objective knowledge in terms of an *inter*relation between predicative practices and predicative self-disclosure. To demonstrate how my critical retrieval leads to such a reframing of the issues, let me conclude with a three-stage review and extension of the truthscape we have examined.

8.1   Holistic Pluralism

Chapter 2 asks whether early Husserl's conception of truth can help us connect propositional and existential truth in a fruitful manner. The chapter concludes that, with suitable revisions, it can. By distinguishing between four concepts of truth, two of them subject-sided and two object-sided, his conception can help us see both the differences and the continuities between truth as it is asserted or claimed and truth as it is experienced or lived.

Yet the revisions I propose in chapter 2 also suggest that the challenge we face is not simply to connect propositional and existential truth. Rather the challenge is to understand how both asserted truth and lived truth belong to a more encompassing whole. If, as I proposed, we expand Husserl's notion of intuitive fulfillment to include many more practices and objects; if we transform his inter-active coincidence (i.e., the act of synthetic evidence) from a single-subject act into an intersubjective process; and if we replace the intuitive "givenness" of objects with their multidimensional availability for human practices, then asserting and claiming become constituents within a wide array of life practices, and the objects about which we make assertions and propositional claims are in the first instance multidimensional life-practical objects. In other words, the distinction between propositional and existential truth begins to blur, such that propositional truth itself seems to become a dimension of existential truth. Or, to say this more carefully, the distinction between propositional and existential truth becomes a placeholder for a more comprehensive idea of truth that would encompass both asserted truth and lived truth and would not be reducible to either.

Precisely this insight into the need for a more comprehensive idea is the great genius of Martin Heidegger's conception of truth as "disclosedness" or "unconcealment."[2] As I discussed in chapter 3, Heidegger's *Being and Time* insists that the disclosedness of Dasein—the essential openness of human existence—is the ontological condition that makes it possible for assertions to be true or false, that is, to be correct or incorrect. So too, the world's disclosedness, relative to Dasein's disclosedness, is the ontological condition that makes possible the "discoveredness" of entities—their capacity for being dis-covered by correct assertions. Both from the side of Dasein's asserting, then, and from the side of an entity's being asserted, so-called propositional truth derives from and depends on the more comprehensive truth that Heidegger calls "disclosedness," as do all the other practices and experiences whose ontological structure he summarizes as understanding (*Verstehen*), attunement (*Befindlichkeit*), and talk (*Rede*). Thanks to disclosedness, human existence as a whole is, as he says, "in the truth"—and, as it turns out, also in untruth.

Despite my specific criticisms of how Heidegger tries to link ontological disclosedness and assertoric correctness, I think he is right to take a holistic approach. To give an adequate account of what propositional "truth" is and why it is important, one needs to situate it in the larger field of interconnected practices and interrelated entities within which correct assertions occur. In chapter 3 I've tried to do this in two ways.

First, I give an account of the predicative availability and predicative self-disclosure that let us make correct assertions about practical objects. This account allows one to specify the type of discoveredness required for propositional truth without employing a problematic Husserlian concept of "self-givenness," thereby both responding to Ernst Tugendhat's criticisms of Heidegger and challenging one of their primary assumptions. For us to make correct assertions about a practical object, not only must the object be available for our predicative practices but also this predicative availability must align with a relevant way in which the object is nonpredicatively available, whether as felt or perceived or used or imagined, for example. Although more than this is required in order to explain assertoric correctness, my account of predicative self-disclosure preserves Heidegger's holistic anchoring of discoveredness in disclosedness without dissolving the distinctive character of propositional truth.

Second, chapter 3 transforms Heidegger's idea of truth as disclosedness into an internally differentiated yet holistic conception of truth as a dynamic correlation between human fidelity to societal principles, on the one hand, and a life-giving disclosure of society, on the other. Truth on this holistic conception is internally differentiated in two ways. In the first place, as a dynamic correlation, it requires both fidelity and disclosure and cannot be reduced to either. This revises Heidegger's account of disclosedness by replacing his self-related authenticity with other-related fidelity and by replacing the notion of Dasein's ontological openness with society's future-oriented opening. Moreover, truth as a whole now becomes not so much an ontological structure as a historical process. In the second place, truth on my conception is internally differentiated because it includes an array of societal principles, such as solidarity, resourcefulness, and justice, and an array of cultural practices and social institutions through which people can try to be faithful to these principles. What exactly truth comes to at a certain time and in certain circumstances depends in part on which principles are primarily at stake and which practices and institutions support human fidelity.

Accordingly, the pursuit of propositional truth can be a legitimate and distinct dimension of human "truthing" yet neither the key nor a barrier to truth as a whole, and the insights achieved via this pursuit can be important contributions to human flourishing in a social context. In other words, I have tried to reject an antipropositional reading of Heidegger's *Being and Time* without falling prey to the "logical prejudice" he so effectively challenges. Indeed, I have begun to propose a holistic pluralism with respect to truth: holistic in its overall emphasis on a dynamic correlation between fidelity and disclosure, and pluralistic about the cultural and social domains where this correlation occurs, including domains such as science and the academy where propositional "truth" plays a leading role.[3]

8.2   Encompassing Dynamic

These initial accounts of assertoric correctness and dynamic correlation, offered in response to Husserl and Heidegger, hold direct implications for the account one gives of the relation between propositional truth and discursive justification. Chapters 4 and 5 take up this second issue by examining the relation between comprehensive truth and authentication in Heidegger and Adorno and the relation between propositional truth and discursive justification in Jürgen Habermas's work. Whereas authentication refers to all the ways in which truth in its holistic plurality is borne out, justification refers to the specifically linguistic and logical way in which propositional truth is borne out in discourse. Just as propositional truth can be regarded as a specific domain within the dynamic correlation between fidelity and disclosure, so the discursive justification of propositional truth claims can be considered a specific domain within the comprehensive authentication of truth.

I arrive at this account in the first instance by examining and criticizing Heidegger's account of authenticity and Adorno's account of philosophical experience. Chapter 4 argues that, despite the explicit opposition between *Negative Dialectics* and *Being and Time*, Adorno and Heidegger both think comprehensive truth needs to be comprehensively authenticated, and not simply discursively justified. Both of them also locate the source of such authentication in a publicly inaccessible domain, whether in authenticity (Heidegger) or in emphatic experience (Adorno). This move generates insufficiently democratic understandings of what it means to bear witness to truth. It also undermines their comprehensive conceptions of truth, for whether as ontological disclosedness (Heidegger) or as a historically inter-woven and self-indexing texture (Adorno), comprehensive truth would seem to call for public authentication. If it cannot be publicly authenticated, then one wonders how it can even be truth.

My alternative is to tie comprehensive authentication to cultural practices and social institutions that enable people to bear witness to truth. What they bear witness to is comprehensive truth in one of its manifestations and on specific occasions or in specific situations. For the most part, then, we bear witness to truth as a whole by bearing witness to truth in one or more of its domains. We bear witness to truth within the very practices and institutions that make authentication possible. Such witness-bearing cannot properly be publicly inaccessible, for it occurs within and is supported by the social and cultural fabric of public life. Authentication is also invitational, I suggest. It invites a response from others, such that the democratic expectations of freedom, recognition, and participation are built into the very process of bearing witness to truth.

Yet truth and authentication are distinct. Our bearing witness to truth might not be true, and what truth requires might not be borne out. Accordingly, I describe authentication as an extension of truth on which the unfolding of truth relies. Bearing witness, in the face of systemic racism, to the correlation between justice and human flourishing, for example, could, if the witness were true, help bring about what this correlation requires. Yet bearing witness is not the same as the dynamic correlation to which witness is borne.

If this account of comprehensive authentication is on the right track, then it can shed light on the contested relation between propositional truth and discursive justification. If propositional truth is a domain within holistic truth, and if discursive justification is a domain within comprehensive authentication, then the relation between propositional truth and discursive justification should echo the relation between holistic truth and authentication. Specifically, discursive justification should in some sense be an extension of propositional truth on which the unfolding of propositional truth relies.

I explore what this specific relation comes to in chapter 5, where I examine the pragmatic realist conception in Habermas's *Truth and Justification*. While appreciative of Habermas's recent attempts to steer a path between alethic realism and antirealism, I argue that the link between truth and justification needs to be more robust than he allows it to be. To offer a more robust link, I revise his accounts of the relation between propositions and facts and of the relation between propositional truth and discursive justification.

Addressing the first relation, I distinguish between beliefs, assertions, and propositions. Then I suggest that "propositional truth" is an umbrella term for what should be more carefully distinguished as the reliability of beliefs, the correctness of assertions, and the accuracy of propositions. Correlatively, I also distinguish between practical objects, facts, and states of affairs, claiming that the notion of "fact" refers to the predicative self-disclosure of practical objects when language users refer to them and predicate about them. Such reference and predication occur whenever we communicate in language, and not only when we make assertions. States of affairs, by comparison, are decontextualized facts—decontextualized predicative self-disclosures. They arise in relationship to propositions, which are the decontextualized content of assertoric practices.[4] The accuracy of propositions pertains to the degree to which they disclose decontextualized facts in a decontextualized way. Propositional "truth" in the strict sense (i.e., accuracy) is a matter of decontextualized disclosure.

Employing this account of propositions and facts, I then argue that discursive justification does not aim simply to establish the acceptability of the truth claims we raise in assertions and other speech acts. Discursive justification also presents and tests the insights offered by the propositions we assert—decontextualized insights, to be sure, but insights nonetheless. It does so with an appeal to the societal principle of logical validity. Via more or less logical argumentation, we try to discover the reach of the propositional insights we assert or could assert. Discursive justification is a way to authenticate the accuracy of the propositions we assert. By allowing us to bear witness in this way, discursive justification allows propositional truth to unfold. When successful, discursive justification can be an extension of propositional truth.

All of this implies significant differences between my own emerging conception of propositional truth and many standard accounts. In the first place, propositional truth in my account has greater internal differentiation than minimalist and deflationary accounts would recognize, and it also belongs to a differentiated array that includes both pre- and post-propositional modes of truth. In the second place, I think typical debates between epistemic and nonepistemic conceptions bypass the specific way in which propositional truth manifests the dynamic correlation between fidelity and disclosure that comprises truth as a whole. They also bypass the wider alethic significance of the specific correlation between discursive fidelity to the societal principle of logical validity and propositional disclosure of practical objects and other matters.

Because this is a specific correlation, and because it occurs within a more encompassing dynamic, two further implications follow. First, propositional truth can be neither divorced from nor reduced to discursive justification and, second, truth as a whole can be neither divorced from nor reduced to either propositional truth or discursive justification. Instead, propositional truth plays an important role, but not an all-important role, in the life-giving disclosure of society, as does discursive justification in the pursuit of fidelity to societal principles. It makes a difference to human flourishing, for example, to have accurate insights into the causes of poverty, just as it makes a difference to the pursuit of justice to have public settings and procedures where we can present our purported insights into such causes and test the validity of our claims about them. Societally, propositional truth matters, as does the pursuit of discursive justification.

8.3   Predicative Interrelations

The alternative posed by my critical retrieval of Husserl, Heidegger, and the Frankfurt School is not either (Heideggerian) disclosure or (Habermasian) validity, not either (Heideggerian) ontology or (Adornian) critique.[5] Rather, the alternative brings these poles together and, in their gathering, aims to recognize how propositional truth and discursive justification participate in a more encompassing dynamic between truth as a whole and its authentication. Such recognition suggests a different approach to questions about objectivity and knowledge, which chapter 6 takes up with reference to early Husserl's concepts of objective identity and synthetic evidence. Rather than start by asking what sorts of (monothetic) evidence can justify propositional beliefs as true, Husserl suggests that we start by asking what sorts of synthetic acts make it possible for us to experience truth as objective identity, and how objective identity makes it possible for us to have true beliefs. A response to these questions would then provide a basis for understanding the more delimited "truth" of beliefs, assertions, and propositions, in relationship to the "intuited" objects in which their meaning is fulfilled. For Husserl, knowledge is more than justified true belief, and what can be known is more than simply facts or states of affairs.

In my own terms, what early Husserl understands, and what Heidegger and Adorno articulate, each in his own way, is this: *interrelations* between life practices and practical objects are the key to objective knowledge in general. So too, specific *interrelations* between disclosive predicative practices and the predicative self-disclosure of practical objects are crucial to the role propositional truth plays in the attainment of objective knowledge. By "objective knowledge" in this context I mean a human disclosure of practical objects that does justice to what they are and what they mean in their sociohistorical contexts.

Clearly, if one construes objective knowledge in this broad way, there will be more to it than justified true belief. For the disclosure of practical objects involves, at a minimum, how we feel toward them, how we perceive them, how we use them, and how we creatively interpret them, for example, in the stories we tell and the images we construct.[6] Moreover, although such experiences and practices usually do not occur in isolation from linguistic communication and logical thought, feeling, perception, usage, and creative interpretation cannot be reduced to matters of language and logic. They are distinct practices of the sort that the early Husserl might call qualitatively distinct kinds of intentional acts, and they provide a lived basis for what he would call signitive acts. They help make up what the later Husserl calls "pre-predicative experience."[7]

Justified true belief—the focus of so much contemporary epistemology—enters the epistemic scene, so to speak, after prelinguistic and prelogical practices like these have set the stage. The "truth bearers" privileged by so many truth theorists—beliefs, assertions, propositions, and the like—do not, for the most part, occur in isolation from such stage-setting and pre-predicative practices. To be "truth bearers" within objective knowledge—to be capable of the reliability, correctness, and accuracy that make up the differentiated range of "propositional truth"—beliefs, assertions, and propositions need to be properly interrelated with such pre-predicative practices. They also need to be properly interrelated with practical objects whose predicative self-disclosure involves an alignment between predicative and nonpredicative availability. As early Husserl understood, there is more to the so-called correspondence between "proposition" and "fact" than is dreamt of by either epistemic or nonepistemic philosophers.

My attempt to go beyond the debate between epistemic and nonepistemic conceptions of propositional truth suggests that analytic debates over "truth makers" need to be recast. A strong truth-maker theory such as David Armstrong's, for example, while it insists upon the existence of nonpropositional states of affairs by virtue of which propositions are true, does not really account for how states of affairs make propositions true.[8] Conversely, a strong rejection of the notion of facts as nonpropositional truth makers, such as Donald Davidson's famous slingshot argument,[9] which insists on the linguistic assignment of predicates to whatever sentences are about, does not explain how the nonlinguistic features of objects either permit or inhibit the linguistic assignment of predicates.

Although this is not the occasion to sort out such debates,[10] they indicate, it seems to me, that one needs a more robust account of both propositions and facts, as well as of their interrelation, if one wants to explain both the "truth-making" capacity of nonpropositional states of affairs and the availability of practical objects for linguistic predication. One needs an account, somewhat like Husserl's, in which the pre-predicative perception of practical objects, for example, neither reduces to the perception of propositions nor precludes an intimate connection between distinctly perceptual and distinctly linguistic and logical practices. One also needs an account of practical objects that both recognizes their multidimensionality and explains how they can be simultaneously available for both predicative and pre-predicative practices and, in such availability, disclose themselves as truth-making facts and states of affairs.

On such an account, it will not suffice to posit a "mind-independent" world and then simply claim we have a language capable of reference to it and predication about it. One needs to acknowledge the *interdependence* between practical objects and human practices, including linguistic practices. One also needs to indicate what, from the object side, allows linguistic reference and predication to get off the ground. The multidimensionality of human experience and of what we experience, as well as the interdependence between human practices and practical objects, call for a thick rather than a thin understanding of propositional truth.

Both Martin Heidegger and Max Horkheimer recognize the need for such an understanding, despite and within the opposition between their conceptions of truth in the two essays chapter 7 discusses. Whereas Heidegger's "On the Essence of Truth" anchors the correctness of propositions in freedom as *Gelassenheit* and in the un/concealment of beings as a whole, Horkheimer's "On the Problem of Truth" anchors it in an open-ended and praxis-oriented mediation between sociohistorical reality and theoretical thought. Both approaches imply that truth as a whole unfolds historically—indeed that history itself is an unfolding of truth—even though they have dramatically different visions of the historical process.

This holistic and historical emphasis, which I share, requires that one relativize propositional truth claims to the unfolding of truth as a whole without simply relativizing them to particular contexts, communities, or circumstances. Accordingly, in my own dialectical appropriation of Heidegger and Horkheimer, I retain an emphasis on the bivalence of truth—which Heidegger calls into question—and I link it with normativity in social life—which Horkheimer hesitates to address. If propositional truth were not bivalent, involving a fundamental contrast between "true" and "false" (i.e., reliable/unreliable or correct/incorrect or accurate/inaccurate), then the idea of objective knowledge would become unintelligible. For it would become impossible to understand what it means to do cognitive justice (or injustice) to practical objects and not simply to satisfy (or not satisfy) the expectations of one's cognitive peers. Similarly, if the pursuit of propositional truth were not linked to fidelity to societal principles and a life-giving disclosure of society, then the pursuit of objective knowledge would lose its larger point. For it would become very difficult to grasp how propositionally "getting things right" not only contributes to freedom as flourishing but also helps constitute what freedom is.

At the same time, however, like Heidegger and Horkheimer, each in his own way, I recognize that objective knowledge, while important, is never enough. By itself, the most accurate propositional insight into practical objects need not expose distortions in how people interrelate, and the most rigorous justification of objective knowledge claims need not resist oppression or give voice to suffering. In this sense, the pursuit of objective knowledge cannot be an end in itself. It properly belongs to a more comprehensive process, namely, the historical unfolding of truth as a dynamic correlation between human fidelity and societal disclosure.

This process both enfolds us and calls on us to help it unfold. To help truth unfold is to pursue societal transformation toward heightened fidelity and greater flourishing—and to seek objective knowledge *within* that pursuit. As Horkheimer and Adorno recognized, the pursuit of societal transformation is not external to the alethic process. Rather, truth itself calls for societal transformation and, in authentication, takes concrete shape within the cultural practices and social institutions of contemporary society. Whether one seeks to justify a propositional truth claim or lodges a protest against pollution and poverty, one tries to bear witness to what truth requires. Truth needs authentication in order to unfold.

That is why the 1965 appendix to Habermas's early work *Knowledge and Human Interests* has not lost its relevance. Taking issue with Husserl, Habermas claims that "the truth of statements is based on anticipating the realization of the good life." Propositional truth, he says, is linked in the final analysis "to the intention of the good and true life"—not because pure theory provides sure guidance for life but because knowledge is intrinsically tied to human interests.[11] Even though the later Habermas shies away from such formulations,[12] and even though he presents them as criticisms of Husserl, they summarize the central insight about truth that I have tried to retrieve from Husserl, Heidegger, and the Frankfurt School. Truth and goodness intersect. The task of philosophy is to show why and how they do.[13]

Notes

1 Introduction: Critical Retrieval

1. For a more extensive account of these issues and of my responses to them, see Lambert Zuidervaart, "Holistic Alethic Pluralism: A Reformational Research Program," *Philosophia Reformata* 81, no. 2 (2016): 156–178.

2. Prior to articulating his theory of validity claims, Habermas engaged in a famous debate with Gadamer over what Habermas called the "hermeneutic claim to universality," a debate that has generated its own extensive secondary literature. Several of the original contributions from Gadamer and Habermas, as well as a masterful critical appropriation of their debate by Paul Ricoeur, can be found in *The Hermeneutic Tradition: From Ast to Ricoeur*, ed. Gayle L. Ormiston and Alan D. Schrift (Albany: SUNY Press, 1990). See in particular Paul Ricoeur, "Hermeneutics and the Critique of Ideology," in *The Hermeneutic Tradition*, 298–334.

3. See Theodor W. Adorno et al., *The Positivist Dispute in German Sociology*, trans. Glyn Adey and David Frisby (London: Heinemann, 1976).

4. See in this connection Richard J. Bernstein, *The Pragmatic Turn* (Cambridge: Polity Press, 2010).

5. "Die Ausführung legitimiert Methode, und das verwehrt deren Supposition." Theodor W. Adorno, *Ästhetische Theorie*, GS 7, 2nd ed. (Frankfurt am Main: Suhrkamp, 1972), 530. This quote comes from the book's "Draft Introduction," in a passage where Adorno explains why his aesthetics cannot and should not begin with a general methodology. In Hullot-Kentor's translation, the sentence reads: "The fulfillment of this proof [of objective artistic content in artworks] legitimates method at the same time that it precludes its supposition." Theodor W. Adorno, *Aesthetic Theory*, trans. Robert Hullot-Kentor (Minneapolis: University of Minnesota Press, 1997), 357.

6. Lambert Zuidervaart, *Adorno's Aesthetic Theory: The Redemption of Illusion* (Cambridge, MA: MIT Press, 1991), xix–xx. As I indicate there, my approach derives both from Hegel's *Phenomenology of Spirit* and from Adorno's own work.

7. Zuidervaart, *Adorno's Aesthetic Theory*, xx. For an account of how immanent criticism relates to metacritique, see "Metacritique: Adorno, Vollenhoven, and the Problem-Historical Method," in Lambert Zuidervaart, *Religion, Truth, and Social Transformation: Essays in Reformational Philosophy* (Montreal: McGill-Queen's University Press, 2016), 183–204.

8. Pierre Keller, *Husserl and Heidegger on Human Experience* Cambridge: Cambridge University Press, 1999); see especially chapter 4, 84–110.

9. Nikolas Kompridis, *Critique and Disclosure: Critical Theory between Past and Future* (Cambridge, MA: MIT Press, 2006). Although Kompridis embraces Heidegger's notion of disclosure, he thinks Heidegger was seriously mistaken to identify disclosure with truth. As will become apparent in subsequent chapters, I do not share Kompridis's assessment.

10. Mark A. Wrathall, *Heidegger and Unconcealment: Truth, Language, and History* (Cambridge: Cambridge University Press, 2011). See especially chapter 2, "The Condition of Truth in Heidegger and Davidson," 40–56.

11. Denis McManus, *Heidegger and the Measure of Truth* (Oxford: Oxford University Press, 2012). For a more detailed comparison of Heidegger and Wittgenstein, see Stephen Mulhall, *On Being in the World: Wittgenstein and Heidegger on Seeing Aspects* (London: Routledge, 1990).

12. William D. Blattner, *Heidegger's Temporal Idealism* (Cambridge: Cambridge University Press, 1999); Steven Crowell, *Husserl, Heidegger and the Space of Meaning: Paths toward Transcendental Phenomenology* (Evanston, IL: Northwestern University Press, 2001); Steven Crowell, *Normativity and Phenomenology in Husserl and Heidegger* (Cambridge: Cambridge University Press, 2013); John Haugeland, *Dasein Disclosed: John Haugeland's Heidegger*, ed. Joseph Rouse (Cambridge, MA: Harvard University Press, 2013); Stephen Mulhall, *The Routledge Guidebook to Heidegger's* Being and Time (London: Routledge, 2013)—a revised edition of Mulhall's *Heidegger and* Being and Time (1996, 2005).

13. An instructive comparison could be made in this connection with the very fine book by Barry Allen, *Truth in Philosophy* (Cambridge, MA: Harvard University Press, 1993). After discussing classical and modern approaches to the idea of truth, Allen examines challenges to these approaches by Friedrich Nietzsche and William James. Then he looks at the subsequent responses by Heidegger, Derrida, Wittgenstein, and Foucault. Husserl and critical theory receive hardly any attention, however, and Allen takes explicit issue with robust conceptions of truth such as I hope to retrieve.

14. Although better known as a literary theorist and critic, Walter Benjamin also drew substantially from Husserlian phenomenology, alongside the neo-Kantianism of the Marburg School, as is documented in the introduction to "Experience and Infinite Task: Knowledge, Language, and Messianism in the Philosophy of Walter Benjamin" by Tamara Tagliacozzo (unpublished manuscript, 2015)—a translation of her *Esperienza e compito infinito nella filosofia del primo Benjamin* (Macerata: Quodlibet, 2003).

15. Herbert Marcuse, *Hegels Ontologie und die Grundlegung einer Theorie der Geschichtlichkeit* (Frankfurt am Main: Klostermann, 1932). Klostermann published a second, unrevised edition of this work in 1968, and it has appeared in English as *Hegel's Ontology and the Theory of Historicity*, trans. Seyla Benhabib (Cambridge, MA: MIT Press, 1987).

16. Theodor Wiesengrund-Adorno, review of Herbert Marcuse, *Hegels Ontologie und die Grundlegung einer Theorie der Geschichtlichkeit*, in *Zeitschrift für Sozialforschung* 1 (1932): 409–410, my translation.

17. I provide more details about Adorno's work on Husserl in chapter 2.

18. Cited by John Abromeit, *Max Horkheimer and the Foundations of the Frankfurt School* (Cambridge: Cambridge University Press, 2011), 58–59.

19. Max Horkheimer and Theodor W. Adorno, *Dialectic of Enlightenment: Philosophical Fragments* (1947), ed. Gunzelin Schmid Noerr, trans. Edmund Jephcott (Stanford, CA: Stanford University Press, 2002), 18–19, 257n30.

20. See especially chapters 5 and 6 in Jürgen Habermas, *The Philosophical Discourse of Modernity: Twelve Lectures*, trans. Frederick Lawrence (Cambridge, MA: MIT Press, 1987), 106–160. Tellingly, the chapters are titled "The Entwinement of Myth and Enlightenment: Horkheimer and Adorno" and "The Undermining of Western Rationalism through the Critique of Metaphysics: Martin Heidegger." It is also instructive to note that in the next chapter, a critique of Jacques Derrida, Habermas zeroes in on Derrida's reading of Husserl's theory of meaning in the *Logical Investigations*. I take up Derrida's reading in chapter 2.

21. See Richard J. Bernstein, *Beyond Objectivism and Relativism: Science, Hermeneutics, and Praxis* (Philadelphia: University of Pennsylvania Press, 1983).

22. As we shall see in chapters 2 and 7, Adorno and Horkheimer frame their critiques of "bourgeois" philosophers in these terms—Adorno with respect to Husserl and Heidegger, and Horkheimer with respect to Hegel.

23. In addition to the works discussed at greater length in this book, see, for example, Edmund Husserl's posthumous *The Crisis of European Sciences and Transcendental Phenomenology: An Introduction to Phenomenological Philosophy* (1954), trans. David

Carr (Evanston, IL: Northwestern University Press, 1970); Martin Heidegger, *The Question Concerning Technology and Other Essays*, trans. William Lovitt (New York: Harper Torchbooks, 1977); Horkheimer and Adorno, *Dialectic of Enlightenment* (1947); and Jürgen Habermas's early *Knowledge and Human Interests* (1968), trans. Jeremy J. Shapiro (Boston: Beacon Press, 1971).

24. See in this connection three contrasting but equally magisterial responses to the so-called secularization thesis: Hans Blumenberg, *The Legitimacy of the Modern Age* (1966, 1976), trans. Robert M. Wallace (Cambridge, MA: MIT Press, 1983); Charles Taylor, *A Secular Age* (Cambridge, MA: Belknap Press of Harvard University Press, 2007); and Enrique Dussel, *Ethics of Liberation: In the Age of Globalization and Exclusion* (1998), trans. Eduardo Mendieta et al., ed. Alejandro A. Vallega (Durham, NC: Duke University Press, 2013).

25. Kenneth Baynes, James Bohman, and Thomas McCarthy, eds., *Philosophy: End or Transformation?* (Cambridge, MA: MIT Press, 1987).

2   Propositional and Existential Truth: Edmund Husserl

1. Ernst Tugendhat, *Der Wahrheitsbegriff bei Husserl und Heidegger* (1967), 2nd ed. (Berlin: Walter de Gruyter, 1970), 1. Unfortunately, this book has never appeared in English translation. The translations in this chapter and subsequent chapters are my own.

2. Ibid., 2–3. In fairness to Tarski, one should note that he developed his semantic conception of truth with a view to formal languages like mathematics and logic, not with a view to "natural" languages like English and German. Yet this has not prevented other truth theorists from applying his conception to natural languages, most notably Donald Davidson, who uses Tarski's Convention T to generate a theory of linguistic meaning. See Alfred Tarski, "The Concept of Truth in Formalized Languages," in *Logic, Semantics, Metamathematics*, trans. J. H. Woodger (Oxford: Clarendon Press, 1956), 152–273; Alfred Tarski, "The Semantic Conception of Truth and the Foundations of Semantics," *Philosophy and Phenomenological Research* 4 (1944): 341–376; and Donald Davidson, *Inquiries into Truth and Interpretation* (Oxford: Clarendon Press, 1984).

3. Tugendhat, *Der Wahrheitsbegriff*, 3.

4. Ibid., 4.

5. Ibid., 1.

6. Ibid., 5–6.

7. Although I use "tm" in this chapter and in chapter 6 to indicate when I have modified J. N. Findlay's translation of Husserl's *Logical Investigations*, the following changes occur without indication: I use the American spellings for "fulfill(s)," "ful-

fillment," and "fullness," and I translate "Erkennen" as "knowledge" (rather than Findlay's "recognition"), "Veranschaulichung" as "rendering intuitive" or "intuitional rendering" (Findlay: "intuitive illustration"), and "Evidenz" as "evidence" (Findlay: "self-evidence").

8. This is not to deny that Husserl made significant revisions as he later took up questions of transcendental constitution, intersubjectivity, and the lifeworld, nor is it to suggest that these revisions are irrelevant to the critical retrieval initiated in this chapter. To take up these revisions, however, would require a detailed and separate discussion. Husserl's most important later writings on the concept of truth are *Formal and Transcendental Logic* (1929), trans. Dorion Cairns (The Hague: Martinus Nijhoff, 1969), and the posthumous *Experience and Judgment: Investigations in a Genealogy of Logic* (1939, 1948), ed. and rev. Ludwig Landgrebe, trans. James S. Churchill and Karl Ameriks (Evanston, IL: Northwestern University Press, 1973). In my judgment, Tugendhat's *Der Wahrheitsbegriff bei Husserl und Heidegger*, which considers the entire range of Husserl's early and later writings, remains the best comprehensive account of his conception of truth.

9. "In Heidegger's eyes, Husserl's *Logical Investigations* and the analysis of truth it contains are not merely the high point of philosophical reflection on logic in the early twentieth century. They represent a genuine 'breakthrough.' ... Husserl's breakthrough is precisely the recognition that western philosophical conceptions of truth and being are ultimately matters of intuition or perception, and not of judgment." Daniel O. Dahlstrom, *Heidegger's Concept of Truth* (Cambridge: Cambridge University Press, 2001), 49–50.

10. Here "post-Heideggerian" indicates not only that each author develops a reading subsequent to Heidegger's highly influential appropriation of Husserl in *Sein und Zeit* but also that each reads Husserl with an eye to Heidegger's appropriation. I regard my own approach to Husserl as post-Heideggerian in this sense.

11. For historical details, see the "Translator's Foreword" by André Orianne in Emmanuel Levinas, *The Theory of Intuition in Husserl's Phenomenology* (1930, 1963) (Evanston, IL: Northwestern University Press, 1973), xi–xxviii, especially xxiv–xxvii; originally published as *Théorie de l'intuition dans la phénoménologie de Husserl* (Paris: Alcan, 1930) and republished by Vrin in 1963.

12. Theodor W. Adorno, "Die Transzendenz des Dinglichen und Noematischen in Husserls Phänomenologie," in Adorno's *Gesammelte Schriften* 1 (Frankfurt: Suhrkamp, 1973), 7–77.

13. Theodor W. Adorno, *Against Epistemology: A Metacritique; Studies in Husserl and the Phenomenological Antinomies*, trans. Willis Domingo (Cambridge, MA: MIT Press, 1982). The now standard German edition is in Adorno's *Gesammelte Schriften* 5 (Frankfurt: Suhrkamp, 1970), 7–245; hereafter cited as GS 5.

14. Jacques Derrida, *Speech and Phenomena: Introduction to the Problem of Signs in Husserl's Phenomenology*, in *Speech and Phenomena and Other Essays on Husserl's Theory of Signs*, trans. David B. Allison (Evanston, IL: Northwestern University Press, 1973), 1–104; originally published as *La voix et le phénomène: Introduction au problème du signe dans la phénoménologie de Husserl* (Paris: Presses Universitaires de France, 1967). The same publisher issued a second, corrected edition in 1998.

15. If we expand the list to include Gilbert Ryle, who published an essay on Husserlian thought titled simply "Phenomenology," *Proceedings of the Aristotelian Society, Supplementary Volume* 11 (1932): 63–83, we can see that leading figures in four of the most influential strands of Western philosophical thought after World War II undertook a serious engagement with Husserl's work: ordinary language philosophy (Ryle), critical theory (Adorno), deconstruction (Derrida), and Levinasian ethics. Ryle wrote the following about *The Concept of Mind* (1949), his most influential book: "The book could be described as a sustained essay in phenomenology, if you are at home with that label." Gilbert Ryle, *Collected Papers* (London: Hutchinson, 1971), 188. For reasons to include Ryle among the ordinary language philosophers, see Stephen P. Schwartz, *A Brief History of Analytic Philosophy from Russell to Rawls* (Oxford: Wiley-Blackwell, 2012), 119–159.

16. In addition to *Logische Untersuchungen*, Levinas examines three writings: "Philosophie als strenge Wissenschaft" (1910), "Ideen zu einer reinen Phänomenologie und phänomenologische Forschung" (1913), and "Husserls Vorlesungen zur Phänomenologie des inneren Zeitbewusstsein" (1928).

17. Levinas, *The Theory of Intuition*, xxxiv, xxxvi.

18. Ibid., 89.

19. Ibid., 92.

20. Ibid., 94. Levinas devotes an entire chapter, titled "The Intuition of Essences" (97–119), to refuting the familiar charge, made by Victor Delbos and others, that Husserl's critique of psychologism, especially in volume 1 of the *Logical Investigations*, falls prey to "logicism" and "Platonic realism." Yet here, too, Levinas suggests that "one can reproach Husserl for his intellectualism" (119), explicitly appealing to Heidegger when he makes this suggestion.

21. Ibid., 155.

22. Adorno, *Against Epistemology*, 1; GS 5, 9. Although the secondary literature has largely overlooked this work, one year before his death in 1969 Adorno still regarded it as his most important book alongside *Negative Dialectics*, according to Rolf Tiedemann (*Against Epistemology*, 241; GS 5, 386).

23. See in this connection Theodor W. Adorno, "Husserl and the Problem of Idealism," *Journal of Philosophy* 37, no. 1 (1940): 5–18.

24. See Georg Lukács, *History and Class Consciousness: Studies in Marxist Dialectics* (1923, 1968), trans. Rodney Livingstone (London: Merlin Press, 1971), especially the central and long essay "Reification and the Consciousness of the Proletariat," 83–222. Adorno cites a footnote in the "Reification" essay where Lukács says that, in Husserl's phenomenological method, "the whole terrain of logic is ultimately transformed into a 'system of facts' [*Faktizität*] of a higher order" (Lukács, *History*, 212n14)—see Adorno, *Against Epistemology*, 58; GS 5, 65. Lukács's note occurs in a section of the "Reification" essay titled "The Antinomies of Bourgeois Thought"—a clear precedent for Adorno's focus on the "idealist" antinomies in Husserlian phenomenology.

25. Adorno, *Against Epistemology*, 89; GS 5, 96, tm.

26. I should note, however, that Adorno does not actually discuss the four concepts of truth laid out in Husserl's Sixth Investigation, chapter 5. Instead he quotes extensively from chapter 6 and aims his criticisms at the concept of categorial intuition, simultaneously taking aim at Husserl's (and, indirectly, Heidegger's) concept of being. See *Against Epistemology*, 200–212; GS 5, 203–215.

27. Adorno, *Against Epistemology*, 72; GS 5, 78–79, tm.

28. It is telling that the section titled "Concept of Intuition" (*Against Epistemology*, 45–47; GS 5, 52–54) in Adorno's chapter on Husserl's logical absolutism does not take up Husserl's concept of sensuous intuition—it is devoted entirely to a critique of Henri Bergson. Husserl could easily have endorsed the central claim in this critique: "Intuition is not a simple antithesis to logic" (*Against Epistemology*, 46; GS 5, 54).

29. Derrida, *Speech and Phenomena*, 99.

30. Ibid., 98.

31. Derrida's deconstruction of Husserl's theory of signs primarily focuses on Husserl's First Investigation, titled "Expression and Meaning."

32. Derrida, *Speech and Phenomena*, 98: "The purification of the formal is guided by a concept of *sense* which is itself determined on the basis of a *relation with an object*. ... Apparently independent from fulfilling intuitions, the 'pure' forms of signification, as 'empty' or canceled sense, are always governed by the epistemological criterion of the relation with objects."

33. See Levinas, *The Theory of Intuition*, 65–84—the first two-thirds of Levinas's central chapter 5, titled "Intuition." According to Levinas, Husserl does not regard intuition as "a mode of immediate knowledge" but rather as "the very course of thought toward truth" (92).

34. Of course, this was impossible in the case of Levinas, who first published his book in 1930, long before the other two books appeared in 1956 and 1967, respectively. One can safely assume that Levinas either did not know of the twenty-one-year-old Adorno's doctoral dissertation of 1924 or did not have access to it.

35. Derrida, *Speech and Phenomena*, 3–4. Derrida also correctly notes that here Husserl assumes, but does not provide, a concept of "the *structure of the sign in general*." Instead, Husserl focuses on "the logical character of signification" and from the outset "is already resolutely engaged in one of the modifications of the general structure of the *Zeigen*: *Hinzeigen* and not *Anzeigen*" (23–24). Husserl himself points out that "absurd" attempts to understand purely symbolic mathematical procedures in terms of "imaginary" entities led him to consider "the signitive [*das Signative*]" and "the purely linguistic aspects" of thought and "forced [him] to carry out general 'investigations,' which concerned universal clarification of the sense, the proposed delimitation, and the unique accomplishment of formal logic." Edmund Husserl, *Introduction to the Logical Investigations: A Draft of a Preface to the Logical Investigations (1913)*, trans. Philip J. Bossert and Curtis H. Peters (The Hague: Martinus Nijhoff, 1975), 33.

36. See Gottlob Frege, "Über Sinn und Bedeutung," *Zeitschrift für Philosophie und philosophische Kritik* 100 (1892): 25–50; translated by Max Black as "On Sense and Reference," in *Translations from the Philosophical Writings of Gottlob Frege*, ed. Peter Geach and Max Black, 3rd ed. (Oxford: Blackwell, 1980), 56–78.

37. In later writings Husserl incorporates the notion of "matter" into the notion of "noema." I shall not attempt to clarify the relationship between these two notions, since noema is the topic of extensive debate in the secondary literature. I also leave aside the additional complication that in the *Logical Investigations* Husserl distinguishes between the *matter* of an intentional experience and the *sensations* experienced. *Ideas I* reworks the distinction between matter and sensation into one between noematic and hyletic moments. According to John Drummond, who argues that Husserl's primarily "noetic" or act-oriented concept of meaning in the *Logical Investigations* gives way to a "noematic" or object-oriented concept of meaning in his later writings, "Husserl distinguishes three moments in the full noema: the thetic characteristic (the noematic correlate of the act-quality), the noematic sense (the assimilation into the intentional contents of … 'act-matter'), and the determinable *X* (i.e., the 'innermost moment' of the noema)." The noematic sense, inclusive of the determinable *X* that makes up its core, provides Husserl's later concept of meaning. See John J. Drummond, "Pure Logical Grammar: Identity Amidst Linguistic Differences," in *Husserl's Logical Investigations in the New Century: Western and Chinese Perspectives*, ed. Kwok-Ying Lau and John J. Drummond (Dordrecht: Springer, 2007), 53–66; quotation from 57.

38. The conceptual background to this argument lies in the mereology Husserl propounds in the Third Investigation, titled "On the Theory of Wholes and Parts."

39. Although Husserl writes here of a coincidence between an intending and a fulfilling act, both of which are perceptual, it is unclear whether sensation, which, strictly speaking, is not an act, is built into the fulfilling act. He says that the purely perceptual content (*Gehalt*) of "external" perception is "the 'sensed' content [*der*

'empfundende' Inhalt]" in the purely perceptual apprehension (*Auffassung*) that immediately belongs to this content. "In the ideal, limiting case of adequate perception, this sensed or self-presenting content [*dieser empfundende oder selbstdarstellende Inhalt*] coincides with the perceived object" (LU II.2, 590; LI 2, 221, tm). Subsequently, he points out that, in the fulfillment of perceptions, there are "components that cannot be called intentions" because they "only fulfill" and do not themselves require fulfillment. These are "self-presentations [*Selbstdarstellungen*], in the strict sense," of the intended object (LU II.2, 595; LI 2, 224, tm).

40. See chapter 6 in this book for a more extensive account of Husserl's notion of fullness.

41. Chapter 6 in this volume discusses these two types of adequation at greater length.

42. According to Dahlstrom, *Heidegger's Concept of Truth*, 67, Martin Heidegger is particularly drawn to this point and "stresses this conception of the originally unthematic experience of the truth not least because his own account of truth essentially builds upon it." See in this connection the following two excerpts from longer works by Heidegger: "My Way to Phenomenology" and "The Fundamental Discoveries of Phenomenology, Its Principle, and the Clarification of Its Name," in *The Phenomenology Reader*, ed. Dermot Moran and Timothy Mooney (London: Routledge, 2002), 251–256 and 257–277, respectively. Implicitly appropriating Husserl's concepts of truth as objective identity and as inter-active coincidence, Heidegger writes: "This act of bringing into coincidence is in touch with the subject matter; it is precisely through this particular intentionality of being-in-touch-with-the-subject-matter [*Bei-der-Sache-sein*] that this intentionality, itself unthematic in its performance, is immediately and transparently experienced as true. This is the phenomenological sense of saying that in evident perception I do not thematically study the truth of this perception itself, but rather live *in* the truth" (276).

43. Chapter 6 in the current volume discusses this refinement at greater length.

44. For a clear and succinct exposition of this concept, see Dieter Lohmar, "Categorial Intuition," in *A Companion to Phenomenology and Existentialism*, ed. Hubert L. Dreyfus and Mark A. Wrathall (Oxford: Blackwell, 2006), 115–126.

45. My two examples attempt to render more intuitive Husserl's abstract discussion of (1) how we perceive α as a part of A and (2) how we perceive (that) A is to the right of B. See LU II.2, 681–684; LI 2, 287–288.

46. For a summary of the criticisms raised in *Der Wahrheitsbegriff bei Husserl and Heidegger*, see Ernst Tugendhat, "Heidegger's Idea of Truth," in *The Heidegger Controversy: A Critical Reader*, ed. Richard Wolin (New York: Columbia University Press, 1991), 245–263. I take up Tugendhat's criticisms of Heidegger in the next two chapters.

47. Gadamer's comment on some of Husserl's later writings could also apply to *Logical Investigations*: "To me, however, he still seems dominated by the one-sided-

ness [of the scientific idealization of experience] that he criticizes, for he projects the idealized world of exact scientific experience into the original experience of the world, in that he makes perception, as something directed toward merely external physical appearances [*Körperlichkeit*], the basis of all other experience." Hans-Georg Gadamer, *Truth and Method*, 2nd, rev. ed., trans. rev. Joel Weinsheimer and Donald G. Marshall (New York: Crossroad, 1989), 347; *Wahrheit und Methode: Grundzüge einer philosophischen Hermeneutik*, 4th ed. (Tübingen: J. C. B. Mohr [Paul Siebeck], 1975), 330.

48. Later Husserl seems to recognize this as well, as is suggested by the emphasis on historicity and the lifeworld in his posthumous and incomplete *The Crisis of European Sciences and Transcendental Phenomenology: An Introduction to Phenomenological Philosophy* (1954), trans. David Carr (Evanston, IL: Northwestern University Press, 1970).

49. Husserl, *Formal and Transcendental Logic*, chapter 6, 232–266.

50. Husserl, *Experience and Judgment*, introduction, 9–68. The editor, Ludwig Landgrebe, points out in his foreword to the 1948 German edition that the introduction stems from Landgrebe's own rendering of Husserl's ideas in his published works, manuscripts, and verbal discussions.

51. Ibid., 49 (italics removed).

52. Ibid., 57–58. See also *Formal and Transcendental Logic*, §96, "The Transcendental Problems of Intersubjectivity and of the Intersubjective World," where Husserl tries to explain how "my transcendental ego," as the "primitive basis for everything that I accept as existent," can constitute within itself "another transcendental ego, and then too an open plurality of such egos—'other' egos, absolutely inaccessible to my ego in their original being, and yet cognizable (for me) as existing and as being thus and so" (239–240). Husserl works out his notion of "monadological intersubjectivity" in the Fifth Meditation of his *Cartesian Meditations: An Introduction to Phenomenology* (1931), trans. Dorion Cairns (The Hague: Martinus Nijhoff, 1960), 89–151.

53. Subject-sided truth in this sense is not the same as discursive justification, nor is it the same as authentication, the larger process of bearing witness to truth to which justification belongs.

54. See, for example, Adorno, ND 183–186/184–187, and chapter 2 in Brian O'Connor, *Adorno's Negative Dialectic: Philosophy and the Possibility of Critical Rationality* (Cambridge, MA: MIT Press, 2004), 45–69.

55. I leave aside the question whether identification is the only type of synthetic practice that can be true with respect to objects. I also leave aside the question whether the truth of identification provides a sufficiently ample basis for generating a more expansive, life-oriented conception of truth. My concern right now is to reframe Husserl's concept of truth in such a way that it does not preclude generating an existential concept of truth and yet does justice to propositional truth.

56. The next chapter explains the concepts of "predicative availability" and "predicative self-disclosure" at greater length.

57. An earlier version of this chapter was presented as an invited keynote lecture at the annual conference of the Canadian Society for Continental Philosophy in Toronto on October 12, 2013, and revised versions were presented at DePaul University, Kalamazoo College, and Grand Valley State University in 2015. I wish to acknowledge the instructive and thought-provoking comments I received on these occasions.

3 Truth as Disclosure: Martin Heidegger

1. SZ 226, tm.

2. See Daniel O. Dahlstrom, *Heidegger's Concept of Truth* (New York: Cambridge University Press, 2001). By "logical prejudice" Dahlstrom means a widespread assumption that assertions, propositions, sentences, and the like are the site of truth on which the truth of anything else depends. It is "the tendency to conceive truth in terms of a specific sort of discourse, namely, in terms of claims, assertions, and judgments, that are formed as indicative, declarative sentences. … For those who cling to this 'model of propositional truth,' 'the predicates "true," "false," are paradigmatically attributes of sentences, statements, claims, judgments, assertions, propositions, and the like'" (Dahlstrom, *Heidegger's Concept of Truth*, 17, citing an article by Carl Friedrich Gethmann). I should add that the logical prejudice is not peculiar to correspondence theories of truth, even though Heidegger's own conception is intended as an alternative to correspondence theories. It can also be found in coherence, consensus, and pragmatic theories of truth as well as more recent primitivist and deflationary accounts.

3. Lambert Zuidervaart, *Artistic Truth: Aesthetics, Discourse, and Imaginative Disclosure* (Cambridge: Cambridge University Press, 2004), 6.

4. "Self-referential incoherence" is my cryptic formulation for the "paradox of thematization" so carefully described by Dahlstrom, *Heidegger's Concept of Truth*, 202–210, 236–242, 252–255, 264–268, 433–456. I do not take up Heidegger's crucial notion of authenticity here, even though that would be required for a complete account of his conception of truth, but address it in chapter 4 instead. Nor do I trace permutations to his conception in Heidegger's subsequent lectures and writings, although his subsequent essay "On the Essence of Truth" is discussed in chapter 7. Yet the current chapter does try to do justice to the textual fabric within which *Sein und Zeit* weaves a comprehensive conception of truth.

5. Although traditional theories of truth as adequation differ in significant respects from modern theories of truth as a correspondence between propositions and facts, for convenience I refer to all of them as correspondence theories.

6. To avoid confusion with Habermas's notion of discourse (*Diskurs*), I use terms other than "discourse" to render Heidegger's "*Rede*"—usually "talk" or "conversation." Despite the originality and significance of Heidegger's discussion of attunement, especially with regard to fear (*Furcht*) and anxiety (*Angst*) in sections 30 and 40, I restrict my summary to understanding and talk, since these have a more direct bearing on Heidegger's explicit critique of traditional theories of truth.

7. Here and elsewhere I ignore the distinction between *Zeitlichkeit* ("temporality") and *Temporalität* ("Temporality") in *Sein und Zeit*. Karin de Boer gives a detailed account of this distinction in *Thinking in the Light of Time: Heidegger's Encounter with Hegel* (Albany: SUNY Press, 2000).

8. Denis McManus shows just how important the emphasis on futural projection is to Heidegger's conception of truth and how this emphasis revises the relation between empty and fulfilled intentions in Husserl's conception of truth. See Denis McManus, *Heidegger and the Measure of Truth* (Oxford: Oxford University Press, 2012), especially 103–114.

9. Stambaugh translates *die Aussage* as "statement." I follow Macquarrie and Robinson in translating it as "assertion."

10. My formulation here ignores Heidegger's careful distinctions between intelligibility (*Verständlichkeit*), meaning (*Sinn*), the totality of significations (*Bedeutungsganze*), and significations (*Bedeutungen*). "Meaning" refers to that which can be articulated (*das Artikulierbare*) in talk, just as "intelligibility" refers to that which can be understood and interpreted. The "totality of significations" refers to the entirety of what is articulated in talk. With this term, Heidegger draws attention to the claim that discrete articulations or "significations" belong to a larger totality. Similarly, although words accrue to discrete significations, this occurrence belongs to a larger process: "The totality of significations ... *is put into words*" (SZ, 161), and the totality of those words is language, in which talk gets expressed. (For more on the concept of "meaning," see SZ, 150–153, 156, and 323–325.)

11. Contrary to my formulation, Heidegger would not say that falling prey is restricted to a mass society—idle talk, for example, "does not first originate through certain conditions which influence Dasein 'from the outside'" (SZ, 177)—rather, falling prey "reveals an *essential*, ontological structure of Dasein itself" (SZ, 179). Nevertheless, his characterization of falling prey is clearly indebted to and descriptive of a social condition in which the structure and principle of publicity (*Öffentlichkeit*) hold sway. In that sense, despite his disclaimer that the term "does not express any negative value judgment" (SZ, 175), it is hard to read his account of "falling prey" or "entanglement" as anything other than a critique of mass society and of the democratic tendencies within it.

12. My paraphrase from SZ, 218, is closer to the Macquarrie and Robinson translation than to the Stambaugh translation. Heidegger writes that the discoveredness

(*Entdecktheit*) of an entity "bewährt sich darin, dass sich das Ausgesagte, das ist das Seiende selbst, *als dasselbe* zeigt." A few lines later he writes: "Die Aussage *ist wahr*, bedeutet: sie entdeckt das Seiende an ihm selbst."

13. In this context Heidegger says that his definition of truth provides "the *necessary* interpretation of what the oldest tradition of ancient philosophy primordially surmised and even understood in a pre-phenomenological way." That is to say, his definition recaptures the alethic sense in which apophantic reason and discourse (*logos*) can be true, namely, "to let beings be seen in their unconcealment [*Unverborgenheit*] (discoveredness [*Entdecktheit*]), taking them out of their concealment [*Verborgenheit*]" (SZ, 219). (See also the discussion of the concepts of *logos* and *aletheia* in Heidegger's introduction, SZ, 32–34.)

14. Note the three characterizations of truth in SZ, 226: "disclosedness, discovering, and discoveredness."

15. I take the clue for this dialectical line of critical interpretation from Adorno's discussion of Heidegger in *Negative Dialectics*, even though I think Adorno misinterprets Heidegger's attempt to interrelate Dasein, truth, and Being. See Adorno, ND, 59–131/67–136. Here are some representative passages from Adorno: "The concept of 'existential' things [*des Existentiellen*] ... is governed by the idea that the measure of truth is not its objectivity, of whichever kind, but the pure being-that-way and actingthat-way of the thinker. ... But truth, the constellation of subject and object in which both penetrate each other, can no more be reduced to subjectivity than to that Being whose dialectical relation to subjectivity Heidegger tends to blur [*zu verwischen trachtet*]" (ND, 127/132–133). "[Heidegger's notion of] historicality immobilizes history in the unhistorical realm, heedless of the historical conditions that govern the inner composition and constellation of subject and object" (ND, 129/135).

16. Another way to put the point is to say that meaning does not determine reference. This formulation is central to the critique of Heidegger's allegedly relativistic reification of language in Cristina Lafont, *Heidegger, Language, and World-Disclosure*, trans. Graham Harman (Cambridge: Cambridge University Press, 2000).

17. This predicative manner of taking something is to be contrasted with the manner of taking entities as something-as-which in pre-predicative interpretation. Cf. SZ, 148–149, 157–158.

18. The translation of the first sentence in this quotation is somewhat misleading. The point of this particular sentence is not that some entity changes from being at hand into something else, but rather that a change-over (*Umschlag*) occurs in Dasein's fore-having, from a circumspect "with which" to an assertoric "about which": "Das *zuhandene womit* des Zutunhabens, der Verrichtung, wird zum '*Worüber*' der aufzeigenden Aussage" (SZ, 158). It is correlatively to this change-over in Dasein's fore-having that the entity also undergoes a change: its handiness

becomes veiled, its objective presence gets discovered, and it gets defined (*bestimmt*) as a "what" rather than being interpreted as a "with which."

19. A similar ambiguity returns in Heidegger's subsequent account of the truth of assertion. On the one hand, confirming the truth of an assertion depends on whether the asserted entity "shows itself *as [that] very same thing. Confirmation* [of an assertion] means *the being's showing itself in its self-sameness.* Confirmation is accomplished on the basis of the being's showing itself" (SZ, 218). On the other hand, the truth of an assertion simply is the assertion's capacity to *discover* the entity in its (specific) identity: "To say that [an assertion] is *true* means that it discovers the beings in themselves [*sie entdeckt das Seiende an ihm selbst*]. It asserts, it shows, it lets beings 'be seen' (*apophansis*) in their discoveredness. The *being true* (*truth*) of the [assertion] must be understood as *discovering* [*entdeckend-sein*]" (SZ, 218). I take up this ambiguity concerning assertoric truth in the next section.

20. In fact, Heidegger says that all talk, whether assertoric or not, is *about* something. "[Talk] is [talk] about . ... That which [talk] is *about* does not necessarily have the character of the theme of a definite statement; in fact, mostly it does not have it. Even command is given about something; a wish is about something. And so is intercession. ... In all [talk] there is *what is spoken* as such, what is said as such when one actually wishes, asks, talks things over about" (SZ, 161–162).

21. Readers familiar with the ontology developed by the Dutch philosophers Herman Dooyeweerd and D. H. Th. Vollenhoven will recognize the term "predicative availability" as a modification of their notion of a "logical" (or "analytic") "object function" of any entity or event about which we can talk and make assertions. I avoid their particular terminology for two reasons: it presupposes a subject–object paradigm, which both Heidegger and I want to challenge, and the terms "logical" and "analytic" are less precise than "predicative." I recognize, however, that the account of subject–object relations given by Dooyeweerd and Vollenhoven breaks with the epistemological emphasis of the modern subject–object paradigm. For a concise and updated version of this account, see Hendrik Hart, *Understanding Our World: An Integral Ontology* (Lanham, MD: University Press of America, 1984), 221–242. See also Herman Dooyeweerd, *A New Critique of Theoretical Thought* (1953–58), reprint ed., vol. 2, trans. David H. Freeman and H. De Jongste (Philadelphia: Presbyterian and Reformed Publishing, 1969), 386–391.

22. Ernst Tugendhat, "Heideggers Idee von Wahrheit," in *Heidegger: Perspektiven zur Deutung seines Werks*, ed. Otto Pöggeler (Cologne: Kiepenheuer & Witsch, 1970), 286–297; translated by Richard Wolin as "Heidegger's Idea of Truth," in *The Heidegger Controversy: A Critical Reader*, ed. Richard Wolin (New York: Columbia University Press, 1991), 245–263. My modifications to this translation (indicated by square brackets) are intended to maintain some consistency with the Stambaugh translation of *Being and Time.* A longer version of Tugendhat's critique occurs in his semi-

nal study *Der Wahrheitsbegriff bei Husserl und Heidegger* (1967), 2nd ed. (Berlin: Walter de Gruyter, 1970).

23. Tugendhat, "Heidegger's Idea," 250–252; "Heideggers Idee," 288–289. The three formulations, all of them on SZ, 218, are: (1) The assertion is true if it discovers the entity "*just as* it is in itself." (The word "just" appears in the Macquarrie and Robinson translation, 261, but not in the Stambaugh translation, 201. Heidegger's formulation in German reads "Das gemeinte Seiende selbst zeigt sich *so, wie* es an ihm selbst ist.") (2) The assertion is true if it discovers the entity "in itself." (3) The assertion is true if it discovers the entity. Whereas Tugendhat accuses Heidegger of sliding through these three formulations, Dahlstrom argues that formulations (2) and (3) can be understood as synonyms or metonyms for (1), and he gives textual evidence for this interpretation (*Heidegger's Concept of Truth*, 405–407). I think that Tugendhat could easily concede this reading without giving up his main criticism, however.

24. "Heidegger's Idea," 254; "Heideggers Idee," 290–291. Although Tugendhat applauds Heidegger's "dynamic" conception of assertion as a mode of disclosedness, I wonder how dynamic this conception can be, given Heidegger's emphasis on disclosed*ness* as a state of Being rather than on disclo*sure* as a process of mediation.

25. "Heidegger's Idea," 254; "Heideggers Idee," 291.

26. "Heidegger's Idea," 255; "Heideggers Idee," 291.

27. "Heidegger's Idea," 256; "Heideggers Idee," 292.

28. "Heidegger's Idea," 257; "Heideggers Idee," 293. The translation of Tugendhat's essay does not bring out the close terminological connection between the assertion's correctness (*Richtig*keit) and the assertion's being directed (*gerichtet*) by the entity's self-givenness.

29. This is a general but not an exhaustive stipulation. Not included, for example, would be first-order statements about which one makes second-order statements (assuming for the sake of illustration that first-order statements can properly be called entities). In such cases, the relevant accord might be with other *predicative* aspects of the "entity's" availability.

30. The adjective "systatic" derives from Herman Dooyeweerd's discussion of the "intermodal systasis of meaning" that grounds any "theoretical synthesis." In Dooyeweerd's account, "systasis" refers to the wholeness or integrality with which the "modal aspects" of reality present themselves in ordinary or "pretheoretical" experience. See *A New Critique of Theoretical Thought*, vol. 2, 427–435. My term "systatic availability" refers to the multidimensional "handiness," both predicative and nonpredicative, of the entities with which human beings have dealings.

31. Jürgen Habermas, "Reflections on Communicative Pathology (1974)," in *On The Pragmatics of Social Interaction: Preliminary Studies in the Theory of Communicative Action*, trans. Barbara Fultner (Cambridge, MA: MIT Press, 2001), 129–171.

32. My summary introduces the terms "practice of asserting" and "accomplished assertion" at points where these seem consistent with Heidegger's account.

33. Cf. Theodor W. Adorno, *Against Epistemology: A Metacritique; Studies in Husserl and the Phenomenological Antinomies*, trans. Willis Domingo (Cambridge, MA: MIT Press, 1982), 186–193; *Zur Metakritik der Erkenntnistheorie: Studien über Husserl und die phänomenologischen Antinomien*, GS 5 (Frankfurt am Main: Suhrkamp, 1970), 190–197. In *The Philosophical Discourse of Modernity: Twelve Lectures*, trans. Frederick Lawrence (Cambridge, MA: MIT Press, 1987), Jürgen Habermas argues that, in both earlier and later articulations, Heidegger "remains caught in the problems that the philosophy of the subject in the form of Husserlian phenomenology had presented to him" (136).

34. Heidegger's Idea," 261; "Heideggers Idee," 296.

35. According to Dahlstrom, *Heidegger's Concept of Truth*, 392, Tugendhat tries to retain the "logical prejudice" that Heidegger's conception of truth aims to expose and dismantle.

36. This approach to principles has some similarities to the "international feminism" of Martha Nussbaum, *Women and Human Development: The Capabilities Approach* (Cambridge: Cambridge University Press, 2000). While I support her call to articulate "universal norms of human capability" (35), I have reservations about the Aristotelian elements of her theory and about her embrace of political liberalism. I would also propose a different list of "central human functional capabilities" (78–80), although my list would overlap hers and would share the underlying intuition of there being a limited plurality of central ways in which people in contemporary societies need to be active if they are to flourish as human beings.

37. In *The Genesis of Heidegger's* Being and Time (Berkeley: University of California Press, 1993), Theodore Kisiel introduces "troth" to translate Heidegger's use of *verwahren* (in the early 1920s) for a nontheoretical and practical or even religious sense of truth. The most prominent usages occur in Heidegger's courses on Aristotle's *Nicomachean Ethics* and in his October 1922 typescript titled "Phänomenologische Interpretationen zu Aristoteles (Anzeige der hermeneutischen Situation)." Kisiel suggests that Heidegger's concept of truth as "taking into troth and holding in troth" derives from his appropriation of Christian sources such as Paul, Augustine, and Luther, which "infiltrate Heidegger's understanding of the Aristotelian senses of practical truth" (226). Heidegger, commenting on Aristotle, claims that holding being(s) in troth (*Seinsverwahrung*) is the fundamental experience of truth. Moreover, *nous, sophia, episteme, techne*, and *phronesis* are all modes of "true-ing." In a gloss to Heidegger's handwritten note to the October 1922 typescript, Kisiel con-

nects troth to care as well: "To care is to take into troth and hold in troth, the kind of having … involved in the habits of truth" (537–538n17). See further Kisiel, 227–225, 302–306, 491–492. Michael Bauer, by contrast, translates "verwahren" as "truthful safe-keeping." See Martin Heidegger, "Phenomenological Interpretations with Respect to Aristotle: Indication of the Hermeneutical Situation," *Man and World* 25 (1992): 355–393.

38. This chapter stems from a paper presented by invitation in a lecture series hosted by the Institut für Philosophie at the Freie Universität Berlin on December 1, 1994. I wish to thank Christoph Menke and Ruth Sonderegger for extending their invitation and Axel Honneth and Albrecht Wellmer for sponsoring the research visit to Berlin during which the paper was written.

4   Truth and Authentication: Heidegger and Adorno in Reverse

1. ND, 13/25, tm.

2. Ernst Tugendhat, "Heidegger's Idea of Truth," in *The Heidegger Controversy: A Critical Reader*, ed. Richard Wolin (New York: Columbia University Press, 1991), 258–259; "Heideggers Idee von Wahrheit," in *Heidegger: Perspektiven zur Deutung seines Werks*, ed. Otto Pöggeler (Cologne: Kiepenheuer & Witsch, 1970), 294.

3. Tugendhat, "Heidegger's Idea," 261; "Heideggers Idee," 296.

4. See *Being and Time*, §44, subsection b, especially SZ, 220–223.

5. As Daniel O. Dahlstrom, *Heidegger's Concept of Truth* (Cambridge: Cambridge University Press, 2001), 423–433, points out, the pragmatic readings of Heidegger proposed by Richard Rorty and Mark Okrent overlook the centrality of "authenticity" and "temporality" or "timeliness" (*Zeitlichkeit*) to Heidegger's conception of truth. This limits their usefulness as readings of Heidegger, even though they do provide an important counterweight to Tugendhat's criticisms of Heidegger's conception.

6. It is worth quoting Heidegger's own summary of "authentic being-toward-death" in section 53 (SZ, 260–267). The italics are Heidegger's: "*Anticipation reveals to Dasein its lostness in the they-self, and brings it face to face with the possibility to be itself, primarily unsupported by concern taking care of things, but to be itself in passionate anxious freedom toward death which is free of the illusions of the they, factical, and certain of itself*" (SZ, 266).

7. Heidegger summarizes the threefold existential structure of Dasein's authentic potentiality-of-being as follows: "The disclosedness of Dasein in wanting-to-have-a-conscience is thus constituted by the attunement of *Angst*, by understanding as projecting oneself upon one's ownmost being-guilty, and by [talk] as reticence. We shall call the eminent, authentic disclosedness attested in Dasein itself by its con-

science—the *reticent projecting oneself upon one's ownmost being-guilty which is ready for Angst—resoluteness*" (SZ, 296–297).

8. Heidegger describes this "being-certain" as a "holding-for-true" (*Für-wahr-halten*) in which Dasein both gives itself to the situation and holds itself free for the possibility of taking itself back. In contrast with irresoluteness, "this holding-for-true, as a resolute holding oneself free for taking back, is the *authentic resoluteness to retrieve itself.*" The ultimate certainty here is that resoluteness is constantly certain of death, which resoluteness anticipates. At the same time, anticipatory resoluteness gives Dasein "the primordial certainty of its being closed off," of its being constantly lost "in the irresoluteness of the they" (SZ, 308).

9. In calling this an "existentiell potentiality" (rather than simply a potentiality that is "existentielly attested"), I follow Macquarrie and Robinson's translation. Heidegger's German text reads: "das Vorlaufen ist ... der *Modus* eines im Dasein bezeugten existenziellen Seinkönnens." Macquarrie and Robinson (357) translate: "anticipation is ... a *mode* of an existentiell potentiality-for-Being that is attested in Dasein." Stambaugh (285) translates: "anticipation is ... a *mode* of a potentiality-of-being existentielly attested in Dasein."

10. Adorno was especially allergic to the aura created by Heidegger's "authenticity" talk and the emptiness of what such talk commends. He objected that Heidegger turns the individual's decision to possess itself into the criterion of authenticity. This allows philosophy to ignore the real social conditions that make individuality possible, to avoid asking whether contemporary society actually allows people to be or become themselves, and to forget that "the old evil" (i.e., reification) might be concentrated in the Heideggerian concept of "selfness" (*Selbstheit*): "The societal relation that encapsulates itself in the subject's identity is de-societalized [by Heidegger's philosophy] into something in-itself." Theodor W. Adorno, *The Jargon of Authenticity*, trans. Knut Tarnowski and Frederic Will (London: Routledge & Kegan Paul, 1973), 115, tm; *Jargon der Eigentlichkeit: Zur deutschen Ideologie* (1964), GS 6 (Frankfurt am Main: Suhrkamp, 1973), 489–490.

11. Kevin Aho seems to miss the worrisome proximity of Heidegger's account of authenticity to Nazi ideology. Although I agree that Heidegger's account can be read in a more communalist and less individualist way, as Aho claims, I do not think such a reading removes the most problematic aspects of Heidegger's account. See Kevin Aho, "Why Heidegger Is Not an Existentialist: Interpreting Authenticity and Historicity in *Being and Time*," *Florida Philosophical Review* 3, no. 2 (winter 2003): 5–22. In *Heidegger's Philosophy of Art* (Cambridge: Cambridge University Press, 2001), Julian Young suggests that by the mid-1930s Heidegger's site of authenticity shifts from individual Dasein to "great art," whose task is to secure an authentic "people" that actively appropriates its cultural heritage (52–60). In this connection, see the discussion of Heidegger's "The Origin of the Work of Art" (1935–36) in Lambert

Zuidervaart, *Artistic Truth: Aesthetics, Discourse, and Imaginative Disclosure* (Cambridge: Cambridge University Press, 2004), 101–117.

12. Michael E. Zimmerman, *Eclipse of the Self: The Development of Heidegger's Concept of Authenticity*, rev. ed. (Athens, OH: Ohio University Press, 1986). See especially the appendix, 277–300.

13. Compare in this connection Heidegger's description of Dasein's everydayness as involving idle talk, curiosity, and ambiguity (SZ, §§35–38). Together these make up the "entanglement" of Dasein, its "character of being lost in the publicness of the they" (SZ, 175). Shortly thereafter he uncovers anxiety as the attunement that throws Dasein back on its own "authentic potentiality-for-being-in-the-world" (SZ, 187). In anxiety one feels the "uncanniness" of "not-being-at-home" in the world. Anxiety individualizes by calling up Dasein's fundamental alienation from all that absorbs Dasein in its everydayness. See §40, SZ, 184–191.

14. See Charles Taylor, *Sources of the Self: The Making of the Modern Identity* (Cambridge, MA: Harvard University Press, 1989). Theodor W. Adorno's Habilitationsschrift on Kierkegaard, written partly in response to *Sein und Zeit* and published as a book in 1933, yields important sociocritical insights into Heidegger's emphasis on Dasein's *Innerlichkeit*. See *Kierkegaard: Construction of the Aesthetic*, trans. Robert Hullot-Kentor (Minneapolis: University of Minnesota Press, 1989); *Kierkegaard: Konstruktion des Ästhetischen*, GS 2 (Frankfurt am Main: Suhrkamp, 1979).

15. Iain Macdonald, "Ethics and Authenticity: Conscience and Non-Identity in Heidegger and Adorno, with a Glance at Hegel," in *Adorno and Heidegger: Philosophical Questions*, ed. Iain Macdonald and Krzysztof Ziarek (Stanford, CA: Stanford University Press, 2008), 9.

16. Ibid., 15.

17. Ibid., 17.

18. Ibid., 13.

19. See especially Charles Guignon, "Philosophy and Authenticity: Heidegger's Search for a Ground for Philosophizing," in *Heidegger, Authenticity, and Modernity: Essays in Honor of Hubert L. Dreyfus, Volume 1*, ed. Mark A. Wrathall and Jeff Malpas (Cambridge, MA: MIT Press, 2000), 79–101, and Hubert L. Dreyfus, *Being-in-the-World: A Commentary on Heidegger's* Being and Time, *Division I* (Cambridge, MA: MIT Press, 1991), 299–340.

20. Taylor Carman, *Heidegger's Analytic: Interpretation, Discourse, and Authenticity in* Being and Time (Cambridge: Cambridge University Press, 2003), 139.

21. Ibid., 143.

22. Ibid., 7.

23. Ibid., 268.

24. Ibid., 268–271.

25. Ibid., 293.

26. This part of *Negative Dialectics* is the weakest, in my view. It is susceptible to Brian O'Connor's comment, in his discussion of Adorno's critique of Heidegger, that Adorno sometimes misrepresents Heidegger "beyond recognition." Brian O'Connor, *Adorno's Negative Dialectic: Philosophy and the Possibility of Critical Rationality* (Cambridge, MA: MIT Press, 2004), 151.

27. In the preface, Adorno suggests that the entire introduction to *Negative Dialectics* "expounds the concept of philosophical experience" (ND, xx/10). "Experience" is correctly identified as a "central concept of Adorno's thought" by the editor's introduction in *The Adorno Reader*, ed. Brian O'Connor (Oxford: Blackwell, 2000), 1–19. In his subsequent book, O'Connor reads *Negative Dialectics* as setting out "to provide an account of experience that [Adorno] sees as exclusively expressible by a nonreified rationality." O'Connor, *Adorno's Negative Dialectic*, 13. Unfortunately, O'Connor misinterprets the epigraph to the current chapter—concerning "full, unreduced experience in the medium of conceptual reflection"—as referring to experience, rather than to what Adorno explicitly identifies as "a transformed philosophy" (*eine veränderte Philosophie*). This misinterpretation leads to an account that, unlike Adorno's, renders experience overly conceptual. See, for example, O'Connor, *Adorno's Negative Dialectic*, 3, 79.

28. J. M. Bernstein, *Adorno: Disenchantment and Ethics* (Cambridge: Cambridge University Press, 2001), 115. For a discussion of the multifaceted character of "experience" in Adorno's writings, see Martin Jay, "Is Experience Still in Crisis? Reflections on a Frankfurt School Lament," *Kriterion*, no 100 (December 1999): 9–25. A corrected version of this essay appears in *The Cambridge Companion to Adorno*, ed. Tom Huhn (Cambridge: Cambridge University Press, 2004), 129–147, and is incorporated into the discussion of Adorno in Martin Jay, *Songs of Experience: Modern American and European Variations on a Universal Theme* (Berkeley: University of California Press, 2005), 343–360. See also Roger Foster, *Adorno: The Recovery of Experience* (Albany: SUNY Press, 2007). Foster argues that Adorno's negative dialectics seeks to recover experience that allows particularity to unfold, and he compares Adorno's project with central ideas of Wittgenstein and Benjamin, contrasts it with Husserl and Bergson, and points out its advantages over the approaches of John McDowell and Jürgen Habermas.

29. The need to reconnect rationality with emphatic experience is also central to Adorno's insistence on the possibility and necessity of what he calls "metaphysical experience," which I discuss in chapter 2 of my *Social Philosophy after Adorno* (Cambridge: Cambridge University Press, 2007), 48–76, as well as to his account of autonomous art as social labor and intellectual praxis, which I examine in chapters 5 and 6

of *Adorno's Aesthetic Theory: The Redemption of Illusion* (Cambridge, MA: MIT Press, 1991), 93–141. On "metaphysical experience," see also Bernstein, *Adorno*, 415–456.

30. My account of public authentication is not intended to endorse the conformism that both Heidegger and Adorno challenge, in their distinctive ways. Yet I do mean to suggest that even the most personal refusal, resistance, or protest—if it is to bear witness to truth—must call attention to specific societal principles and to specific needs for societal disclosure. What those principles and needs are, and how to articulate and interpret them, are, of course, always open to contestation and struggle.

31. This discussion of public authentication implies a refusal to privilege discourse in the manner of Habermas's discourse ethics and, albeit less prominently, of his more recent pragmatic conception of truth. See Jürgen Habermas, *Moral Consciousness and Communicative Action*, trans. Christian Lenhardt and Shierry Weber Nicholsen, introduction by Thomas McCarthy (Cambridge, MA: MIT Press, 1990), and *Truth and Justification*, ed. and trans. Barbara Fultner (Cambridge, MA: MIT Press, 2003). I discuss Habermas's conception of truth in chapter 5.

32. An earlier version of this chapter was presented during the conference *Heidegger/ Adorno: Aesthetics, Ethics, Technology* at the Université de Montréal in April 2004. I want to thank the conference organizers Iain Macdonald and Krzysztof Ziarek for their invitation and the participants for their instructive comments. Calvin Seerveld's comments on a first draft encouraged me to refine my formulations about the public authentication of truth. I also wish to acknowledge the collaborative support offered by the students in my graduate seminar Truth and Authenticity: Heidegger's *Being and Time*.

5   Truth and Justification: Jürgen Habermas

1. Jürgen Habermas, "Richard Rorty's Pragmatic Turn," in *Richard Rorty and His Critics*, ed. Robert B. Brandom (Oxford: Blackwell, 2000), 40. The same essay can be found in Jürgen Habermas, *On the Pragmatics of Communication*, ed. Maeve Cooke (Cambridge, MA: MIT Press, 1998), 343–382.

2. Alvin Plantinga, "How to Be an Anti-Realist," *Proceedings and Addresses of the American Philosophical Association* 56, no. 7 (1982): 47–70.

3. Ibid., 47.

4. Ibid., 62.

5. Ibid., 64.

6. Ibid., 66.

7. Ibid., 67–68.

8. Ibid., 68–70.

9. Although this is not the occasion to discuss Plantinga's theistic antirealism in depth, the positions he took in his 1982 presidential address have remained central to his work. Kevin Diller rightly observes that from the 1980s onward Plantinga has consistently identified "creative anti-realism" and "naturalism" as "the primary contemporary rivals to Christian thought, though sometimes giving more emphasis to the offspring of creative anti-realism: 'relativism and anti-commitment.'" Kevin Diller, *Theology's Epistemological Dilemma: How Karl Barth and Alvin Plantinga Provide a Unified Response*, foreword by Alvin Plantinga (Downers Grove, IL: IVP Academic, 2014), 98n13. Plantinga's positions in "How to Be an Anti-Realist" remain important in more recent discussions of truth theory as well. For example, the late William Alston, in a paper prepared for a major analytic anthology on truth, cites Plantinga's paper as a key backup to Alston's own "extensional" argument against Putnam's "ideal justifiability conception" of truth. See William Alston, "A Realist Conception of Truth," in *The Nature of Truth: Classic and Contemporary Perspectives*, ed. Michael Lynch (Cambridge, MA: MIT Press, 2001), 59. Similarly, although without citing Plantinga, David Efird's August 17, 2009, online review of the book *Truth and Truth-Making*, ed. E. J. Lowe and A. Rami, in *Notre Dame Philosophical Reviews*, uses Plantinga's move to explain the (human-) mind-independence of propositional truth: "I propose that a proposition's being true is metaphysically grounded in, or metaphysically explained by, God's knowing that proposition." Hence the 1982 presidential address is a good place to start if one wants to understand Plantinga's own contributions to contemporary truth theory.

10. Michael Lynch, "Realism and the Correspondence Theory: Introduction," in *The Nature of Truth*, 9.

11. Ibid., 11.

12. Plantinga holds something like this with regard to divinely known truth, although he speaks only of God's thinking and believing a proposition, not of God's offering a justification for thinking and believing as God does.

13. That is one reason why Plantinga frames his criticism of Putnam and Rorty's epistemic conceptions in terms of their purported creative antirealism.

14. My brief sketch of Habermas's development leaves out his earlier and more Hegelian Marxist approach in the 1960s, especially in Jürgen Habermas, *Knowledge and Human Interests* (1968), trans. Jeremy J. Shapiro (Boston: Beacon Press, 1971). For a thorough account of Habermas's earlier approach to the idea of truth and how this approach leads to what I identify as the stages of "consensus theory" and "formal pragmatics," see Thomas McCarthy, *The Critical Theory of Jürgen Habermas* (1978), paperback edition (Cambridge, MA: MIT Press, 1981).

15. The consensus theory receives its most expansive articulation in the Christian Gauss Lectures Habermas gave at Princeton University in 1971 and in the seminal article "Wahrheitstheorien" (Truth Theories) published in 1973. See "Reflections on

the Linguistic Foundation of Sociology: The Christian Gauss Lectures (Princeton University, February–March 1971)," in Habermas's *On the Pragmatics of Social Interaction: Preliminary Studies in the Theory of Communicative Action*, trans. Barbara Fultner (Cambridge, MA: MIT Press, 2001), 1–103, and "Wahrheitstheorien," in *Wirklichkeit und Reflexion: Walter Schulz zum 60. Geburtstag*, ed. Helmut Fahrenbach (Pfullingen: Günther Neske, 1973), 211–265. Habermas has never allowed "Wahrheitstheorien" to be published in an English translation. He indicates his subsequent reservations about his "consensus theory" in the 1983 additions he inserted into the footnotes to both the Gauss Lectures and "Wahrheitstheorien" in his *Vorstudien und Ergänzungen zur Theorie des kommunikativen Handelns* (Frankfurt: Suhrkamp, 1984).

16. In the writings under consideration, Habermas identifies "intelligibility" as a fourth unavoidable validity claim, but in subsequent writings he drops it from the list and treats it instead as a general condition for communicative action as such.

17. Habermas, *On the Pragmatics of Social Interaction*, 89.

18. Jürgen Habermas, *The Theory of Communicative Action*, trans. Thomas McCarthy, 2 vols. (Boston: Beacon Press, 1984, 1987).

19. The shift to a formal pragmatics of meaning is apparent in Habermas's 1976 essay "What Is Universal Pragmatics?" in Jürgen Habermas, *Communication and the Evolution of Society*, trans. Thomas McCarthy (Cambridge: Polity Press, 1984), 1–68, 208–219. Although it does not thematize truth, this essay marks a transition from stage 1 to stage 2 in his theory of truth.

20. Habermas, *The Theory of Communicative Action*, vol. 1, 277.

21. Ibid., 318.

22. Barbara Fultner, "The Redemption of Truth: Idealization, Acceptability and Fallibilism in Habermas' Theory of Meaning," *International Journal of Philosophical Studies* 4, no. 2 (1996): 238.

23. Hilary Putnam, *Reason, Truth, and History* (Cambridge: Cambridge University Press, 1981), 55.

24. Habermas, "Richard Rorty's Pragmatic Turn," 40. It is worth noting that Brandom chose Rorty's "Universality and Truth" (1–30), Habermas's essay, and Rorty's "Response to Jürgen Habermas" (56–64) to open *Richard Rorty and His Critics*. Despite their disagreements about truth, Rorty was highly appreciative of Habermas's democratic politics and his emphasis on the communicative character of rationality.

25. Ibid., 41.

26. Jürgen Habermas, *Truth and Justification*, ed. and trans. Barbara Fultner (Cambridge, MA: MIT Press, 2003), hereafter cited as TJ. With the exception of two essays, this book is a translation of Habermas's *Wahrheit und Rechtfertigung: Philosophische Aufsätze* (Frankfurt: Suhrkamp, 1999). My commentary focuses on the book's "Intro-

duction: Realism after the Linguistic Turn" (TJ, 1–49/7–64). The German title of this essay speaks not of the "linguistic" turn but of the "language-pragmatic" (*sprachprag-matisch*) turn.

27. In the passage under consideration (TJ, 33–36/44–48), Habermas does not explicitly mention his formal pragmatic conception of meaning. But it is implied throughout. Habermas appears to have been persuaded by Albrecht Wellmer and especially by Cristina Lafont that one must give up the tendency in the German hermeneutical tradition to think that meaning determines reference. See Cristina Lafont, *The Linguistic Turn in Hermeneutic Philosophy*, trans. José Medina (Cambridge, MA: MIT Press, 1999).

28. Habermas uses Hilary Putnam's theory of direct reference to account for such constancy of reference.

29. "Argumentation remains the only *available* medium of ascertaining truth since truth claims that have been problematized cannot be tested in any other way. There is no unmediated, discursively unfiltered access to the truth conditions of empirical beliefs" (TJ, 38/51).

30. These are not the only questions needing better answers, of course. In addition to the writings by Barbara Fultner and Cristina Lafont cited earlier, see James Swindal, *Reflection Revisited: Jürgen Habermas's Discursive Theory of Truth* (New York: Fordham University Press, 1999); Maeve Cooke, "Meaning and Truth in Habermas's Pragmatics," *European Journal of Philosophy* 9 (April 2001): 1–23; and Albrecht Wellmer, "The Debate about Truth: Pragmatism without Regulative Ideas," in *The Pragmatic Turn in Philosophy: Contemporary Engagements between Analytic and Continental Thought*, ed. William Egginton and Mike Sandbothe (Albany, NY: SUNY Press, 2004), 93–114.

31. I have explored these conceptions on other occasions and do not repeat the details here. In addition to chapters 3, 4, 7, and 8 in the current volume, see "Unfinished Business: Toward a Reformational Conception of Truth," *Philosophia Reformata* 74 (2009): 1–20, and "Religion in Public: Passages from Hegel's *Philosophy of Right*," *University of Toronto Journal for Jewish Thought* 1 (April 2010), http://tjjt.cjs.utoronto.ca/articles-2/. Both of these essays now appear in Lambert Zuidervaart, *Religion, Truth, and Social Transformation: Essays in Reformational Philosophy* (Montreal: McGill-Queen's University Press, 2016).

32. Habermas, "Richard Rorty's Pragmatic Turn," 41.

33. Habermas, *On the Pragmatics of Social Interaction*, 86; cf. "Wahrheitstheorien," 211–212.

34. Although the content of what one asserts could be called an "assertion," it is easy to confuse this usage with our using the term *assertion* to indicate a practice or speech act. So, like Habermas, I adopt the well-established convention of calling the content

asserted a *proposition*. This distinction between "assertion" as a speech act and "proposition" as the content asserted expresses in a different way the distinction made in chapter 3 between "asserting" as a practice and the accomplished "assertion."

35. See also Zuidervaart, "Unfinished Business," 15–18.

36. An earlier version of this chapter was presented as a keynote lecture titled "How Not to Be an Anti-Realist: Habermas, Truth, and Justification" at an international conference on *Truth Matters* at the University of Toronto in August 2010. I presented a revised version to the Philosophy Colloquium at Grand Valley State University in April 2013. I want to thank the audiences at both occasions for their helpful comments and questions.

6   Synthetic Evidence and Objective Truth: Husserl Revisited

1. LU II.2, 654–655; LI 2, 265, tm.

2. As in chapter 2, here I use the term "early" to refer to Husserl's conception of truth in the *Logical Investigations*.

3. Louis Dupré, "The Concept of Truth in Husserl's *Logical Investigations*," *Philosophy and Phenomenological Research* 24, no. 3 (1964): 354.

4. Dallas Willard, *Logic and the Objectivity of Knowledge: A Study in Husserl's Early Philosophy* (Athens, OH: Ohio University Press, 1984), 237.

5. Lee Hardy, *Nature's Suit: Husserl's Phenomenological Philosophy of the Physical Sciences* (Athens, OH: Ohio University Press, 2013), 4. Of course, instrumentalism in the philosophy of science is a narrower position than epistemological idealism in general; presumably one could be an instrumentalist with respect to science and a realist with respect to other domains of knowledge, just as Hardy claims Husserl to be with respect to scientific laws and scientific theories, respectively. Typically, however, instrumentalism's background assumptions about knowledge and its objects resist or challenge epistemological realism.

6. Ibid., 79.

7. Among the commentators discussed by Hardy who give an epistemic construal and who seem to reduce truth to evidence are Günther Patzig, "Husserl on Truth and Evidence," in *Readings on Edmund Husserl's* Logical Investigations, ed. J. N. Mohanty (The Hague: Martinus Nijhoff, 1977), 179–196, and Henry Pietersma, "Husserl's Views on the Evident and the True," in *Husserl: Expositions and Appraisals*, ed. Frederick A. Elliston and Peter McCormick (Notre Dame, IN: University of Notre Dame Press, 1977), 38–53.

8. Hardy, *Nature's Suit*, 81.

9. Ibid., 82.

10. Hardy devotes a separate chapter (chapter 4) to the question of how, according to Husserl, we can be justified in believing that theoretical entities exist despite their lack of perceptual givenness. I do not have the space here to take up Hardy's provocative discussion.

11. Hardy, *Nature's Suit*, 89.

12. Ibid., 85.

13. Ibid., 90, 93.

14. Ibid., 93–97.

15. Ibid., 96. See also Elisabeth Ströker, "Husserl's Principle of Evidence: The Significance and Limitations of a Methodological Norm of Phenomenology as a Science," in *Husserlian Foundations of Science*, ed. Lee Hardy (Lanham, MD: Center for Advanced Research in Phenomenology and University Press of America, 1987), 34.

16. Ströker, "Husserl's Principle," 38. Ströker finds support for this interpretation in Ernst Tugendhat's study *Der Wahrheitsbegriff bei Husserl und Heidegger* (Berlin: Walter de Gruyter, 1970).

17. Patzig, "Husserl on Truth and Evidence," completely misses this prepropositional sense of the "experience of truth," perhaps because, as Ströker points out, he "relies primarily on certain passages of the *Logical Investigations* that do not sufficiently reflect the Sixth Logical Investigation" (168n1). In fact, Patzig focuses almost exclusively on volume 1 of the *Logical Investigations*.

18. This review assumes and expands the account of Husserl's phenomenology of knowledge in the second section of chapter 2 in this book.

19. The flip side to fulfillment is frustration (*Enttäuschung*), and the reverse of identification is conflict (*Widerstreit*). Yet, for Husserl, frustration and conflict are neither nonsynthetic nor antisynthetic: "The experience of conflict institutes [*setzt in*] relations and unity: it is a form of *synthesis*" (LU II.2, 575; LI 2, 212; tm).

20. Husserl indicates in a footnote that from here on he will use the terms "significative," "signitive," and "symbolic" interchangeably to talk about acts of meaning-intention and meaning-conferral (LU II.2, 567; LI 2, 356n5). I follow this usage. John Drummond points out, however, that in later works Husserl distinguishes between *significative* intentions and *signitive* intentions. Whereas significative intentions "belong to objectifying acts," signitive intentions belong to "expressive acts." "The former present an object with a certain significance, whereas the latter are the intentions belonging to the act expressing in words the sense belonging to the objectifying act." This refinement, which is connected to Husserl's introducing the notion of a "noematic sense," clarifies somewhat the relation between acts of meaning-intention and language usage. See the entry titled "Objectifying Act" in John J.

Drummond, *Historical Dictionary of Husserl's Philosophy* (Lanham, MD: Scarecrow Press, 2008), 150–151.

21. Early Husserl's account of images and imagination is fairly traditional. He does not take up issues of creative imagination (e.g., Immanuel Kant's account of productive imagination as a source of "aesthetic ideas"), and he clearly would have had serious disagreements with Nelson Goodman's antimimetic account of pictorial representation. See, for example, Nelson Goodman, *Languages of Art: An Approach to a Theory of Symbols* (Indianapolis, IN: Bobbs-Merrill, 1968), 3–43.

22. My summary omits Husserl's sophisticated discussion of gradations among mediate fulfillments, mediate presentations (*mittelbare Vorstellungen*), and presentations of presentations (*Vorstellungsvorstellungen*). Two points are important to take away from this discussion. First, every mediate fulfillment eventually ends in an immediate intuition (LU II.2, 602; LI 2, 230). Second, the authentic intuitional rendering (*eigentliche Veranschaulichung*) of a signitive intention occurs only when a coincidence occurs between the matters of the signitive and intuitive acts in question, "so that the intuitively appearing object itself comes to the fore [*dasteht*] as the object intended in the [act of] meaning." Only in such cases of authentic *Veranschaulichung* is the thought "realized in the manner of perception or illustrated in the manner of imagination" (LU II.2, 605–606; LI 2, 232, tm).

23. Not every such synthesis involves an increase in fullness, however, insofar as "partial fulfillment and partial emptying [*Entfüllung*] can go hand in hand." That is why we must distinguish between acts of "mere identification" and acts of fulfillment: acts of identification can lack fulfillment because the synthesized acts lack any fullness, or identification can involve a fulfillment together with simultaneous emptying, such that no emphatic and pure consciousness of an increase in fulfillment occurs (LU II.2, 616; LI 2, 239–240, tm).

24. I leave aside the additional refinements that Husserl introduces in order to fill in the structure of objectifying acts. If I understand him correctly, he replaces his initial concepts of "matter" and (intuitive) "content" with the notion of an act's "representation" (*Repräsentation*) and then distinguishes among the representation's interpretative form, interpretative sense, and interpretative content, all of which are distinct from the intentional object as such, which is the object of interpretation (*Gegenstand der Auffassung*) (LU II.2, 621–622; LI 2, 242–243). Only by taking this entire structure into account, Husserl says, can we adequately describe the phenomenological differences between signitive and intuitive acts of objectification as well as their relationships within acts of identification and fulfillment.

25. Husserl also distinguishes between intuitions that have simple and complex relations to their objects, either of which can be adequate or inadequate (LU II.2, 627–628; LI 2, 247–248).

26. I omit Husserl's brief but instructive use of this distinction (between adequate and objectively complete intuitional rendering) to account for cases where the intuitional rendering conflicts with a signitive meaning and the signitive meaning is at least partially frustrated. See LU II.2, 630–631; LI 2, 248–249. I also pass over Husserl's discussion of the possibility and impossibility of meanings in chapter 4, titled "Verträglichkeit und Unverträglichkeit," even though it is important for his philosophy of logic and has implications for the (im)possibility of a dialectical logic. Although Findlay translates "Verträglichkeit" as "consistency," "compatibility" (the term Findlay uses to translate "Vereinbarkeit") is closer to what Husserl has in mind. He intends to lay out a conception of meanings in their (ideal) compatibility or incompatibility with an "objectively complete *Veranschaulichung*," and that is a different matter from logical consistency or inconsistency.

27. Husserl says that, for the most part, a perception does not offer a genuine presence (*ein wahrhaftes Gegenwärtigensein*) but only a present appearance (*ein gegenwärtig Erscheinen*), in which the object's presence—the objective presence (*die gegenständliche Gegenwart*)—displays various degrees (*Abstufungen*). For the perceiver, a perception's variegated fullness counts (*gilt uns*) as the "definitive presentation [*endgültige Präsentation*] of the corresponding objective element: [this fullness] offers itself [*gibt sich*] as identical with [the objective element], not as a mere representative [*Repräsentant*] but as [the objective element itself] in the absolute sense" (LU II.2, 646–647; LI 2, 260, tm). If the reader compares my summary of this passage with Findlay's translation at LI 2, 260, many departures from his word choices will become apparent. I have tried to capture some of the overlap and resonances among Husserl's German terms.

28. Findlay's translation omits the next sentence, which says that in such a case the representing and the represented content are identical: "Repräsentierender und repräsentierter Inhalt sind hier identisch eines" (LU II.2, 647).

29. This account of adequation, which regards perceptions as the site for the final fulfillment of all objectifying intentions, prompts a possible objection. How can universal conceptual intentions and analytically correct assertions find final fulfillment in *perception*, given Husserl's treatment of sensuous perception as being directed at what is "individually singular" (*das individuell Einzelne*)? At a minimum, would not *imagination* need to be the site of final fulfillment for such intentions? Husserl acknowledges the potential problem here, but he defers a solution until later, when he will expand the concepts of perception and intuition to include the nonsensuous elements of categorial intuition (LU II.2, 649–650; LI 2, 261–262)—see my discussion of categorial intuition in chapter 2.

30. Husserl uses the phrase "die gegenständliche Seite der Akte" (LU II.2, 654; LI 2, 265). Because the term "objective" can be misleading in this context, I have decided to use the term "object side" instead.

31. Aristotle, *Metaphysics*, Book IV, 1011b, 26–27.

32. In this sense, the passage about Husserl's first concept of truth that I quoted earlier from Ströker, "Husserl's Principle," 38, is too restrictive: Husserl understands "true" as a predicate of *objective identity*, not simply, in Ströker's words, "as a predicate of the state of affairs."

33. In line with this, Husserl suggests two different ways to understand the domain of judgment (*Urteil*). A broad understanding would equate it with positing (and objectifying) acts in general (*setzende Akt überhaupt*), which could be either assertoric or nonassertoric and to which broad concepts of (subject-sided) truth and falsity would apply. A narrow understanding would restrict judgment to the assertion and its possible fulfillments—that is, to certain relational positing acts—for which narrower concepts of truth and falsity would apply (LU II.2, 655; LI 2, 266). Misleadingly, Findlay translates *setzende* as "assertive" rather than "positing" in this passage.

34. Hardy, *Nature's Suit*, 215n14, summarizing Tugendhat, *Der Wahrheitsbegriff*, 94.

35. Tugendhat, *Der Wahrheitsbegriff*, 94. Tugendhat adds that this approach to evidence would make the third concept of truth (as intuitive fullness) more fundamental and more comprehensive than the first and fourth concepts (as objective identity and signitive correctness)—*Der Wahrheitsbegriff*, 95.

36. Hardy, *Nature's Suit*, 89.

37. Tugendhat, *Der Wahrheitsbegriff*, 98–99.

38. Ibid., 99–100.

39. "Die Bedeutung von Husserls Analysen liegt nicht in Resultaten, auf die unmittelbar aufzubauen ware, sondern in den neu auszuarbeitenden Möglichkeiten, die sie eröffnen." Ibid., 101.

40. I presented a precursor to chapter 6 in the Philosophy Department Colloquium at Calvin College in March 2014 and received helpful comments there. I wish to thank Lee Hardy and Andrew Spear for their astute remarks on a subsequent draft of this chapter.

7   Transforming Truth: Heidegger and Horkheimer in Dialectical Disclosure

1. G. W. F. Hegel, *Phenomenology of Spirit*, trans. A. V. Miller (Oxford: Oxford University Press, 1977), 10.

2. In German the first word of each title also differs. "On" translates "Vom" in Heidegger's title and "Zur" in Horkheimer's.

3. Horkheimer and several other members of the Institute of Social Research had settled in New York by 1935, but most of them continued to write in German until

the 1940s. The *Zeitschrift für Sozialforschung* changed its name to *Studies in Philosophy and Social Science* in 1939–1940 and ceased publication in 1941.

4. Daniel O. Dahlstrom, *Heidegger's Concept of Truth* (Cambridge: Cambridge University Press, 2001).

5. Throughout this chapter I use the term "propositional correctness" as a synonym for "propositional truth," without employing the distinctions introduced in chapter 5 among the reliability of beliefs, the correctness of assertions, and the accuracy of propositions.

6. In this chapter I use "bivalence" more broadly than is typical in contemporary truth theories. Kirkham, for example, describes the "principle of bivalence" as the position that "every meaningful declarative sentence is either true or false, none is neither." Those who deny this principle claim either "that some sentences are 'indeterminate' in their truth value" or "that some sentences simply have no truth value." Richard L. Kirkham, *Theories of Truth: A Critical Introduction* (Cambridge, MA: MIT Press, 1992), 175. Heidegger's challenge to bivalence goes deeper than this, for he asks whether untruth is of the essence of truth.

7. My condensation of Heidegger's formulation stems from the following passage:

Die Aussage über das Geldstück bezieht "sich" aber auf dieses Ding, indem sie es vor-stellt und vom Vor-gestellten sagt, wie es mit ihm selbst nach der je leitenden Hinsicht bestellt sei. Die vorstellende Aussage sagt ihr Gesagtes so vom vorgestellten Ding, wie es als dieses ist. ... Vor-stellen bedeutet hier ... das Entgegenstehenlassen des Dinges als Gegenstand. Das Entgegenstehende muss als das so Gestellte ein offenes Entgegen durchmessen und dabei doch in sich als das Ding stehenbleiben und als ein Ständiges zich zeigen. Dieses Erscheinen des Dinges im Durchmessen eines Entgegen vollzieht sich innerhalb eines Offenen, dessen Offenheit ... je nur als ein Bezugsbereich bezogen und übernommen wird. (ET, 141/183–184)

8. Heidegger adds "As standing in the openness" (ET, 141/184) in the marginalia to the essay's third edition (1954), probably to allay any suggestion that human beings can simply initiate such standing.

9. The notion of a pregiven standard does important work here, but Heidegger does not really explain it. He suggests that properly open human comportment must accept or "take over" this standard (*dieses Mass sich anweisen lassen*), not establish or impose it. The standard in question is "what is opened up" (*Offenbares*) (ET, 142/182). This notion reflects Heidegger's ongoing attempts to articulate a "measure of truth," as explained by Denis McManus, *Heidegger and the Measure of Truth* (Oxford: Oxford University Press, 2012).

10. The addition of the phrase *"as the correctness of a statement"* in the *Gesamtausgabe* edition indicates that for Heidegger freedom is not the true essence of truth in its most comprehensive sense.

11. Marginalia to the essay's first published edition (1943) characterize this letting-be as the "granting—preservation" (*gewähren—Wahrnis*) of beings and the "heeding" (*achten*) or "taking heed" (*er-achten*) of Being (*Sein*) (ET, 144/188).

12. Heidegger's term here is "ek-sistent," which, as the translator's note mentions, "indicates the ecstatic character of freedom, its standing outside itself" (ET, 372n10).

13. See John Abromeit, *Max Horkheimer and the Foundations of the Frankfurt School* (Cambridge: Cambridge University Press, 2011), 301–393. Abromeit argues that Horkheimer's early critical theory provides a nuanced historical and social-psychological account of the development of bourgeois society in modern Europe, and that this account should be seen as the background to Horkheimer and Adorno's *Dialectic of Enlightenment* and their other writings after 1940. Although, as Abromeit suggests, "bourgeois society" is a more inclusive and accurate label for the topic of Horkheimer's investigations, I shall use the terms "capitalism" and "capitalist society."

14. Horkheimer lists three aspects of dialectical presentation: the direction of thought, the selection of materials (*des inhaltlichen Materials*), and linguistic usage (PT, 186/331). As examples of uncritical interest and partisanship, he mentions Hegel's insufficiently historical conceptions of peoples (*Völker*) and freedom (*Freiheit*) (PT, 187/331–332).

15. "Traditional and Critical Theory" (1937), in Max Horkheimer, *Critical Theory: Selected Essays*, trans. Matthew J. O'Connell et al. (New York: Continuum, 1972), 188–243.

16. Horkheimer specifically mentions the role played in both empirical research and theory verification by the direction of our attention, the subtlety of our methods, and the structure of our categories (PT, 190/335).

17. By theoretical verification, Horkheimer means how a view can be completely borne out (*kann sich ohne Rest bewähren*) insofar as the objective relationships claimed to exist are confirmed (*sich finden*) "on the basis of experience and observation" through the use of unobjectionable methods and inferences (PT, 196/342).

18. I omit discussion of Horkheimer's response to Max Scheler's critique of pragmatism: it adds little to Horkheimer's account of truth and corroboration. See PT, 200–203/346–349.

19. I leave aside the difficult question of whether Horkheimer's materialist dialectic is applicable to so-called nature.

20. Max Horkheimer, "Materialism and Morality" (1933), in *Between Philosophy and Social Science: Selected Early Writings*, trans. G. Frederick Hunter et al. (Cambridge, MA: MIT Press, 1993), 15–47.

21. Horkheimer mentions such principles in passing when he connects the proclamation of truth with the struggle to actualize "better principles of society" (PT,

197/342), but he gives no example of what could count as a "better principle." That leaves open the question whether the principles would be better because they are pursued "in truth," or whether to pursue them "in truth" one must already recognize what makes them better—for example, in what ways they would be more conducive to human flourishing.

22. See especially ND, 241–245/240–243, where Adorno declares that the most advanced theory is the only authority (*Instanz*) for right practice and the good. I question Adorno's stance in the last chapter of *Social Philosophy after Adorno* (Cambridge: Cambridge University Press, 2007), 163–165.

23. This chapter derives from a keynote lecture presented at *Phenomenology and Critical Theory*, the Twenty-Fifth Annual Symposium hosted by the Simon Silverman Phenomenology Center at Duquesne University in March 2007. I wish to thank the symposium organizers for their generous hospitality, my fellow panelists Cristina Lafont, David Rasmussen, and Joel Whitebook for their insightful comments, and the audience for their provocative questions. I also want to thank Matt Klaassen for his research assistance.

8   Conclusion: Truth and Goodness Intersect

1. Jürgen Habermas, *Knowledge and Human Interests* (1968), trans. Jeremy J. Shapiro (Boston: Beacon Press, 1971), 317.

2. "Disclosedness" (*Erschlossenheit*) and "unconcealment" (*Unverborgenheit*) are largely synonymous in Heidegger's writings, although Mark Wrathall suggests that, in the later writings, "unconcealment" has a wider extension. See Mark Wrathall, *Heidegger and Unconcealment: Truth, Language, and History* (Cambridge: Cambridge University Press, 2011), especially 11–39.

3. It is not uncontroversial, of course, to assign propositional truth a leading role in academic work. See, for example, Joseph Rouse, *Knowledge and Power: Toward a Political Philosophy of Science* (Ithaca, NY: Cornell University Press, 1987). Taking issue with Rouse's deflationary approach and his pragmatist interpretation of Heidegger's conception of truth, I have argued elsewhere that the pursuit of propositional truth is central to academic work. See "Science, Society, and Culture: Against Deflationism," in my *Religion, Truth, and Social Transformation: Essays in Reformational Philosophy* (Montreal: McGill-Queen's University Press, 2016), 298–313.

4. Here I set aside questions about the propositional content of beliefs and of speech acts that are not assertoric.

5. In refusing the "either/or," I take inspiration from the work of Nikolas Kompridis, even though he and I have quite different approaches to the idea of truth. See Nikolas Kompridis, *Critique and Disclosure: Critical Theory between Past and Future* (Cambridge, MA: MIT Press, 2006).

6. For an account of creative interpretation as one practice within the intersubjective aesthetic process I call "imagination," see chapter 3 in my *Artistic Truth: Aesthetics, Discourse, and Imaginative Disclosure* (Cambridge: Cambridge University Press, 2004), 55–73.

7. See part 1 in Edmund Husserl, *Experience and Judgment: Investigations in a Genealogy of Logic* (1939, 1948), ed. and rev. Ludwig Landgrebe, trans. James S. Churchill and Karl Ameriks (Evanston, IL: Northwestern University Press, 1973), 69–194.

8. D. M. Armstrong, *Truth and Truthmakers* (Cambridge: Cambridge University Press, 2004). Armstrong calls his position "Truthmaker Necessitarianism and Truthmaker Maximalism" (5), and he says it yields the following theory concerning the nature of truth: "p (a proposition) is true if and only if there exists a T (some entity in the world) such that T necessitates that p and p is true in virtue of T" (17).

9. Donald Davidson, "True to the Facts" (1969), in *Inquiries into Truth and Interpretation* (Oxford: Clarendon Press, 1984), 37–54. For a succinct and illuminating survey of such arguments as criticisms directed at correspondence theories of truth, see Pascal Engel, *Truth* (Montreal: McGill-Queen's University Press, 2002), 14–26.

10. I plan to discuss analytic truth theories at much greater length in a subsequent volume.

11. Habermas, *Knowledge and Human Interests*, 314, 317. Habermas indicates that this appendix, titled "Knowledge and Human Interests: A General Perspective," stems from his inaugural lecture at the Goethe University in Frankfurt am Main in 1965.

12. This is partly due to criticisms of his theory of human interests. See in this connection Jürgen Habermas, "A Postscript to *Knowledge and Human Interests*," *Philosophy and the Social Sciences* 3 (1973): 157–189, where Habermas takes up these criticisms and other objections to his epistemology. This document is not included in the English translation of *Knowledge and Human Interests*. It first appeared as "Nachwort (1973)" in the second German edition of Jürgen Habermas, *Erkenntnis und Interesse* (Frankfurt am Main: Suhrkamp, 1973), 367–417.

13. Perhaps more than anything else, the retention of this insight distinguishes my proposed critical retrieval from the more Foucauldian and Rortian appropriation of continental philosophy proposed by Barry Allen. Allen dismisses Habermas's linking truth with goodness as emblematic of an "old faith." Truth has no value, Allen says, "apart from whatever is built, destroyed, sustained, or impeded with what passes for true. Truth has … no utopian potential, no affinity for good, and will not make us free." Barry Allen, *Truth in Philosophy* (Cambridge, MA: Harvard University Press, 1993), 182.

Works Cited

Abromeit, John. *Max Horkheimer and the Foundations of the Frankfurt School*. Cambridge: Cambridge University Press, 2011.

Adorno, Theodor W. *Aesthetic Theory* (1970). Trans. Robert Hullot-Kentor. Minneapolis: University of Minnesota Press, 1997.

Adorno, Theodor W. *Against Epistemology: A Metacritique; Studies in Husserl and the Phenomenological Antinomies* (1956). Trans. Willis Domingo. Cambridge, MA: MIT Press, 1982.

Adorno, Theodor W. *Ästhetische Theorie. Gesammelte Schriften* 7. 2nd ed. Frankfurt am Main: Suhrkamp, 1972.

Adorno, Theodor W. "Die Transzendenz des Dinglichen und Noematischen in Husserls Phänomenologie." In *Gesammelte Schriften* 1, 7–77. Frankfurt am Main: Suhrkamp, 1973.

Adorno, Theodor W. "Husserl and the Problem of Idealism." *Journal of Philosophy* 37, no. 1 (1940): 5–18.

Adorno, Theodor W. *Jargon der Eigentlichkeit: Zur deutschen Ideologie*. In *Gesammelte Schriften* 6, 413–526. Frankfurt am Main: Suhrkamp, 1973.

Adorno, Theodor W. *The Jargon of Authenticity* (1964). Trans. Knut Tarnowski and Frederic Will. London: Routledge & Kegan Paul, 1973.

Adorno, Theodor W. *Kierkegaard: Construction of the Aesthetic* (1933). Trans. Robert Hullot-Kentor. Minneapolis: University of Minnesota Press, 1989.

Adorno, Theodor W. *Kierkegaard: Konstruktion des Ästhetischen. Gesammelte Schriften* 2. Frankfurt am Main: Suhrkamp, 1979.

Adorno, Theodor W. *Negative Dialectics* (1966, 1967). Trans. E. B. Ashton. New York: Seabury Press, 1973.

Adorno, Theodor W. *Negative Dialektik*. In *Gesammelte Schriften* 6, 7–412. Frankfurt am Main: Suhrkamp, 1973.

Adorno, Theodor W. "Review of Herbert Marcuse, *Hegels Ontologie und die Grundlegung einer Theorie der Geschichtlichkeit.*" *Zeitschrift für Sozialforschung* 1 (1932): 409–410.

Adorno, Theodor W. *Zur Metakritik der Erkenntnistheorie: Studien über Husserl und die phänomenologischen Antinomien.* In *Gesammelte Schriften* 5, 7–245. Frankfurt am Main: Suhrkamp, 1970.

Adorno, Theodor W., Hans Albert, Ralf Dahrendorf, Jürgen Habermas, Harald Pilot, and Karl R. Popper. *The Positivist Dispute in German Sociology.* Trans. Glyn Adey and David Frisby. London: Heinemann, 1976.

Aho, Kevin. "Why Heidegger Is Not an Existentialist: Interpreting Authenticity and Historicity in *Being and Time.*" *Florida Philosophical Review* 3, no. 2 (winter 2003): 5–22.

Allen, Barry. *Truth in Philosophy.* Cambridge, MA: Harvard University Press, 1993.

Alston, William. "A Realist Conception of Truth." In *The Nature of Truth: Classic and Contemporary Perspectives,* ed. Michael Lynch, 41–66. Cambridge, MA: MIT Press, 2001.

Arato, Andrew, and Eike Gebhardt, eds. *The Essential Frankfurt School Reader.* New York: Urizen Books, 1978.

Armstrong, D. M. *Truth and Truthmakers.* Cambridge: Cambridge University Press, 2004.

Baynes, Kenneth, James Bohman, and Thomas McCarthy, eds. *Philosophy: End or Transformation?* Cambridge, MA: MIT Press, 1987.

Bernstein, J. M. *Adorno: Disenchantment and Ethics.* Cambridge: Cambridge University Press, 2001.

Bernstein, Richard J. *Beyond Objectivism and Relativism: Science, Hermeneutics, and Praxis.* Philadelphia: University of Pennsylvania Press, 1983.

Bernstein, Richard J. *The Pragmatic Turn.* Cambridge: Polity Press, 2010.

Blattner, William D. *Heidegger's Temporal Idealism.* Cambridge: Cambridge University Press, 1999.

Blumenberg, Hans. *The Legitimacy of the Modern Age* (1966, 1976). Trans. Robert M. Wallace. Cambridge, MA: MIT Press, 1983.

Carman, Taylor. *Heidegger's Analytic: Interpretation, Discourse, and Authenticity in Being and Time.* Cambridge: Cambridge University Press, 2003.

Cooke, Maeve. "Meaning and Truth in Habermas's Pragmatics." *European Journal of Philosophy* 9 (April 2001): 1–23.

Crowell, Steven. *Husserl, Heidegger and the Space of Meaning: Paths toward Transcendental Phenomenology.* Evanston, IL: Northwestern University Press, 2001.

Crowell, Steven. *Normativity and Phenomenology in Husserl and Heidegger.* Cambridge: Cambridge University Press, 2013.

Dahlstrom, Daniel O. *Heidegger's Concept of Truth.* Cambridge: Cambridge University Press, 2001.

Davidson, Donald. *Inquiries into Truth and Interpretation.* Oxford: Clarendon Press, 1984.

Davidson, Donald. "True to the Facts" (1969). In *Inquiries into Truth and Interpretation,* 37–54. Oxford: Clarendon Press, 1984.

de Boer, Karin. *Thinking in the Light of Time: Heidegger's Encounter with Hegel.* Albany: SUNY Press, 2000.

Derrida, Jacques. *Speech and Phenomena: Introduction to the Problem of Signs in Husserl's Phenomenology* (1967, 1998). In *Speech and Phenomena and Other Essays on Husserl's Theory of Signs,* trans. David B. Allison, 1–104. Evanston, IL: Northwestern University Press, 1973.

Diller, Kevin. *Theology's Epistemological Dilemma: How Karl Barth and Alvin Plantinga Provide a Unified Response.* Foreword by Alvin Plantinga. Downers Grove, IL: IVP Academic, 2014.

Dooyeweerd, Herman. *A New Critique of Theoretical Thought* (1953–58). 4 vols. Trans. David H. Freeman et al. Rpt ed. Philadelphia: Presbyterian and Reformed Publishing, 1969.

Dreyfus, Hubert L. *Being-in-the-World: A Commentary on Heidegger's* Being and Time, *Division I.* Cambridge, MA: MIT Press, 1991.

Drummond, John J. *Historical Dictionary of Husserl's Philosophy.* Lanham, MD: Scarecrow Press, 2008.

Drummond, John J. "Pure Logical Grammar: Identity Amidst Linguistic Differences." In *Husserl's Logical Investigations in the New Century: Western and Chinese Perspectives,* ed. Kwok-Ying Lau and John J. Drummond, 53–66. Dordrecht: Springer, 2007.

Dupré, Louis. "The Concept of Truth in Husserl's *Logical Investigations.*" *Philosophy and Phenomenological Research* 24, no. 3 (1964): 354.

Dussel, Enrique. *Ethics of Liberation: In the Age of Globalization and Exclusion* (1998). Ed. Alejandro A. Vallega. Trans. Eduardo Mendieta et al. Durham, NC: Duke University Press, 2013.

Efird, David. Review of *Truth and Truth-Making,* ed. E. J. Lowe and A. Rami. *Notre Dame Philosophical Reviews,* August 17, 2009. http://ndpr.nd.edu/news/24127-truth-and-truth-making.

Engel, Pascal. *Truth.* Montreal: McGill-Queen's University Press, 2002.

Foster, Roger. *Adorno: The Recovery of Experience*. Albany: SUNY Press, 2007.

Frege, Gottlob. 1980. "On Sense and Reference" (1892). In *Translations from the Philosophical Writings of Gottlob Frege*, 3rd. ed., trans. Max Black, ed. Peter Geach and Max Black, 56–78. Oxford: Blackwell.

Frege, Gottlob. "Über Sinn und Bedeutung." *Zeitschrift für Philosophie und philosophische Kritik* 100 (1892): 25–50.

Fultner, Barbara. "The Redemption of Truth: Idealization, Acceptability, and Fallibilism in Habermas' Theory of Meaning." *International Journal of Philosophical Studies* 4, no. 2 (1996): 233–251.

Gadamer, Hans-Georg. *Truth and Method* (1960). 2nd rev. ed. Trans. rev. by Joel Weinsheimer and Donald G. Marshall. New York: Crossroad, 1989.

Gadamer, Hans-Georg. *Wahrheit und Methode: Grundzüge einer philosophischen Hermeneutik*. 4th ed. Tübingen: J. C. B. Mohr (Paul Siebeck), 1975.

Goodman, Nelson. *Languages of Art: An Approach to a Theory of Symbols*. Indianapolis, IN: Bobbs-Merrill, 1968.

Guignon, Charles. "Philosophy and Authenticity: Heidegger's Search for a Ground for Philosophizing." In *Heidegger, Authenticity, and Modernity: Essays in Honor of Hubert L. Dreyfus*, vol. 1, ed. Mark A. Wrathall and Jeff Malpas, 79–101. Cambridge, MA: MIT Press, 2000.

Habermas, Jürgen. *Erkenntnis und Interesse*. 2nd ed. Frankfurt am Main: Suhrkamp, 1973.

Habermas, Jürgen. *Knowledge and Human Interests* (1968). Trans. Jeremy J. Shapiro. Boston: Beacon Press, 1971.

Habermas, Jürgen. *Moral Consciousness and Communicative Action*. Trans. Christian Lenhardt and Shierry Weber Nicholsen. Cambridge, MA: MIT Press, 1990.

Habermas, Jürgen. *The Philosophical Discourse of Modernity: Twelve Lectures* (1985). Trans. Frederick Lawrence. Cambridge, MA: MIT Press, 1987.

Habermas, Jürgen. "A Postscript to *Knowledge and Human Interests*." *Philosophy of the Social Sciences* 3 (1973): 157–189.

Habermas, Jürgen. "Reflections on Communicative Pathology" (1974). In Jürgen Habermas, *On the Pragmatics of Social Interaction: Preliminary Studies in the Theory of Communicative Action*, trans. Barbara Fultner, 129–171. Cambridge, MA: MIT Press, 2001.

Habermas, Jürgen. "Reflections on the Linguistic Foundations of Sociology: The Christian Gauss Lectures (Princeton University, February–March 1971)." In Jürgen Habermas, *On the Pragmatics of Social Interaction: Preliminary Studies in the Theory of Communicative Action*, trans. Barbara Fultner, 1–103. Cambridge, MA: MIT Press, 2001.

Habermas, Jürgen. "Richard Rorty's Pragmatic Turn." In *Richard Rorty and His Critics*, ed. Robert Brandom, 31–55. Oxford: Blackwell, 2000.

Habermas, Jürgen. *The Theory of Communicative Action* (1981). Trans. Thomas McCarthy. 2 vols. Boston: Beacon Press, 1984, 1987.

Habermas, Jürgen. *Truth and Justification*. Ed. and trans. Barbara Fultner. Cambridge, MA: MIT Press, 2003.

Habermas, Jürgen. *Vorstudien und Ergänzungen zur Theorie des kommunikativen Handelns*. Frankfurt am Main: Suhrkamp, 1984.

Habermas, Jürgen. "Wahrheitstheorien." In *Wirklichkeit und Reflexion: Walter Schulz zum 60. Geburtstag*, ed. Helmut Fahrenbach, 211–265. Pfullingen: Günther Neske, 1973.

Habermas, Jürgen. *Wahrheit und Rechtfertigung: Philosophische Aufsätze*. Frankfurt am Main: Suhrkamp, 1999.

Habermas, Jürgen. "What Is Universal Pragmatics?" In Jürgen Habermas, *Communication and the Evolution of Society*, trans. Thomas McCarthy, 1–68, 208–219. Cambridge: Polity Press, 1984.

Hardy, Lee. *Nature's Suit: Husserl's Phenomenological Philosophy of the Physical Sciences*. Athens, OH: Ohio University Press, 2013.

Hart, Hendrik. *Understanding Our World: An Integral Ontology*. Lanham, MD: University Press of America, 1984.

Haugeland, John. *Dasein Disclosed: John Haugeland's Heidegger*. Ed. Joseph Rouse. Cambridge, MA: Harvard University Press, 2013.

Hegel, G. W. F. *Phenomenology of Spirit*. Trans. A. V. Miller. Oxford: Oxford University Press, 1977.

Heidegger, Martin. *Being and Time* (1927). Trans. John Macquarrie and Edward Robinson. New York: Harper & Row, 1962.

Heidegger, Martin. *Being and Time* (1927). Trans. Joan Stambaugh. Albany: SUNY Press, 1996.

Heidegger, Martin. "On the Essence of Truth" (1930). Trans. John Sallis. In Martin Heidegger, *Pathmarks*, ed. William McNeill, 136–154. Cambridge: Cambridge University Press, 1998.

Heidegger, Martin. "Phenomenological Interpretations with Respect to Aristotle: Indication of the Hermeneutical Situation." *Man and World* 25 (1992): 355–393.

Heidegger, Martin. *The Question Concerning Technology and Other Essays*. Trans. William Lovitt. New York: Harper Torchbooks, 1977.

Heidegger, Martin. *Sein und Zeit*. 15th ed. Tübingen: Max Niemeyer, 1979.

Heidegger, Martin. "Vom Wesen der Wahrheit." In Martin Heidegger, *Wegmarken*, 3rd ed., 177–202. Frankfurt am Main: Klostermann, 1996.

Horkheimer, Max. "Materialism and Morality" (1933). In Max Horkheimer, *Between Philosophy and Social Science: Selected Early Writings*, trans. G. Frederick Hunter et al., 15–47. Cambridge, MA: MIT Press, 1993.

Horkheimer, Max. "On the Problem of Truth" (1935). In Max Horkheimer, *Between Philosophy and Social Science: Selected Early Writings*, trans. G. Frederick Hunter et al., 177–215. Cambridge, MA: MIT Press, 1993.

Horkheimer, Max. "Traditional and Critical Theory" (1937). In Max Horkheimer, *Critical Theory: Selected Essays*, trans. Matthew J. O'Connell et al., 188–243. New York: Continuum, 1972.

Horkheimer, Max. "Zum Problem der Wahrheit." *Zeitschrift für Sozialforschung* 4 (1935): 321–364.

Horkheimer, Max, and Theodor W. Adorno. *Dialectic of Enlightenment: Philosophical Fragments* (1947). Ed. Gunzelin Schmid Noerr. Trans. Edmund Jephcott. Stanford, CA: Stanford University Press, 2002.

Huhn, T., ed. *The Cambridge Companion to Adorno*. Cambridge: Cambridge University Press, 2004.

Husserl, Edmund. *Cartesian Meditations: An Introduction to Phenomenology* (1931). Trans. Dorion Cairns. The Hague: Martinus Nijhoff, 1960.

Husserl, Edmund. *The Crisis of European Sciences and Transcendental Phenomenology: An Introduction to Phenomenological Philosophy* (1954). Trans. David Carr. Evanston, IL: Northwestern University Press, 1970.

Husserl, Edmund. *Experience and Judgment: Investigations in a Genealogy of Logic* (1939, 1948). Ed. and rev. Ludwig Landgrebe. Trans. James S. Churchill and Karl Ameriks. Evanston, IL: Northwestern University Press, 1973.

Husserl, Edmund. *Formal and Transcendental Logic* (1929). Trans. Dorion Cairns. The Hague: Martinus Nijhoff, 1969.

Husserl, Edmund. *Introduction to the Logical Investigations: A Draft of a Preface to the Logical Investigations (1913)*. Trans. Philip J. Bossert and Curtis H. Peters. The Hague: Martinus Nijhoff, 1975.

Husserl, Edmund. *Logical Investigations* (1900–1901). 2 vols. Trans. J. N. Findlay, with a new preface by Michael Dummett, ed. Dermot Moran. London: Routledge, 1970, 2001.

Husserl, Edmund. *Logische Untersuchungen*. 2 vols. *Husserliana*, vols. 18 and 19. The Hague: Martinus Nijhoff, 1975, 1984.

Jay, Martin. "Is Experience Still in Crisis? Reflections on a Frankfurt School Lament." *Kriterion*, no. 100 (December 1999): 9–25.

Jay, Martin. *Songs of Experience: Modern American and European Variations on a Universal Theme*. Berkeley: University of California Press, 2005.

Keller, Pierre. *Husserl and Heidegger on Human Experience*. Cambridge: Cambridge University Press, 1999.

Kirkham, Richard L. *Theories of Truth: A Critical Introduction*. Cambridge, MA: MIT Press, 1992.

Kisiel, Theodore. *The Genesis of Heidegger's* Being and Time. Berkeley: University of California Press, 1993.

Kompridis, Nikolas. *Critique and Disclosure: Critical Theory between Past and Future*. Cambridge, MA: MIT Press, 2007.

Lafont, Cristina. *Heidegger, Language, and World-Disclosure*. Trans. Graham Harman. Cambridge: Cambridge University Press, 2000.

Lafont, Cristina. *The Linguistic Turn in Hermeneutic Philosophy*. Trans. José Medina. Cambridge, MA: MIT Press, 1999.

Levinas, Emmanuel. *The Theory of Intuition in Husserl's Phenomenology* (1930, 1963). Evanston, IL: Northwestern University Press, 1973.

Lohmar, Dieter. "Categorial Intuition." In *A Companion to Phenomenology and Existentialism*, ed. Hubert L. Dreyfus and Mark A. Wrathall, 115–126. Oxford: Blackwell, 2006.

Lukács, Georg. *History and Class Consciousness: Studies in Marxist Dialectics* (1923, 1968). Trans. R. Livingstone. London: Merlin Press, 1971.

Lynch, Michael, ed. *The Nature of Truth: Classic and Contemporary Perspectives*. Cambridge, MA: MIT Press, 2001.

Macdonald, Iain. "Ethics and Authenticity: Conscience and Non-Identity in Heidegger and Adorno, with a Glance at Hegel." In *Adorno and Heidegger: Philosophical Questions*, ed. Iain Macdonald and Krzysztof Ziarek, 6–21. Stanford, CA: Stanford University Press, 2008.

Marcuse, Herbert. *Hegels Ontologie und die Grundlegung einer Theorie der Geschichtlichkeit*. Frankfurt am Main: Klostermann, 1932.

Marcuse, Herbert. *Hegel's Ontology and the Theory of Historicity*. Trans. Seyla Benhabib. Cambridge, MA: MIT Press, 1987.

McCarthy, Thomas. *The Critical Theory of Jürgen Habermas* (1978). Cambridge, MA: MIT Press, 1981.

McManus, Denis. *Heidegger and the Measure of Truth*. Oxford: Oxford University Press, 2012.

Moran, Dermot, and Timothy Mooney, eds. *The Phenomenology Reader*. London: Routledge, 2002.

Mulhall, Stephen. *On Being in the World: Wittgenstein and Heidegger on Seeing Aspects*. London: Routledge, 1990.

Mulhall, Stephen. *The Routledge Guidebook to Heidegger's Being and Time*. London: Routledge, 2013.

Nussbaum, Martha C. *Women and Human Development: The Capabilities Approach*. Cambridge: Cambridge University Press, 2000.

O'Connor, Brian, ed. *The Adorno Reader*. Oxford: Blackwell, 2000.

O'Connor, Brian. *Adorno's Negative Dialectic: Philosophy and the Possibility of Critical Rationality*. Cambridge, MA: MIT Press, 2004.

Ormiston, Gayle L., and Alan D. Schrift, eds. *The Hermeneutic Tradition: From Ast to Ricoeur*. Albany: SUNY Press, 1990.

Patzig, Günther. "Husserl on Truth and Evidence." In *Readings on Edmund Husserl's Logical Investigations*, ed. J. N. Mohanty, 179–196. The Hague: Martinus Nijhoff, 1977.

Pietersma, Henry. "Husserl's Views on the Evident and the True." In *Husserl: Expositions and Appraisals*, ed. Frederick A. Elliston and Peter McCormick, 38–53. Notre Dame, IN: University of Notre Dame Press, 1977.

Plantinga, Alvin. "How to Be an Anti-Realist." *Proceedings and Addresses of the American Philosophical Association* 56, no. 7 (1982): 47–70.

Putnam, Hilary. *Reason, Truth, and History*. Cambridge: Cambridge University Press, 1981.

Ricoeur, Paul. "Hermeneutics and the Critique of Ideology." In *The Hermeneutic Tradition: From Ast to Ricoeur*, ed. Gayle L. Ormiston and Alan D. Schrift, 298–334. Albany: SUNY Press, 1990.

Rorty, Richard. "Universality and Truth." In *Richard Rorty and His Critics*, ed. Robert Brandom, 1–30. Oxford: Blackwell, 2000.

Rouse, Joseph. *Knowledge and Power: Toward a Political Philosophy of Science*. Ithaca, NY: Cornell University Press, 1987.

Ryle, Gilbert. *Collected Papers*. London: Hutchinson, 1971.

Ryle, Gilbert. *The Concept of Mind*. New York: Barnes & Noble, 1949.

Ryle, Gilbert. "Phenomenology." *Proceedings of the Aristotelian Society, Supplementary Volume* 11 (1932): 63–83.

Schwartz, Stephen P. *A Brief History of Analytic Philosophy from Russell to Rawls.* Oxford: Wiley-Blackwell, 2012.

Ströker, Elisabeth. "Husserl's Principle of Evidence: The Significance and Limitations of a Methodological Norm of Phenomenology as a Science." In *Husserlian Foundations of Science*, ed. Lee Hardy, 31–53, 168–172. Lanham, MD: Center for Advanced Research in Phenomenology and University Press of America, 1987.

Swindal, James. *Reflection Revisited: Jürgen Habermas's Discursive Theory of Truth.* New York: Fordham University Press, 1999.

Tagliacozzo, Tamara. *Esperienza e compito infinito nella filosofia del primo Benjamin.* Macerata: Quodlibet, 2003.

Tagliacozzo, Tamara. "Experience and Infinite Task: Knowledge, Language and Messianism in the Philosophy of Walter Benjamin." Unpublished manuscript, 2015.

Tarski, Alfred. "The Concept of Truth in Formalized Languages." In *Alfred Tarski, Logic, Semantics, Metamathematics*, trans. J. H. Woodger, 152–273. Oxford: Clarendon Press, 1956.

Tarski, Alfred. "The Semantic Conception of Truth and the Foundations of Semantics." *Philosophy and Phenomenological Research* 4 (1944): 341–376.

Taylor, Charles. *A Secular Age.* Cambridge, MA: Belknap Press of Harvard University Press, 2007.

Taylor, Charles. *Sources of the Self: The Making of the Modern Identity.* Cambridge, MA: Harvard University Press, 1989.

Tugendhat, Ernst. *Der Wahrheitsbegriff bei Husserl und Heidegger* (1967). 2nd ed. Berlin: Walter de Gruyter, 1970.

Tugendhat, Ernst. "Heidegger's Idea of Truth." In *The Heidegger Controversy: A Critical Reader*, ed. Richard Wolin, 245–263. New York: Columbia University Press, 1991.

Tugendhat, Ernst. "Heideggers Idee von Wahrheit." In *Heidegger: Perspektiven zur Deutung seines Werks*, ed. Otto Pöggeler, 286–297. Cologne, Berlin: Kiepenheuer & Witsch, 1970.

Wellmer, Albrecht. "The Debate about Truth: Pragmatism without Regulative Ideas." In *The Pragmatic Turn in Philosophy: Contemporary Engagements between Analytic and Continental Thought*, ed. William Egginton and Mike Sandbothe, 93–114. Albany, NY: SUNY Press, 2004.

Willard, Dallas. *Logic and the Objectivity of Knowledge: A Study in Husserl's Early Philosophy.* Athens, OH: Ohio University Press, 1984.

Wrathall, Mark A. *Heidegger and Unconcealment: Truth, Language, and History.* Cambridge: Cambridge University Press, 2011.

Young, Julian. *Heidegger's Philosophy of Art*. Cambridge: Cambridge University Press, 2001.

Zimmerman, Michael E. *Eclipse of the Self: The Development of Heidegger's Concept of Authenticity*, rev. ed. Athens, OH: Ohio University Press, 1986.

Zuidervaart, Lambert. *Adorno's Aesthetic Theory: The Redemption of Illusion*. Cambridge, MA: MIT Press, 1991.

Zuidervaart, Lambert. *Artistic Truth: Aesthetics, Discourse, and Imaginative Disclosure*. Cambridge: Cambridge University Press, 2004.

Zuidervaart, Lambert. "Holistic Alethic Pluralism: A Reformational Research Program." *Philosophia Reformata* 81, no. 2 (2016): 156–178.

Zuidervaart, Lambert. "How Not to Be an Anti-Realist: Habermas, Truth, and Justification." *Philosophia Reformata* 77 (2012): 1–18.

Zuidervaart, Lambert. "Propositional and Existential Truth in Edmund Husserl's *Logical Investigations*." *Symposium: Canadian Journal of Continental Philosophy* 20, no. 1 (spring 2016): 150–180.

Zuidervaart, Lambert. "Religion in Public: Passages from Hegel's *Philosophy of Right*." *University of Toronto Journal for Jewish Thought* 1 (April 2010). http://tjjt.cjs.utoronto.ca/articles-2/.

Zuidervaart, Lambert. *Religion, Truth, and Social Transformation: Essays in Reformational Philosophy*. Montreal: McGill-Queen's University Press, 2016.

Zuidervaart, Lambert. *Social Philosophy after Adorno*. Cambridge: Cambridge University Press, 2007.

Zuidervaart, Lambert. "Truth Matters: Heidegger and Horkheimer in Dialectical Disclosure." *Telos*, no. 145 (winter 2008): 131–160.

Zuidervaart, Lambert. "Unfinished Business: Toward a Reformational Conception of Truth." *Philosophia Reformata* 74 (2009): 1–20.

Index